MARTIN RITT

INTERVIEWS

CONVERSATIONS WITH FILMMAKERS SERIES
PETER BRUNETTE, GENERAL EDITOR

Photo credit: Photofest

MARTIN RITT
INTERVIEWS

EDITED BY GABRIEL MILLER

UNIVERSITY PRESS OF MISSISSIPPI / JACKSON

www.upress.state.ms.us

Copyright © 2002 by University Press of Mississippi
All rights reserved
Manufactured in the United States of America

∞
Library of Congress Cataloging-in-Publication Data

Ritt, Martin, 1914–1990.
　　Martin Ritt : interviews / edited by Gabriel Miller.
　　　p. cm.—(Conversations with filmmakers series)
　　Filmography: p.
　　Includes index.
　　ISBN 1-57806-433-3 (cloth : alk. paper)—ISBN 1-57806-434-1 (pbk. : alk. paper)
　　1. Ritt, Martin, 1914–1990—Interviews. 2. Motion picture producers and directors—United States—Interviews. I. Miller, Gabriel, 1948– II. Title. III. Series.

PN1998.3.R578 A5 2003
791.43′0233′092—dc21   2002069125

British Library Cataloging-in-Publication Data available

CONTENTS

Introduction *vii*

Chronology *xvii*

Filmography *xxi*

Ritt for the Record on Direction 3
  HOWARD THOMPSON

American Film Institute Seminar: Conversation with Martin Ritt 6
  AMERICAN FILM INSTITUTE

Dialogue with Martin Ritt and Abraham Polonsky 34
  ABRAHAM POLONSKY

Norma Rae's Big Daddy 53
  BRUCE COOK

Dialogue on Film: Martin Ritt 63
  AMERICAN FILM INSTITUTE

"I Don't Ask Questions. If It Works, It Works!" 71
  PHYLLIS R. KLOTMAN

Working Class Hero: An Interview with Martin Ritt 87
  LYN GOLDFARB AND ANATOLI ILYASHOV

Martin Ritt: A Shaper of the Medium Is Now Its Critic 95
  STAN BERKOWITZ

Ritt Large   105
PATRICK MCGILLIGAN

Martin Ritt and the Group Theatre   121
STEWART STERN

A Conversation with Martin Ritt   148
RONALD DAVIS

The Long, Hot Career   186
CARRIE RICKEY

True Ritt   194
JULIA CAMERON

Index   207

INTRODUCTION

MARTIN RITT WORKED STEADILY and successfully within the Hollywood system for over thirty years. He was a highly regarded professional—one who regularly brought in a completed film on time and either on or under budget. Ritt liked the term professional and applied it to himself. He was not a proponent of the auteur theory; although he acknowledged that the director was in charge, he refused to put his name above the title even when he had the clout and prestige to do so.

This attitude explains in part why Martin Ritt's name is not well known among filmgoers even though he had a sterling reputation in the film community and every "A list" actor wanted to work with him. Another reason for his lack of fame was an approach to filmmaking that highlighted the actor's performance instead of the director's technique. Ritt was also an accomplished teacher of acting, and ironically, his love for his actors and their craft accentuated their artistry and cost him recognition before the public. His actors received twelve Academy Award nominations while Ritt received only one.

Because Ritt did not sign his films visually—Walter Bernstein noted that Ritt made "integrity into a style"—he has become an interesting case. Despite one of the most productive careers as a Hollywood director—directing or producing and directing twenty-six films in thirty-three years—he remains nearly anonymous. Almost everyone has seen or admired *The Long Hot Summer, Hud, Hombre, The Spy Who Came in from the Cold, The Front,* and *Norma Rae,* yet few know the director who made these films.

Ritt's attitude toward his role as director and the theatrical/cinematic enterprise in general was influenced by his three years as a member of the Group Theatre (1937–40) and the life lessons inculcated in him by its directors, notably Harold Clurman. Almost fifty years after his Group Theatre days, Ritt would still remember Clurman as "a deeply passionate man, committed to humanism, committed to America, committed to the importance of the artist, and I loved him" (Stern). In that same interview he called *Golden Boy*, directed by Clurman, "the best acted play I've ever seen."

In 1931 Clurman wrote, "We believe that the individual can achieve his fullest stature only through the identification of his own good with the good of his group, a group which he himself must help to create...."[1] Ritt adhered to this philosophy throughout a career that included acting and directing in the theater, television, and the movies. He rejected the cult of the director and embraced the notion of "group" and community. This was not only a working philosophy; the creation of community became a thematic thread that runs throughout his work. As a film director, Ritt liked to surround himself with people he trusted and valued: Sidney Levin, John Alonzo, Tambi Larson, Walter Scott Herndon, and James Wong Howe worked with him through much of his film career. Ritt liked to speak of a "shorthand" he developed with close associates that made the work easier, but there was also a deep-seated appreciation of the talents of these people that came out of the "group" philosophy. During the AFI Seminar, he speaks rather wistfully about not being able to work with John Alonzo on "First Blood," a project he later abandoned—it would eventually become a great success for Sylvester Stallone—and he referred to hiring a new cameraman as a "new love affair."

This attitude extended to writers as well. Ritt loved working with Irving Ravetch and Harriet Frank Jr., who wrote the screenplays for eight of his twenty-six films, and with Walter Bernstein, who wrote three others, including two of Ritt's most personal works, *The Front* and *The Molly Maguires*. Ravetch and Bernstein also co-produced a number of films with Ritt. Writers liked working with Ritt because he respected their work, recognizing the writer as integral to the creative process. Unlike most Hollywood directors of his era, he liked having writers around for the entire creative process.

The Group Theatre's approach to acting also influenced Ritt. Lee Strasberg, one of the Group's co-founders, adapted the teachings of Konstantin Stanislavsky to hone an acting technique that brought to the American stage an

---

1. Wendy Smith, *Real Life Drama* (New York: Knopf, 1990), 6.

emotional realism and psychological depth unprecedented in its history. Likewise, the best performances in Ritt's films exhibit an emotional and intellectual unity with the material—the actors are not only one with their roles but also with the meticulously rendered world of the film. The coupling of these organic performances with Ritt's uncanny ability to recreate an environment gives these films a documentary-like effect. Paul Newman, Sally Field, Cicely Tyson, Paul Winfield, Richard Burton, Joanne Woodward, James Earl Jones, Jon Voight, Robert DeNiro, and Jane Fonda all did some of their best work in Ritt's films. Ritt commented often that casting the right actor is 80 percent of the success of directing, but he was also an astute teacher of acting who developed effective exercises and techniques to bring out the proper emotions in his actors (see AFI Seminar, Cameron, Cook).

He was both impatient with actors who squandered their talent and genuinely respectful of those who "make the most of their equipment" (see Cameron, AFI, SMU). He especially admired Paul Newman, who constantly pushed himself to expand his acting range and discipline his talent, as well as Sally Field and Jane Fonda, who impressed him with their work ethic and dedication to craft. He came to appreciate Robert DeNiro's method, although it initially put him off, because Ritt recognized him as an artist and a student. He spoke often of misjudging Cicely Tyson in the role of Rebecca Morgan in *Sounder* and of how much he learned from watching her act. Conversely, he had little patience for actors who dissipated their ability including Richard Burton and Orson Welles. Still, he elicited one of Burton's best screen performances, in *The Spy Who Came in from the Cold*, and he managed to coax an intriguing performance out of Welles in *The Long, Hot Summer*.

The Group Theatre further shaped Ritt's overriding vision as an artist, defining what would become the focus of his life's work. In the SMU interview he recalled, " . . . they were totally committed to doing American work, American plays. . . . it was in the true tradition of what they conceived to be a democratic America, and what they conceived to be serious work, creative work." This was Clurman's professed aim in choosing to present contemporary plays by American writers that confronted "the essential moral and social preoccupations of our time" responding to the "profoundest spiritual needs" of their audience."[2]

Ritt's films are almost exclusively focused on America and American his-

---

2. Ibid., 8.

tory. Of his twenty-six films, only three take place in foreign settings: *Five Branded Women*, a film Ritt deliberately left off of his filmography because it was the only one he had made for money; *The Spy Who Came in from the Cold;* and *Paris Blues*, which actually deals with American issues from a remote setting. Most of his films directly confront the "moral and social preoccupations" of American society. Ritt dealt forcefully and perceptively with the perversion of the agrarian ideal and the debilitating effects of industrialism in *Hombre*, *The Molly Maguires*, *Norma Rae*, and *Cross Creek*. He exposed the dehumanization of American power by dissecting the corporate ethic in *The Brotherhood*, *Hud*, and *The Spy Who Came in from the Cold*. Many of his films developed from historical subjects or true stories: *Hemingway's Adventures of a Young Man*, *The Molly Maguires*, *The Great White Hope*, *The Front*, *Norma Rae*, *Cross Creek*, and *Conrack*.

One of his central subjects—and one that he is often questioned about in the interviews collected here—is race and racism. Few white directors have made as many films confronting this problem as Ritt did. His very first film, *Edge of the City*, touches on it, as does *Paris Blues*. Later works such as *The Great White Hope*, *Conrack*, and especially *Sounder*—one of the most eloquent of all American films on the subject—explore this in greater detail.

Ritt stated that he made movies about blacks because "I have to. . . . I feel deeply about the dilemma of Black people. I always have" (McGilligan). Yet in many of the interviews he expresses anger, hurt, and defensiveness about criticisms he received from the black community for his films. He resented the suggestion that *Conrack* was about a "white Jesus" and the condemnation he suffered for depicting a sharecropping family in *Sounder*. Much of the early exchange in the AFI Seminar is Ritt's defense of his emphasis on what the white schoolteacher gives to the blacks in *Conrack* rather than on what the black community teaches him. His schooling in the realities of commercial Hollywood—another persistent theme in these interviews—led him to react with impatience, arguing that because opportunities to make serious films don't come along very often, even making compromises is "better than not doing it." He remained proud of the fact that he had tackled these difficult subjects and of his record on race and integration. He often replied to his detractors that when they got the opportunity, they should make the films they want to make; meanwhile, he would persist in making the films he wanted to make.

Throughout his career, Ritt was labeled a maverick, a radical, and a political filmmaker, but in reality he was a very astute player in the film business. Often in these interviews he talks about the cost of making movies, the commercial realities of Hollywood, and the need to keep an eye on the bottom line if one is to succeed within the system. The artist in Ritt was insistent on the value of content, but the survivor in him always knew how to play the game. He liked to consider himself a "professional," an essential distinction in Hollywood, where making personal films is more difficult than in Europe. In many of these interviews, Ritt remarks that it is almost impossible to make issue-oriented films in Hollywood—though sometimes he concedes that it has become easier—and he remained surprised and delighted that he was able to make *The Front,* a film about the blacklist.

Ritt valued the primacy of content above all considerations in his films, but as a practicing realist he chose to deal with issues within the context of a story that would appeal to a wide audience. From his earliest days in television, he remembered the excitement of dealing with quality material, including works by Ernest Hemingway, Willa Cather, and John Updike. He also registered the difficulty of making worthwhile films within a general culture that values "junk." In his interview with Patrick McGilligan he talks about a culture addicted to comic books and fast food and a film industry committed to making a "size twelve dress that everyone will buy," concluding that the artist must resist the temptation to cater to studio perceptions of popular taste. His conversation with Abraham Polonsky, published here for the first time, is a record of two filmmakers' commitment to serious, uplifting, and issue-oriented material and the extreme difficulty of getting that material made.

Ritt did quarrel, however, with being labeled a political filmmaker. Journalists had hung that label on him because of the leftist leanings of his films, which often tackled issues like racism, unions, the blacklist, informing, and the incursions of government and big business on the life of the individual. Although he acknowledged often that he was a political animal and left of Hollywood in general, he told Bruce Cook that he considered only *The Molly Maguires* and *The Front* to be political films. *Norma Rae,* which a number of journalists and critics had pigeonholed as a film about unionism, Ritt considered to be primarily about "a woman who changed her life" (Cineaste).

The central focus of Ritt's films is the evolution of character. All of his great films are grounded in complex stories presenting strong protagonists who struggle against powerful social forces. He considered his subject in general terms to be "the human condition"; his "humanism" was what distinguished his films. This is a point he returns to frequently in these interviews. For Ritt, all great artists find "their way back to humanism, because there's nothing else" (McGilligan). In his remarks at Ritt's memorial service, Walter Bernstein said that Ritt's films are "eulogies to the human spirit, people fighting to remain human, to become more human."

This credo is similar to that of another of Ritt's great teachers and influences, Elia Kazan, who first brought him into the Group Theatre. Kazan commented, "I admire the filmmakers I admire for the same reason I admire other artists . . . because of the degree of humanity, the amount of human feeling they have."[3] Ritt would certainly agree with Kazan that the purpose of art is to make man confront his humanity. This, of course, was the communal purpose of the Group, which shaped both Ritt and Kazan. Both of them made socially oriented films, and both preferred location shooting. Both had unadorned styles and favored linear narrative lines. And because of their Group training, both emerged as superior teachers of acting and became known as actors' directors.

Although Ritt and Kazan started their careers as close friends, their relationship was shattered by the House Committee on Un-American Activities investigations into film and television and the resulting blacklists, events that shaped both their careers and lives. In his interview with Patrick McGilligan, Ritt refuses to discuss Kazan, yet he opened up a bit about him to Stewart Stern and Ronald Davis, perhaps because these remarks were not intended for publication in a magazine. Rejecting the explanation given by Kazan and others about political struggles within the Group Theatre, Ritt insist that he knew of no Communist cabals to take over the Group. He notes that a few members were on the left but claims that most were not. Kazan, Ritt felt, was motivated by "appetite"—he was not prepared to give up his success.

Still, Ritt remained admiring of Kazan's talent, calling him the most "inventive" director to come out of the Group and commenting that his greatest quality was "incredible judgment." Even in 1986, speaking about Kazan filled him with emotion and regret: "We were very close. And I've never really gotten over that because he was a great influence in my life"

---

3. William Baer, ed., *Elia Kazan: Interviews* (Jackson: University Press of Mississippi, 2000), 116.

(Stern). And while Ritt maintained that Kazan "shouldn't be forgiven," one gets the feeling that he was willing to hedge a little, as he did with Clifford Odets (see McGilligan).

Ritt was insistent, however, that informing ruined both Odets's career and Kazan's. "I consider [Kazan] one of the great tragedies of the McCarthy period, because he was easily the most talented director of my time. And he's produced nothing since then" (Stern). If this judgment seems overly harsh, statements Ritt made in various interviews show that he regarded informing as a dramatic violation of the artist's essential being: "For an artist, it is the most dangerous thing in the world you can do. You can't deny who you are or what you are" (McGilligan).

The HUAC investigations and subsequent blacklist were seminal events in Ritt's life; the subject of informing became a recurrent theme in many of his films through 1975. Ritt recounted his own experience of being blacklisted from television in the fifties for numerous interviewers, and that subject is covered in most of the interviews reprinted here. Ritt usually described his firing from CBS in comic/absurdist terms. He spoke of being summoned to Donald Davis's office and told, "You haven't been renewed." When Ritt asked why, Davis replied, "I have no idea." But unlike many victims of HUAC, Ritt was never subpoenaed and never testified. His name appeared on some lists primarily because he had directed a play for a trade union.

Ritt was occasionally told that he could work again if he would name names, even the names of dead people. He was fond of emphasizing that the committees who offered such deals were primarily interested in thought control, because the value of the names meant nothing to them. In *The Front*—written by Ritt's close friend an fellow blacklisted victim, Walter Bernstein, it was the first Hollywood film to deal with this subject—the request to name dead people is utilized to great ironic effect when Howard Prince (Woody Allen) is finally called before the committee. The absurd invitation to commit a meaningless betrayal provokes Prince to walk away from the hearings and accept a prison term. (Irwin Winkler presented a similar incident years later in his film *Guilty by Suspicion*.) Informing would also be an important motif in other Ritt films, including *Five Branded Women*, *Edge of the City*, *The Spy Who Came in from the Cold*, *The Brotherhood*, and *The Molly Maguires*.

The one film that Ritt returned to again and again in these interviews was *The Molly Maguires*, his favorite film; its failure haunted him. At times he blamed that failure on the cultural climate in America, which mitigated against complex films on serious subjects. Most often, however, he felt the characterization was too complicated, that he "didn't give the audience a simple enough person to root for. I don't think they knew whose side they should be on" (AFI Seminar). Perhaps he felt that he had "complicated" things too much. He took some comfort from the film's success in France, but its failure in his own country gnawed at him. *The Molly Maguires* is indeed a great neglected film, one that deserves to find a wider audience.

Ritt did not consider himself an intellectual. He felt that his taste reflected that of a broad sampling of America, and he was confident that if he liked a story, many filmgoers would like it as well: "If I really like something I will be able to get it across to most people" (McGilligan). He regarded a story's main virtue to be its ability to move an audience emotionally and to entertain. Interestingly, Ritt did not like agitprop material because it lacked a strong story line.

Above all, these interviews reveal a classic American individualist. Despite his dedication to the ideals of unionism, democracy, and group action, Ritt's films display an idealistic affinity for the individual, the loner who rejects the community's corrupt values. Ritt was a man who maintained his balance within a commercial system and a loyalty to a group of artists within that system, but still managed to create films imbued with his own personal politics. He fought to make projects reflecting the humanistic spirit that is on full view in these pages, and in doing so, he forged a body of work that deserves a place of honor in American film history.

The interviews presented here conform to the policy of the University Press of Mississippi with regard to this series: most have not been edited in any significant way. Five of he interviews published here have never been published before: the AFI Seminar, the dialogue with Abraham Polonsky, the interviews with Stewart Stern and Phyllis R. Klotman, and SMU's Oral History Project conducted by Ronald Davis. These are among the best interviews Ritt ever gave; all are housed in the Martin Ritt Collection at the Margaret Herrick Library of the Motion Picture Academy in Los Angeles. Because these interviews were not originally intended for publication, some personal comments about individuals have been edited out. Some of the interviews were overly long, and at times Ritt went off on tangents. Had these interviews been published previously, some of this material would have been excised editorially in order to make the interview read more fluently. I edited with the same object here.

Otherwise the interviews are presented in chronological order and remain as they were published. (The Polansky interview is undated and Polansky himself did not remember when he had this conversation with Ritt; I'm guessing that it was conducted around 1976.) There is a certain amount of repetition in these interviews, but I believe the overlaps provide extra evidence of integrity for the scholarly reader and offer valuable insight into the recurrent concerns that preoccupied Ritt during a lifetime in television, theater, and film.

I would like to thank Anne Stascavage of the University Press of Mississippi for her patience, advice, and assistance during the preparation of this volume. Another thank-you is due Peter Brunette for his encouragement. Special thanks to Barbara Hall of the Margaret Herrick Library for her help with the previously unpublished interviews and to Jim Verniere for helping me in a variety of ways. Again, I owe a great debt to the late Adele Ritt and her daughter Tina Ritt for helping clear the way so that the unpublished interviews could be published here for the first time. Finally, another thank-you to Lizzie (who typed the chronology and filmography), Jessica, and Kathy for their love and support.

CHRONOLOGY

1914 Born in New York City to Rose and Morris Ritt.

1932 Graduates from DeWitt Clinton High School.

1932–34 Attends Elon College in Burlington, North Carolina, where he plays football and studies literature.

1935 Briefly attends St. John's Law School in Jamaica, New York.

1935–37 Acts in productions with the Theater of Action and the Federal Theater Project in New York City. Wins a prominent role in William Saroyan's *The Time of Your Life* with the Glasgow Theater Company, only to be replaced by Gene Kelly.

1937 Elia Kazan recommends him for the Group Theatre, where he gets a small role in Clifford Odets's *Golden Boy*. He also teaches the show's star, Luther Adler, how to box.

1939 Acts in Irwin Shaw's *The Gentle People* for the Group Theatre.

1940 Marries Adele Wolf. Appears in *Two on an Island* by Elmer Rice.

1943–46 Serves in Air Force. Appears in Moss Harts' *Winged Victory* on Broadway and in George Cukor's film version. Directs his first play, *Yellow Jack* by Sidney Howard, in 1944.

1946 Directs his first Broadway play, *Mr. Peebles and Mr. Hooker*.

1950–52 Acts in, directs, and produces over 100 live television dramas, primarily for the CBS series *Danger*, the *Somerset Maugham Theatre*, *Starlight Theatre*, and *Climax*. Stars in "The Paper Box Kid," written by Walter Bernstein (1952), for which he is acclaimed as a major television actor.

1952–56 Blacklisted from television but works in the theater, notably in Clifford Odets's *The Flowering Peach* as an actor and as director of Arthur Miller's *A View from the Bridge* and *A Memory of Two Mondays* (1955). Also teaches at the Actor's Studio, where his students include Paul Newman, Joanne Woodward, Lee Remick, and Julie Harris.

1957 His first film, *Edge of the City*, is released, as is his first Hollywood film, *No Down payment*.

1958 *The Long Hot Summer*, his first film with Paul Newman and the screenwriting team of Irving Ravetch and Harriet Frank Jr. His film, *The Gladiators*, starring Yul Brynner as Spartacus, is announced with a full-page ad in *Variety*. This project is later abandoned and a version based on different material is produced by Kirk Douglas.

1959 *The Sound and the Fury* and *The Black Orchid*, for which Sophia Loren is cited as Best Actress at the Venice Film Festival.

1960 *Five Branded Women*.

1961 *Paris Blues*, nominated for one Academy Award.

1962 *Hemingway's Adventures of a Young Man* (released in England as *Adventures of a Young Man*). Wins Hollywood Foreign Press Award as Best Director. Forms Salem Films with Paul Newman.

1963 *Hud* (first production of Salem Films), for which he is nominated for an Academy Award as Best Director. Patricia Neal and Melvyn Douglas win Academy Awards as Best Supporting Actress and Actor. Wins Foreign Press Award as Best Director.

1964 *The Outrage*.

1965 *The Spy Who Came in from the Cold*, which he also produces, is nominated for two Academy Awards, including Best Actor (Richard Burton).

1967	*Hombre*, which he also co-produces.
1968	*The Brotherhood*. Awarded an Honorary Doctor of Fine Arts degree by Elon College. Announced as the director of *The Man Who Would Be King* (a project he eventually abandons).
1970	*The Molly Maguires*, co-produced with Walter Bernstein. *The Great White Hope*, for which James Earl Jones and Jane Alexander are nominated for Academy Awards.
1972	*Sounder*, which receives four Academy Award nominations, including Best Picture and Best Actress (Cicely Tyson). *Pete 'n' Tillie*, which receives two Academy Award nominations.
1974	*Conrack*, which he also co-produces. British Film Institute retrospective of his work.
1976	*The Front*, which receives an Academy Award nomination for Best Original Screenplay. Has a starring role in *The End of the Game*, directed by Maximillian Schell.
1978	*Casey's Shadow*.
1979	*Norma Rae*, which receives four Academy Award nominations. Sally Field wins the Academy Award for Best Actress. Entry at Cannes Film Festival. Retrospective at the Museum of Modern Art.
1980	Distinguished Alumni Award from Elon College.
1981	*Back Roads*.
1983	*Cross Creek*, which is nominated for four Academy Awards.
1984	Begins shooting *No Small Affair* with Matthew Broderick and Sally Field, which he is forced to abandon because of poor health.
1985	*Murphy's Romance*, which is nominated for two Academy Awards, including Best Actor (James Garner). Acts in *The Slugger's Wife*, written by Neil Simon and directed by Hal Ashby.
1987	*Nuts*. Lifetime Achievement Award from Boston University.
1990	*Stanley and Iris*. Dies December 8.

FILMOGRAPHY

As Director

1957
EDGE OF THE CITY
Studio: MGM
Director: **Martin Ritt**
Producer; David Susskind
Screenplay: Robert Alan Aurthur, based on his teleplay *A Man Is Ten Feet Tall*
Director of Photography: Joseph Brun
Editor: Sidney Meyers
Art Direction: Richard Sylbert
Music: Leonard Rosenman
Cast: Val Avery (Brother), John Cassavetes (Axel North), David Clarke (Wallace), Ruby Dee (Lucy Tyler), John Kellogg (Detective), William A. Lee (Davis), Kathleen Maguire (Ellen Wilson), Sidney Poitier (Tommy Tyler), Robert G. Simon (Mr. Nordmann), Jack Warden (Charles Malik), Ruth White (Mrs. Nordmann)
85 minutes
Black and White

1957
NO DOWN PAYMENT
Studio: Twentieth Century Fox

Producer: Jerry Wald
Director: **Martin Ritt**
Screenplay: Philip Yordan
Novel: John McPartland
Cinematography: Joseph LaShelle
Editor: Louis R. Loeffler
Art Direction: Herman A. Blumenthal, Lyle R. Wheeler
Music: Leigh Harline
Cast: Joanne Woodward (Leola Boone), Sheree North (Isabelle Flagg), Tony Randall (Jerry Flagg), Jeffrey Hunter (David Martin), Cameron Mitchell (Troy Boone), Patricia Owens (Jean Martin), Barbara Rush (Betty Kreitzer), Pat Hingle (Herman Kreitzer), Robert Harris (Markham), Aki Aleong (Iko), Jim Hayward (Mr. Burton)
105 minutes
Black and White

1958
THE LONG HOT SUMMER
Studio: Twentieth Century Fox
Producer: Jerry Wald
Director: **Martin Ritt**
Screenplay: Irving Ravetch, Harriet Frank Jr. based on *Barn Burning, The Spotted Horses,* and *The Hamlet* by William Faulkner
Photography: Joseph LaShelle
Editor: Louis R. Loeffler
Art Direction: Lyle R. Wheeler, Maurice Ransford
Music: Alex North
Cast: Paul Newman (Ben Quick), Joanne Woodward (Clara Varner), Anthony Franciosa (Jody Varner), Orson Welles (Will Varner), Lee Remick (Eula Varner), Angela Lansbury (Minnie), Richard Anderson (Alan Stewart), Sarah Marshall (Agnes Stewart), Mabel Albertson (Mrs. Stewart), J. Pat O'Malley (Ratliff), William Walker (Lucious), George Dunn (Peabody), Jess Kirkpatrick (Armistead), Val Avery (Wilk), I. Stanford Jolley (Houstin), Nicholas King (Hon Fisher), Lee Erickson (Tom Shortly), Ralph Reed (J. V. Brokright)
115 minutes
Color

1959
THE SOUND AND THE FURY
Studio: Twentieth Century Fox
Producer: Jerry Wald
Director: **Martin Ritt**
Screenplay: Irving Ravetch, Harriet Frank Jr.
Novel: William Faulkner
Director of Photography; Charles G. Clarke
Editor: Stuart Gilmore
Art Direction: Lyle R. Wheeler, Maurice Ransford
Music: Alex North, conducted by Lionel Newman
Cast: Yul Brynner (Jason Compson), Joanne Woodward (Quentin Compson), Margaret Leighton (Caddy Compson), Stuart Whitman (Charles Busch), Ethel Waters (Dilsey), Jack Warden (Ben Compson), Francoise Rosay (Mrs. Compson), John Beal (Howard), Albert Dekker (Earl), Stephen Perry (Luster), William Gunn (T. P.), Roy Glenn (Job).
115 minutes
Color

1959
THE BLACK ORCHID
Studio: Paramount
Producers: Carlo Ponti, Marcello Girosi
Director: **Martin Ritt**
Screenplay: Joseph Stefano
Director of Photography: Robert Burks
Editor: Howard Smith
Art Direction: Hal Pereira, Roland Anderson
Music: Alessandro Cicognini
Cast: Sophia Loren (Rose Bianco), Anthony Quinn (Frank Valente), Mark Richman (Noble), Virginia Vincent (Alma Gallo), Frank Puglia (Henry Gallo), Jimmy Baird (Ralph Bianco), Naomi Stevens (Guilia Gallo), Whit Bissell (Mr. Harmon), Robert Carricart (Priest), Joe De Reda (Joe), Jack Washburn (Tony Bianco), Ina Balin (Mary Valente)
95 minutes
Black and White

1960
FIVE BRANDED WOMEN (JOVANKA E LE ALTRE)
Studio: Paramount
Producer: Dino De Laurentiis
Director: **Martin Ritt**
Screenplay: Ivo Perilli and Michael Wilson, Paul Jarrico (Uncredited)
Novel: Ugo Pirro
Director of Photography: Giuseppe Rotunno
Editor: Jerry Webb
Art Direction: Mario Chiari
Music: Francesco Lavagnino, conducted by Franco Ferrara
Cast: Richard Basehart (Captain Reinhardt), Barbara Bel Geddes (Marja), Sidney Clute (Milan), Harry Guardino (Branco), Van Heflin (Velko), Silvana Mangano (Jovanka), Vera Miles (Daniza), Jeanne Moreau (Ljuba), Alex Nicol (Svenko), Teresa Pellati (Boja), Romolo Valli (Mirko)
100 minutes
Black and White

1961
PARIS BLUES
Studio: United Artists
Executive Producers: George Glass, Walter Seltzer
Producer: Sam Shaw
Director: **Martin Ritt**
Screenplay: Walter Bernstein, Irene Kamp, Lulla Rosenfeld, Jack Sher
Novel: Harold Flender
Director of Photography: Christian Matras
Editor: Roger Dwyre
Art Direction: Alexandre Trauner
Music: Duke Ellington
Cast: Paul Newman (Ram Bowen), Joanne Woodward (Lillian Corning), Sidney Poitier (Eddie Cook), Louis Armstrong (Wild Man Moore), Diahann Carroll (Connie Lampson), Barbara Laage (Marie Seoul), André Luguet (Rene Bernard), Marie Versini (Nicole), Moustache (Drummer), Serge Reggiani (Michel Duvigne)
98 minutes
Black and White

1962
HEMINGWAY'S ADVENTURES OF A YOUNG MAN
Studio: Twentieth Century Fox
Producer: Jerry Wald
Associate Producer: Peter Nelson
Director: **Martin Ritt**
Screenplay: A. E. Hotchner
Based on stories by: Ernest Hemingway
Photography: Lee Garmes
Editor: Hugh S. Fowler
Art Direction: Jack Martin Smith, Paul Groesse
Music: Franz Waxman
Cast: Richard Beymer (Nick Adams), Diane Baker (Carolyn), Corinne Calvet (Contessa), Arthur Kennedy (Dr. Adams), Jessica Tandy (Mrs. Adams), Susan Strasberg (Nurse Rosanna), Eli Wallach (Sergeant), Ricardo Montalban (Major Padula), Dan Dailey (Billposter), Fred Clark (Mr. Turner), Paul Newman (Bugs), James Dunn (Telegrapher), Michael Pollard (George)
145 minutes
Color

1963
HUD
Studio: Paramount
Producers: **Martin Ritt**, Irving Ravetch
Director: **Martin Ritt**
Screenplay: Irving Ravetch and Harriet Frank Jr.
Novel: *Horseman Pass By* by Larry McMurtry
Cinematography: James Wong Howe
Editor: Frank Bracht
Art Direction: Hal Pereira, Tambi Larsen
Music: Elmer Bernstein
Cast: Paul Newman (Hud Bannon), Melvyn Douglas (Homer Bannon), Patricia Neal (Alma), Brandon de Wilde (Lon Bannon), John Ashley (Hermy), Whit Bissell (Burris), Crahan Denton (Jesse), Val Avery (Jose), Sheldon Allman (Thompson), Pitt Herbert (Larker), Peter Brooks (George), Curt Conway (Truman Peters), Yvette Vickers (Lily Peters), George Petrie (Joe Scanlon), David Kent (Donald), Frank Killmond (Dumb Billy)

112 minutes
Black and White

1964
THE OUTRAGE
Studio: Metro-Goldwyn-Mayer
Executive Producer: **Martin Ritt**
Producer: A. Ronald Lubin, Michael Kanin
Director: **Martin Ritt**
Screenplay: Michael Kanin, based on the play *Rashomon* by Fay Kanin and Michael Kanin
Cinematography: James Wong Howe
Editor: Frank Santillo
Art Direction: George W. Davis, Tambi Larsen
Music: Alex North
Cast: Paul Newman (Juan Carrasco), Laurence Harvey (Husband), Claire Bloom (Wife), Edward G. Robinson (Con Man), William Shatner (Preacher), Howard Da Silva (Prospector), Albert Salmi (Sheriff), Thomas Chalmers (Judge), Paul Fix (Indian)
95 minutes
Black and White

1965
THE SPY WHO CAME IN FROM THE COLD
Studio: Paramount
Producer: **Martin Ritt**
Director: **Martin Ritt**
Screenplay: Paul Dehn, Guy Trosper
Novel: John le Carré
Cinematography: Oswald Morris
Editor: Anthony Harvey
Art Direction: Tambi Larsen, Josie MacAvin, Ted Marshall, Hal Pereira
Music: Sol Kaplan
Cast: Richard Burton (Alec Leamas), Oskar Werner (Fiedler), David Bauer (Young Judge), Anne Blake (Miss Crail), Claire Bloom (Nan Perry), Richard Caldicot (Mr. Pitt), Cyril Cusack (Control), Rupert Davies (George Smiley), Marianne Deeming (Frau Floerdke), Scott Finch (German Guide), Walter

Gotell (Holten), Robert Hardy (Carlton), Edward Harvey (Man in the Shop), Michael Hordern (Ashe), Esmond Knight (Old Judge), Bernard Lee (I) (Patmore), Beatrix Lehmann (Tribunal President), Niall MacGinnis (German Checkpoint guard), Warren Mitchell (Mr. Zanfrello), Henk Molenberg (Dutch customs officer), Nancy Nevinson (Mrs. Zanfrello), Steve Plytas (East German Judge), Michael Ripper (Lofthouse), Michael Rittermann (Security officer), Tom Stern (CIA agent), George Voskovec (East German Defense Attorney), Sam Wanamaker (Peters), Peter van Eyck (Hans-Dieter Mundt)
112 minutes
Black and White

1967
HOMBRE
Studio: Twentieth Century Fox
Producers: **Martin Ritt** and Irving Ravetch
Director: **Martin Ritt**
Screenplay: Irving Ravetch and Harriet Frank Jr.
Novel: Elmore Leonard
Cinematography: James Wong Howe
Editor: Frank Bracht
Art Direction: Jack Martin Smith, Robert Emmet Smith
Music: David Rose
Cast: Paul Newman (John Russell), Fredric March (Alexander Favor), Richard Boone (Cicero Grimes), Diane Cilento (Jessie), Cameron Mitchell (Sheriff Frank Braden), Barbara Rush (Audra Favor), Peter Lazer (Billy Lee Blake), Margaret Blye (Doris), Martin Balsam (Henry Mendez), Skip Ward (Steve Early), Frank Silvera (Mexican Bandit), David Canary (Lamar Dean), Val Avery (Delgado), Larry Ward (Soldier)
119 minutes
Color

1968
THE BROTHERHOOD
Studio: Paramount
Producer: Kirk Douglas
Executive Producer: **Martin Ritt**

Director: **Martin Ritt**
Screenplay: Lewis John Carlino
Cinematography: Frank Bracht, Boris Kaufman
Editor: Frank Bracht
Art Direction: Tambi Larsen, Antonio Sarzi-Braga
Music: Lalo Schifrin
Cast: Kirk Douglas (Frank Ginetta), Alex Cord (Vince Ginetta), Irene Papas (Ida Ginetta), Luther Adler (Dominick Bertolo), Susan Strasberg (Emma Ginetta), Murray Hamilton (Jim Egan), Eduardo Ciannelli (Don Peppino), Joe De Santis (Pietro Rizzi), Connie Scott (Carmela Ginetta), Val Avery (Jake Rotherman), Val Bisoglio (Cheech), Alan Hewitt (Sol Levin), Barry Primus (Vido), Michele Cimarosa (Toto), Louis Badolati (Don Turridu)
96 minutes
Color

1970
THE MOLLY MAGUIRES
Studio: Paramount
Producers: **Martin Ritt**, Walter Bernstein
Director: **Martin Ritt**
Screenplay: Walter Bernstein, suggested by a book by Arthur H. Lewis
Photography: James Wong Howe
Editor: Frank Bracht
Art Direction: Tambi Larsen
Set Decoration: Darrell Silvera
Music: Henry Mancini
Cast: Sean Connery (Jack Kehoe), Richard Harris (James McParlan), Samantha Eggar (Mary Raines), Frank Finley (Davies), Anthony Zerbe (Dougherty), Bethel Leslie (Mrs. Kehoe), Art Lund (Frazier), Philip Bourneuf (Father O'Connor), Anthony Constello (Frank McAndrew), Brendan Dillon (Mr. Raines), Frances Heflin (Mrs. Frazier), John Alderson (Jenkins), Malachy McCourt (Bartender), Susan Goodman (Mrs. McAndrew)
124 minutes
Color

1970
THE GREAT WHITE HOPE
Studio: Twentieth Century Fox
Producer: Lawrence Turman

Co-Executive Producer: **Martin Ritt**
Director: **Martin Ritt**
Screenplay: Howard Sackler, from his play
Director of Photography: Burnett Guffey
Editor: William Reynolds
Art Direction: John DeCuir
Music: Lionel Newman
Cast: James Earl Jones (Jack Jefferson), Jane Alexander (Eleanor), Lou Gilbert (Goldie), Joel Fluellen (Tick), Chester Morris (Pop Weaver), Robert Webber (Dixon), Marlene Warfield (Clara), R. G. Armstrong (Cap'n Dan), Hal Holbrook (Cameron), Beah Richards (Mama Tiny), Moses Gunn (Scipio), Lloyd Gough (Smitty), George Ebeling (Fred), Larry Pennell (Frank Bardy), Roy E. Glenn Sr. (Pastor)
103 minutes
Color

1972
SOUNDER
Studio: Twentieth Century Fox
Producer: Robert B. Radnitz
Director: **Martin Ritt**
Screenplay: Lonne Elder III
Novel: William H. Armstrong (winner, 1970 Newbery Medal)
Cinematography: John Alonzo
Editor: Sid Levin
Art Direction: Walter Herndon
Music: Taj Mahal
Cast; Cicely Tyson (Rebecca Morgan), Paul Winfield (Nathan Lee Morgan), Kevin Hooks (David Lee Morgan), Carmen Mathews (Mrs. Boatright), Taj Mahal (Ike), James Best (Sheriff Young), Yvonne Jarrell (Josie Mae Morgan), Eric Hooks (Earl Morgan), Sylvia "Kuumba" Williams (Harriet), Janet MacLachlan (Camille), Teddy Airhart (Mr. Perkins), The Rev. Thomas N. Phillips (The Preacher), Judge William Thomas Bennett (The Judge), Inez Durham, His Court Clerk (Court Clerk), Spencer Bradford (Clarence), Myrl Sharkey (Mrs. Clay)
105 minutes
Color

1972
PETE 'N' TILLIE
Studio: Universal
Executive Producer: Jennings Lang
Producer: Julius J. Epstein
Screenplay: Julius J. Epstein
Director: **Martin Ritt**
Novella: *Witch's Milk* by Peter De Vries
Director of Photography: John Alonzo
Editor: Frank Bracht
Art Direction: George Webb
Music: John T. Williams
Cast: Walter Matthau (Pete), Carol Burnett (Tillie), Geraldine Page (Gertrude), Barry Nelson (Burt), Rene Auberjonois (Jimmy Twitchell), Lee H. Montgomery (Robbie), Henry Jones (Mr. Tucker), Kent Smith (Father Keating), Philip Bourneuf (Dr. Willett), Whit Bissell (Minister), Timothy Blake (Lucy Lund)
111 minutes
Color

1974
CONRACK
Studio: Twentieth Century Fox
Producers: **Martin Ritt** and Harriet Frank Jr.
Director: **Martin Ritt**
Screenplay: Irving Ravetch and Harriet Frank Jr.
Novel: *The Water Is Wide* by Pat Conroy
Editor: Frank Bracht
Director of Photography: John Alonzo
Production Designer: Walter Scott Herndon
Music: John Williams
Cast: Jon Voight (Pat Conroy), Paul Winfield (Mad Billy), Madge Sinclair (Mrs. Scott), Tina Andrews (Mary), Antonio Fargas (Quickfellow), Ruth Attaway (Edna), James O'Reare (Messenger), Gracia Lee (Mrs. Sellers), C. P. MacDonald (Mr. Ryder), Jane Moreland (Mrs. Webster), Thomas Horton (Judge), Nancy Butler (Mrs. Ryder), Robert W. Page (Mr. Spaulding), Hume Cronyn (Skeffington)
107 minutes
Color

1976
THE FRONT
Studio: Columbia Pictures
Producer: **Martin Ritt**
Executive Producer: Charles H. Joffe
Director: **Martin Ritt**
Screenplay: Walter Bernstein
Photography: Michael Chapman
Editor: Sidney Levin
Art Direction: Charles Bailey
Music: Dave Grusin
Cast: Woody Allen (Howard Prince), Zero Mostel (Hecky Brown), Herschel Bernardi (Phil Sussman), Michael Murphy (Alfred Miller), Andrea Marcovicci (Florence Barrett), Remak Ramsay (Hennessey), Marvin Lichterman (Myer Prince), Lloyd Gough (Delaney), David Margulies (Phelps), Joshua Shelley (Sam), Norman Rose (Howard's Attorney), Charles Kimbrough (Committee Counselor), M. Josef Sommer (Committee Chairman), Danny Aiello (Danny La Gattuta), Georgann Johnson (Television Interviewer), Scott McKay (Hampton), David Clarke (Hubert Jackson), I. W. Klein (Bank Teller), John Bentley (Bartender), Julie Garfield (Margo), Murray Moston (Boss), McIntyre Dixon (Harry Stone), Rudolph Wilrich (Tailman), Burt Britton (Bookseller), Albert M. Ottenheimer (School Principal), William Bogert (Parks), Joey Faye (Waiter), Marilyn Sokol (Sandy), John J. Slater (Television Director), Renee Paris (Girl in Hotel Lobby), Gino Gennaro (Stage Hand), Joan Porter (Myer's Wife), Andrew Bernstein, Jacob Bernstein (Alfred's children), Matthew Tobin (Man at Party), Marilyn Persky (His Date), Sam McMurray (Young Man at Party), Joe Jamrog (F.B.I. Man), Michael Miller (F.B.I. Man), Lucy Lee Flippin (Nurse), Jack Davidson (Congressman), Donald Symington (Congressman), Patrick McNamara (Federal Marshall)
94 minutes
Color

1978
CASEY'S SHADOW
Studio: Columbia Pictures
Producer: Ray Stark
Executive Producer: Michael Levee

Director: **Martin Ritt**
Screenplay: Carol Sobieski, based on an article by John McPhee
Photography: John Alonzo
Editor: Sidney Levin
Production Design: Robert Luthardt
Music: Patrick Williams
Cast: Walter Matthau (Lloyd Bourdelle), Alexis Smith (Sarah Blue), Robert Webber (Mike Marsh), Murray Hamilton (Tom Patterson), Andrew A. Rubin (Buddy Bourdelle), Stephan Burnes (Randy Bourdelle), Susan Myers (Kelly Marsh), Michael Hershewe (Casey Bourdelle), Harry Caesar (Calvin Lebec), Joel Fluellen (Jimmy Judson), Whit Bissell (Dr. Williamson), Jimmy Halfy (Donovan), William Pitt (Dr. Pitt), Dean Turpitt (Dean), Sanders Delhomme (Old Cajun), Richard Thompson (Lenny), Galbert Wanoskie (Indian), William Kern (Old Man)
115 minutes
Color

1979
NORMA RAE
Studio: Twentieth Century Fox
Producers: Tamara Asseyev and Alex Rose
Director: **Martin Ritt**
Screenplay: Irving Ravetch and Harriet Frank Jr.
Director of Photography: John A. Alonzo
Production Design: Walter Scott Herndon
Editor: Sidney Levin
Music: David Shire
Cast: Sally Field (Norma Rae), Beau Bridges (Sonny), Ron Leibman (Reuben), Pat Hingle (Vernon), Barbara Baxley (Leona), Gail Strickland (Bonnie Mae), Morgan Paull (Wayne Billings), Robert Broyles (Sam Bolen), John Calvin (Ellis Harper), Booth Colman (Dr. Watson), Lee DeBroux (Lujan), James Luisi (George Benson), Vernon Weddle (Reverend Hubbard), Gilbert Green (Al London), Bob Minor (Lucius White), Jack Stryker (J. J. Davis), Gregory Walcott (Lamar Miller), Noble Willingham (Leroy Mason), Lonnie Chapman (Gardner), Bert Freed (Sam Dakin), Bob E. Hannah (Jed Buffum), Edith Ivey (Louise Pickens), Scott Lawton (Craig), Frank McRae (James Brown), Gerald

Okuneff (Pinkerton Man), Gina Kay Pounders (Millie), Henry Slate (Policeman), Melissa Ann Wait (Alice)
115 minutes
Color

1981
BACK ROADS
Studio: CBS Theatrical Films/Warner Brothers
Producer: Ronald Shedlo
Director: **Martin Ritt**
Screenplay: Gary DeVore
Photography: John A. Alonzo
Editor: Sidney Levin
Art Direction: Walter Scott Herndon
Music: Henry Mancini
Cast: Sally Field (Amy Post), Tommy Lee Jones (Elmore Pratt), David Keith (Mason), Miriam Colon (Angel), Michael Gazzo (Tazio), Dan Shor (Spivey), M. Emmet Walsh (Arthur), Barbara Babcock (Rickey's Mom), Nell Carter (Waitress), Alex Colon (Enrique), Lee de Broux (Red), Ralph Seymour (Gosler), Royce Applegate (Father), Bruce M. Fischer (Ezra), John Dennis Johnston (Gilly), Don "Red" Barry (Pete), Billy Jacoby (boy Thief), Eric Laneuville (Pinball Wizard), Brian Frishman (Bleitz), Diane Sommerfield (Liz), Henry Slate (Grover), Matthew Campion (Stromberg), Tony Ganios (Bartini). Cherie Brantley (Ellen), John Jackson (Merle)
94 minutes
Color

1983
CROSS CREEK
Studio: Universal
Producer: Robert B. Radnitz
Director: **Martin Ritt**
Screenplay: Dalene Young, based on the memoirs of Marjorie Kinnan Rawlings
Photography: John Alonzo
Editor: Sidney Levin
Production Design: Walter Scott Herndon

Music: Leonard Rosenman
Cast: Mary Steenburgen (Marjorie Kinnan Rawlings), Rip Torn (Marsh Turner), Peter Coyote (Norton Baskin), Dana Hill (Ellie Turner), Alfre Woodard (Geechee), Joanna Miles (Mrs. Turner), Ike Eisenmann (Paul), Cary Guffey (Floyd Turner), Toni Hudson (Tim's Wife), Bo Rucker (Leroy), Jay O. Sanders (Charles Rawlings), John Hammond (Tim), Malcolm McDowell (Maxwell Perkins), Norton Baskin (Man in Rocking Chair)
122 minutes
Color

1985
MURPHY'S ROMANCE
Studio: Columbia Pictures
Executive Producer: **Martin Ritt**
Associate Producer: Jim Van Wyck
Director: **Martin Ritt**
Screenplay: Irving Ravetch and Harriet Frank Jr.
Novel: Max Schott
Production Designer: Joel Schiller
Cinematographer: William A. Fraker
Editor: Sidney Levin
Music: Carole King
Cast: Sally Field (Emma Moriarty), James Garner (Murphy Jones), Brian Kerwin (Bobby Jack Moriarty), Corey Haim (Jake Moriarty), Dennis Burkley (Freeman Coverly), Georgann Johnson (Margaret), Dortha Duckworth (Bessie), Michael Prokopuk (Albert), Billy Ray Sharkey (Larry Le Beau), Michael Crabtree (Jim Forrest), Anna Levine (Wanda), Charles Lane (Amos Abbott), Bruce French (Rex Boyd), John C. Beecher (Jesse Pinker), Henry Slate (Fred Hite), Tom Rankin (Ben), Peggy McCay (Mrs. Willis), Carole King (Tillie), Ted Gehring (Auctioneer), Joshua Ravetch (Henry Boss), C. Ray Cook (Voice at Bingo Game), Eugene Cochran (Jonas), Gene Blakely (Lucius Holt), Sherry Lynn Amorosi (Doris), Patricia Ann Willoughby (Lil), Mike Casper (Hay Trucker), Hugh Burrit (Kid in Car Crash), Michael Firel and Ari Royer (Clerks), Merian Gibson (Mrs. Abbott), Irving Ravetch (Customer), Michael Hungerford, Ron Nix, Johnny Ray Anthony and Paul E. Pinni (Auction Bidders), John Higgenbotham (Boy at Barbecue), Drasha Meyer (Ice Cream Lady)
107 minutes
Color

1987
NUTS
Studio: Warner Brothers
Producer: Barbra Streisand
Director: **Martin Ritt**
Screenplay: Tom Topor, Darryl Ponicsan, and Alvin Sargent, based on the play by Tom Topor
Photography: Andrzej Barikowiak
Editor: Sidney Levin
Art Direction: Joel Schiller
Music: Barbra Streisand
Cast: Barbra Streisand (Claudia Draper), Richard Dreyfuss (Aaron Levinsky), Maureen Stapleton (Rose Kirk, Claudia's mother), Karl Malden (Arthur Kirk), Eli Wallach (Dr. Herbert A. Morrison, psychiatrist), Robert Webber (Francis MacMillian, Prosecuting Attorney), James Whitmore (Judge Stanley Murdoch), Leslie Nielsen (Allen Green), William Prince (Clarence Middleton), Dakin Matthews, Paul Benjamin
116 minutes
Color

1990
STANLEY AND IRIS
Studio: Metro-Goldwyn-Mayer
Executive Producers: Patrick J. Palmer and Arlene Sellers
Associate Producers: Jim Van Wyck and Alex Winitsky
Director: **Martin Ritt**
Screenplay: Irving Ravetch and Harriet Frank Jr.
Novel: *Union Street* by Pat Barker
Photography: Donald McAlpine
Editor: Sidney Levin
Art Direction: Joel Schiller
Music: John Williams
Cast: Jane Fonda (Iris King), Robert De Niro (Stanley Cox), Swoosie Kurtz (Sharon), Martha Plimpton (Kelly), Harley Cross (Richard), Jamey Sheridan (Joe), Feodor Chaliapin Jr. (Leonides Cox), Zohra Lampert (Elaine), Loretta Devine (Bertha), Julie Garfield (Belinda), Karen Ludwig (Melissa), Kathy Kinney (Bernice), Laurel Lyle (Muriel), Mary Testa (Joanne), Katherine Cortez

(Jan), Stephen Root (Mr. Hershey), Eddie Jones (Mr. Hagen), Fred J. Scollay (Mr. Delancey), Dortha Duckworth (Librarian), Jack Gill (The Pursesnatcher), Bob Aaron (Bakery Foreman), Gordon Masten (Oscar Roebuck), Richard Blackburn (Park Ranger), B. J. Reed (Park Ranger), Conrad Bergschneider (Apple Picker Foreman), Guy Sanvido (Man in Car), Michael C. Blackburn (Street Kid), Paul Horruzey (Street Kid), Gerry Quigley (Bellhop)
102 minutes
Color

As Actor Only

1944
WINGED VICTORY
Studio: Twentieth Century Fox
Producer: Darryl F. Zanuck
Director: **George Cukor**
Screenplay: Moss Hart (adapted from his play)
Photography: Glen MacWilliams
Editor: Barbara McLean
Art Direction: Lewis H. Creber and Lyle R. Wheeler
Cast: Jane Ball (Jane Preston), Richard Benedict (Drunken Seaman), Lee J. Cobb (Doctor), Jeanne Crain (Helen), Mark Daniels (Alan Ross), Jo-Carroll Dennison (Dorothy Ross), Peter Lind Hayes (O'Brien), Judy Holliday (Ruth Miller), Lon McCallister (Frankie Davis), Jim Nolan (Stranger on street), Edmond O'Brien (Irving Miller), Anthony Ross (Ross), Don Taylor (Danny "Pinkie" Scariano), Ken Terrell (Man), Gary Merrill (Captain McIntyre), Alan Baxter (Major Halper), Geraldine Wall (Mrs. Ross), Red Buttons [Whitey/Andrews Sister (as Corporal Red Buttons)], George Humbert (Mr. Scariano), Barry Nelson [Bobby Crills (as Corporal Barry Nelson)], Rune Hultman (Dave Anderson), Richard Hogan (Jimmy Gardner), Philip Bourneuf (Colonel Gibney), Damian O'Flynn (Colonel Ross), George Reeves (Lieutenant Thompson), George Petrie (Barker), Alfred Ryder (Milhauser), Karl Malden (Adams), **Martin Ritt** (Gleason), Harry Lewis (Cadet Peter Clark), Ray Bidwell (Officer), Henry Rowland (Flight surgeon), Carroll Riddle (Captain Speer), Sascha Brastofff (Carmen Miranda), Archie Robbins (Master of ceremonies), Jack Slate (Andrews Sister), Henry Slate (Andrews Sister), Timmy Hawkins (Irving Jr.), Moyna MacGill (Mrs. Gardner), Don Beddoe (Man), Frances

Gladwin (WAC), Sally Yarnell (Cigarette girl), Kevin McCarthy (Ronnie Meade), Mario Lanza (Chorus member)
130 minutes
Black and White

1976
THE END OF THE GAME (DER RICHTER UND SEIN HENKEG)
Studio: Twentieth Century Fox
Producers: Maximillian Schell and Arlene Sellers
Director: Maximillian Schell
Screenplay: Friedrich Duerrenmatt, Bo Goldmann, Maximillian Schell, based on the novel *The Judge and His Hangman* by Duerrenmatt
Photography: Ennio Guarniari, Robert Gerardi, and Klaus Loenig
Editor: Dagmar Hirtz
Art Direction: Mario Garbuglia
Cast: Jon Voight (Walter Tachonitz), Jacqueline Bisset (Anna Crawley), **Martin Ritt** (Hans Borach), Robert Shaw (Richard Gastmann), Helmut Qualtinger (Von Schwendi), Gabriele Ferzetti (Dr. Lutz), Rita Calderoni (Nadine), Friedrich Duerrenmatt (Friedrich), Willy Huegll (Clanin), Norbert Schiller (Dr. Hungertobel), Guido Cerniglia (Coroner), Margarethe Schell von Noe (Mrs. Schoener), Otto Ryser (Blotter), Rudolf Hunsperger, Edy Hubacher (Guards), Pinchas Zukerman (Violinist), Lil Dagover (Mrs. Gatesman), Toni Roth (Old Lady), Wigland Liebske (Taxi Driver), Anton Netzer (Dr. Schallert), Kathrin Brunner (Cleaning Girl)
106 minutes
Color

1985
THE SLUGGER'S WIFE
Studio: Columbia Pictures
Producer: Ray Stark
Director: Hal Ashby
Screenplay: Neil Simon
Photography: Caleb Deschanel
Editors: George Villasenor and Don Brochu
Production Design: J. Michael Riva
Art Direction: Rich Carter

Music: Quincy Jones, Glen Bellard, Cliff Magness, Carole Bayer-Sager
Cast: Michael O'Keefe (Darryl Palmer), Rebecca De Mornay (Debby Palmer), **Martin Ritt** (Burley De Vito), Randy Quaid (Goose Granger), Cleavani Derricks (Manny Alvarado), Lisa Langlois (Aline Cooper), Loudon Wainwright (Gary), Georgann Johnson (Marie De Vito), Danny Tucker (Coach O'Brien), Lynn Whitfield (Tina Alvarado), Al Garrison (Guard), Nicandra Hood (Nurse), Ginger Taylor (Sherry), Kay McClelland (Peggy), Julie Kemp (Paloma), Tina Kincaid, Martha Harrison and Becky Pate (Baseball Wives), Dennis Burkley (Chuck), Alisha Das (Lola), Dan Biggers (Preacher), Justine Thielemann (Iris Granger), Marc Clement (Mr. Davis), Richard Alan Reiner (Patron at Zelda's), Valerie Mitchell (Waitress at Limelight), Edwin H. Cipot (Cuneo), Stephen H. Stier (Varsity Patron), David R. Yood (Cop in Varsity), Wallace G. Merck (Fan in Limelight), Johnny B. Watson Jr. (Gateman), Alex Hawkins (Hawkins), Mort Scwartz (Man), John B. Sierling (Himself), George Stokes (Stage Manager), Harmon L. Wages (Interviewer), John W. Bradley (Himself), Jerome Olds (Musician), Erby Walker, Philipe Fonranelli (Waiters), Steve Daniels Jr., Henry J. Rountree, George Jack Karman, Colin Fagan, David M. Pallone (Umpires), Kevin James Barnes (Public Address), John Lawhorn (Coach Reckan), Douglas Garland Nave, Bill G. Fite (Catchers), Al Hrobosky, Mark Fidrych (Baseball Players), Pete Van Wiesen, Ernie Johnson (Baseball Narrators), Skip Caray, Nick Charles (Sportscasters), Chico Renvoe, Anthony Peck, Corey B. McPherrin, Paul S. Ryden, Charles Darden, Hohn Buren Solberg, Brad Nessler (Reporters)
105 minutes
Color

MARTIN RITT
INTERVIEWS

Ritt for the Record on Direction

HOWARD THOMPSON/1958

MARTIN RITT says movies, not motion pictures,—and means it. To the surprised interest of Hollywood, and in a relatively short time, the director has firmly established himself as a man to watch, with three films that definitely moved: *Edge of the City, No Down Payment* and the current *The Long, Hot Summer*. The comparative newcomer to the screen has this to say about his work:

"I love the movies. I always have. It's that simple."

Ritt headed West last summer as a well-known actor-director on Broadway and television, steeped in the stagecraft he also taught at the Actors Studio, and proceeded to uncork a real film flair almost overnight. Paradoxically, the man who charged *The Long, Hot Summer* with such genuine, all-Southern electricity is a former butcher's assistant in the Bronx. The native New Yorker also was and looks like a physical education instructor turned star halfback and, briefly, law student (St. John's University, Brooklyn). Ritt is a husky fellow of medium height, whose speech balances imagination with plain horse sense. Levelling a steady glance through horn-rimmed glasses, he talks swiftly, with the leathery articulation of a realistic dreamer.

Although Ritt directed three Broadway plays *(Mr. Peebles and Mr. Hooker, The Man,* and *Set My People Free),* appeared in more than 100 television shows and directed another 100, it was his staging of Arthur Miller's *A View from the*

Originally published in *The New York Times* (June 1, 1958). Reprinted by permission of *The New York Times.*

Bridge that won him a three-year contract at Twentieth Century-Fox. Ritt puts it succinctly:

"Theirs was the best deal," he admits, with a smile and a shrug.

The new directorial pride and joy of Fox stopped briefly in town recently en route to Europe. His itinerary included as a first stop a place "somewhere near" Vienna where he expects to confer with Yul Brynner and Arthur Koestler on the actor's forthcoming independent version of the latter's novel, *The Gladiators*. Upon returning to this country, he will swing through the Deep South starting at Savannah, Ga., scouting locations for an adaptation of William Faulkner's *The Sound and the Fury* (also starring Mr. Brynner).

Was Hollywood, he was asked bluntly, all that he expected—pro and con? "Pretty much," he said after a moment. "The conflict you hear about—the traditional conflict of the real creators and the money-handlers—is partially true. But it makes a director work harder than, say, here on Broadway, where the traditional rehearsals for a play are such a tremendous help. Hollywood is a commercial place; but so is any successful business. The important thing, creatively, is for a director to have fun. I mean just that—to enjoy what he's doing. I've managed to do so in all my pictures so far, but I love pictures anyway. There's your compensation for any drawbacks. There's no comparison between the visual scope of movies and the stage—what you can actually show with a camera and what you can only suggest in front of the footlights."

Ritt wryly admits that the fate of his first picture, Metro-Goldwyn-Mayer's *Edge of the City*, came close to cooling his present enthusiasm after its production here in 1956. Ritt directed the waterfront drama on a one-picture deal.

"The studio didn't even want to release it," he recalls. "It wasn't even on the release list. The reviews were good, though, and I was particularly pleased when the picture and Sid (Sidney Poitier) were nominated by the London Academy. I liked the picture, too. Why? Well, it moved me; I like anything that moves me to laughter or tears."

"I'll tell you something about *Summer*," he said, smiling. "A lot of people didn't realize there was a hell of a lot of bravura acting in that picture. It didn't seem so because the performances fitted into each other—even Orson Welles, a brilliant, moody player who's usually his own island. Most of the young people were former Actors Studio students, using a certain kind of training. We understood each other—that was the advantage—like orchestra players knowing the tastes of a conductor."

He was asked to analyze the Oscar-winning talents of Joanne Woodward, who had previously worked for him in *No Down Payment*. What she has, as a player and a person, is a sort of dead honesty. She's a star. In the old days all you had to have was sex appeal; now a star has to work hard. It's not easy." "As for *Sound and the Fury*, I've always been a real Faulkner bug. We've now made it a conventional story but preserved the basic quality." Was it indicative that all three of his pictures to date were fairly grim in content? "I don't agree," he said equably. "Take *Summer*, now—it's juicy and funny and adult. A perfect subtitle would have been 'in praise of appetite.' Is that grim? I like all kinds of material, but I'd like to find something deeply sunny. I like to reflect what I feel in my pictures. To me, that's why people like Arthur Miller and Tennessee Williams are great artists: their work reflects their own personalities. The same holds true, invariably, for the best American movie directors—Willie Wyler, Kazan—and foreigners like Fellini. When this happens—and it takes years to get your own real perspective—you realize what the movies can do like nothing else: open up a gate to nature.

American Film Institute Seminar: Conversation with Martin Ritt

AMERICAN FILM INSTITUTE/1974

JAMES POWERS: *Leroy McDonald knows Mr. Ritt well from working on one of his films, Leroy is chairing the seminar. Leroy?*
LEROY McDONALD: I'd just had the good fortune as Jim pointed out of spending about six months working with Mr. Ritt on the production of *Conrack*. One of the things that I discovered was that I could ask him anything and he always tried to answer them. I'd like to first of all ask you Marty, what is it that actually attracts you to your material? On what basis do you actually make your choices about what you want to do?
MARTIN RITT: The most important thing I think for any creative person is that he or she must be moved either emotionally—preferably emotionally—or intellectually. There is some material that in the course of my career has affected intellectually, that I decided to do because I felt it was serious material. Although when it has really failed commercially, when it has failed to get to a mass audience, it has failed primarily because it didn't get them emotionally or gut-wise. I think that's the best. You pick up something, which affects you. You read it. And that's the picture you should make. What affects you. The whole key to the creative process is the release of the subjective, because the subjective is the only thing any of us have that's genuinely original. And any cerebral idea that we come up with, we've either gotten from other films, other novels, other plays, somewhere in the civilized world. What is terribly personal is the subjective and the release of the subjective is

---

Reprinted by permission of the American Film Institute.

the key to any artist, because it is totally *his* interior, totally *his* darkness, totally his light and therefore, when I pick up a piece of material which moves me, which gets to me, I feel that that is the material that will release me and therefore, that is what I choose to do. Release is the game. When you see a very good singer of songs, a very good dancer working and you see the music literally course through their veins, you know that they have made a total relation to the object and the subjective is coming out. And that is style at its best, because it is not superimposed. It does not come from an idea, which no matter how clever, you have somehow cribbed in your life experience from somebody else. It comes from something which has affected you and which in a certain way, you have no control over, which is what makes it great. When actors are at their best, when writers are at their best, when directors are at their best, it's when that happens. Yes?

TED LANGE: *Being that today is 1974 and attitudes have changed, people have gone through an evolution here in this country, what particularly do you see that released your subconscious, that hit you, that made you want to do this response, made you want to make this film, [Conrack] especially being how attitudes are of black people towards white people and the whole white god concept of someone coming in.*

MARTIN RITT: I've been around a long time and I've been a very political fellow in my lifetime and I know that politics change and I don't remember who it was that said that fashion is the bastard son of the arts, but it's a very apt phrase. I don't try to be fashionable or to go with the current political thought or current artistic thought. I really don't try. I have learned to trust myself. But if I feel that it's right and I feel that it's human and I feel that it's perceptive, then it can't be wrong. It may not suit the purpose of everybody at the particular time that I make the film, but I can't go any further than that. If I felt, because I had a sense that this might come up in relation to *Conrack,* if I felt really that it was injurious or bad, if I didn't feel in some cases it was black special plea, all that rubble, I wouldn't have done the film. I was aware that this might come in, in this kind of discussion might erupt out of this film, but I felt that fundamentally the film was so full of love that a partisan point of view on the black level or the white level would be special pleading and I really wasn't interested.

TED LANGE: *But it's one side of it and that's a distortion. That love is distorted.*
MARTIN RITT: I don't think it's one-sided because I think he commits himself to the kids, as he did. And they commit themselves to him. There's nothing one-sided about that. The film is a love story between twenty-one black kids and a white man.

TED LANGE: *I never saw a give and take relationship between the black children and the white man. I saw this white man giving knowledge to ignorant blacks on how to spell, how to talk, how to listen to music and interpret what is the current thought and what halloween is, but I never saw what this white man learned from the children. Where was the communication? I saw a one-sided thing. Could you elaborate on what you were trying to do there?*
MARTIN RITT: Yes, I feel that with a bunch of kids that are totally deprived, a man came in and committed himself to them. He gave them love and he gave them understanding. And taught them that they could be loved by a white man, that a white man would commit himself to their cause, as this boy did, aware all the time that there was an incipient paternalism in the relationship. I was aware of that. And yet, I decided to do the film, because I think it was better than not doing it, because I do know that I also know certain things about Conrack, things that he's done subsequently. But I'll tell you, I worked around a play called *Death of a Salesman*. It was one of my first jobs. And I remember—there were many, many stories—but I do remember one specific thing that happened opening night. A couple did walk out on that play—I presume you all know that play—and the husband turned to his wife and said, "I always told you that New England territory was no good." That's what he got out of the play. Now, what you're getting out of the picture, it comes again from your subjective and from your life style and everything you feel about it and I don't—

TED LANGE: *—it comes from twenty—or ten or fifteen—years of watching movies, first as a person and then, seeing images of black kids depicted on a screen and me, looking for my images, as an actor, when I was an actor, or as an actor, being interested in films and theatre. What I'm talking about is, your film is, I think it's a very polished film. I think it's technically a very beautiful film. However also, I think it's a very degrading film for blacks and I respond only from what I see over the years. I mean, we talk about black exploitation films. I think this is a white exploitation film for white people, to come see and feel very good about a white*

man that goes into the South to educate some black kids out of the kindness of his heart. Then after he gets fired, he leaves and there is a little bit about Beethoven, never discussing that Beethoven was black or that black people feel that Beethoven was black, never really exploring the black experience or what these kids—
MARTIN RITT: —that's another picture. Which you should make, if you can make and if you can get the—

TED LANGE: —if you were producing, maybe I would make it. I'm not opposed to white people going in and teaching blacks, but I am opposed to a one-sided view of the greatness of me, stepping down to—
MARTIN RITT: —this film could be made with a black teacher going into white Appalachia, because the same conditions exist there.

TED LANGE: They did it with To Sir, with Love, but then, you explore the kids. You explore Sidney Poitier and then, you show the kids. He had a beautiful, beautiful opening with the thirteen-year-old girl coming from her element and him, coming from his, with the music and the flowers and this girl, waking up in a shack and going out and taking crabs out of the sea, but they never came together. I saw what this white man gave this black girl. He taught her how to cook and he taught her values. He gave her some values, but she already had a history of her own. And I'm sure she must have given this man something.
MARTIN RITT: Don't you think he got something from the midwife he spoke with early?

TED LANGE: Yes, but you see, it was never shown. And that's what my argument is. It was never shown in the film what this man got from the community.
MARTIN RITT: I don't believe that. I don't feel it.

TED LANGE: Could you say to me what was shown?
MARTIN RITT: As I say, I don't want to make a polemic about the film.

TED LANGE: I don't either, but I just want you to say to me so that—
MARTIN RITT: Yes, I felt that it was a love story. And in all successful love stories and the few that I've been associated with in my life, personal and artistic, when there wasn't some give and take, they didn't work. And if there was no give and take in the film, then the film didn't work. That is not what happens to audiences who see the film, black audiences included. I mean,

we have had quite a few black people who have come to see the film, who have not had—

TED LANGE: —*I'm not asking that. You said that you felt that you showed it. I would like you to tell me how you showed it. I'm saying that I didn't see it and maybe you could show me where I missed something and the next time I view the film, I'll say, "Oh, I should—"*
MARTIN RITT: —well, he did go in and confront the authority in terms of their rights to do certain things. He did commit himself on that level and they really didn't show him a great deal. I think that is true. I don't know what it is they could have shown him. If you're talking about the culture of the island, for instance which in some ways you reflect by speaking about the way she awakened. The culture of the island was really quite degrading. I didn't want to spend any time with it.

JAMES FONER: —*Did Conrack change as a result of his*—
MARTIN RITT: Yes, I think he did change.

ALEX LASKER: *I think he was the same when he came and the same when he left. The same man.*
MARTIN RITT: No, I think he did change. I think finally he was much more aware of the situation. He didn't know anything when he came to that island. He had no notion of what he was going to encounter. He was actually a middle-class Catholic from a Marine family, who would go to the Citadel and play basketball there and met a Jewish boy there who said to him when he found out that we were cutting him out of the picture, he said, "The picture can't be any goddamn good, if I'm not in it." And Bernie . . . is his name, because he's in the material, if you happen to read the book. And I think he did learn. He did learn. He had no notion. He had never taken a position in his life, which would cost him a job. He went back into Beaufort—that's where the end of the film is—that was before the book came out and got any kind of press in the New York *Times*—and lived in that town and finished his biography in a year and we bought it.

TED LANGE: *I think that's a beautiful Horatio Alger story. I think I should go live in Beverly Hills and write a book about my experience with white kids and*

publish a book on it and leave Beverly Hills forever and make a mint. But you see, what I'm saying is—
MARTIN RITT: —well, if you can do it—

TED LANGE: —*in most stories, you do see a change and if he was as moved as he was, he would have come back on weekends at least to help them love Mozart.*
MARTIN RITT: What he did was take every penny he got and left it for all the kids when they reached majority, so they could go to college. Every one of those kids got a thousand dollars out of the money he got for the book. Now, we didn't want to carry it any further because we'd have him on a cross by that time, which is your assumption anyway.

LEROY McDONALD: *When dealing with a film based on fact, how much do you feel obligated to change those facts or re-arrange them for dramatic purposes? In other words, I'm asking you, how much leeway did you have?*
MARTIN RITT: We took a great deal of leeway, because it was a biography and it was not a dramatic piece of writing and so, we took a great deal of leeway on that level. The other kind of leeway, there's a limit to what you can take, because you're going to be sued. There's a limit to what you can say if people are alive, one of the reasons why I have never done a biography is that there is a limit to what you can say about people who are alive and whose lives you are depicting. But I don't mean to cop a plea on that basis. It's not because we didn't want to say—we said what we wanted to say. I think the film will be judged on that basis and I think it will either fail or succeed on that basis.

LEROY McDONALD: *There was a point when I think I came to you and asked you, did you want to consider maybe getting into accents more in terms of dealing with that kind of thing that was a prevalent language off the coast of South Carolina, on the island. And you said no. What was your reason for not wanting to deal with that?*
MARTIN RITT: When I started to do *Sounder* and I had Ken Hooks in the film and the first week's rehearsal I asked him to play around with a southern accent and I so inhibited the kid that I decided at that point that I wouldn't waste any time and if I had to sacrifice anything in order to maintain the relationship with his father and mother and keep everything truthful, I would. In this film I immediately removed the parts that had been written

and I named every kid in the film by his own name. So I had immediate contact. If I said, Susie, she answered. If I said, Jimmy, he answered. So I would not under any stretch of the imagination with unprofessional people try to force them into a theatrical straitjacket, which would be an accent or anything else on that level. So that they were all able to do what they were about. So whatever personalities they had, they could get a release on, as I mentioned earlier on, and we would see what the sweetness was or anger or whatever. That's why I would never bother. Those are highly sophisticated things to do, even for experienced actors. I would never bother inexperienced or amateurs, in this case. Absolute amateurs. But with those problems, they never would have been able to play the part.

NEIL SENTURIA: *Could you discuss story structure? The structure of the film, particularly* Hud *and* Conrack. *My question about* Hud *is about the last twenty minutes. The shape of the film in the screenplay, what you did with it, and the total piece, meaning wherever it hits the curve, the highlights, the punch.*

MARTIN RITT: I'm not sure I remember that clearly, but I'll try to tell you what we did do with that film. We had decided that we were going to take—that was the old kind of film that Gable played a shitheel for the first half of the film and then always turned around to be a rather decent guy. We said, "Let's carry that man, addicted to appetite, which is a very strong American type, right through to its logical conclusion. And we couldn't get the picture off the ground. We had Paul Newman and we couldn't get it off the ground. MCA, who was then handling Paul, said, "You can't play this guy. He's a heel." Somehow or other, because of my ineffable charm, I finally seduced Mr. Newman into playing that part, but the structure of that—Hud was not a character by the way, in the book. The book was a lyric novel, rather beautifully written about the growing up of a boy and his experience with his grandfather. And somewhere hidden in the novel, in one chapter, was a guy, kind of a brawling, Hud, who hung around the barracks. He was one of the hands. And the weakness in that screenplay, in my opinion, was the fortuitous death of the father—of the grandfather—and we had to get to a situation where it was that split. We had to split the generation of Hud and the kid.

NEIL SENTURIA: *When you say fortuitous death, for me, the death is fine. My question is the last twenty minutes. I had the feeling that the placement of the death—I don't know whether it was right or wrong; that isn't what I'm talking about. But you must have had a reason for putting it where you did. Somehow, the last ten minutes, I wanted more. That's what I meant. I'm not objecting to the death but where it was.*

MARTIN RITT: There was no way that we could break the kid off from Hud, without an act of that magnitude. And I had a terrible experience with that film. When the film was finished and it was a success, I got lots of letters from kids in the United States, supporting Hud. And if I had been really smart, I would have understood what was going on in this country and would have been able to deal with the next ten years, which I've dealt with rather ineffectively on certain levels, except with my own kids. I thought we were creating a major heel and the kids all said Hud was right. They didn't like the kid; they didn't like the grandfather. They liked the picture, because of that heel, right in the middle of the picture. Again it's not at all what I intended and that's really what happened. That insolent, appetite-ridden, but of course, terribly attractive. Now the reason he was terribly attractive, we felt we would never make the film work, if he had been played by anybody darker in interior terms than Paul Newman. We felt he would be such a heel that we wouldn't be able to maintain him in the early part of the film.

GREY McCARTY: *That was interesting, whose point of view Hud was from. It was from the boy's point of view I guess, right?*
MARTIN RITT: Yes.

GREG McCARTY: *But it's kind of interesting, at the end, you end it with Hud, going back into the house when the boy is gone. For some reason, that left me with Hud. And that's kind of why I stayed with him, rather than the boy.*
MARTIN RITT: It's very difficult, particularly today and it's one of the things I do like about *Conrack* very much, it's very difficult to make an affirmative film, without making a namby-pamby film. It's very difficult, because the real vigor in the world and in the country is against the establishment. It's not for the establishment. And even though the kid himself was not for the establishment, he was a lyric note and we felt if we made a lyric film at that point, two million, four, we'd never make another film. We could have stayed with the boy. We chose the other way, because also, we felt the other was more original. And we wanted to make this film work. We wanted it to be a success. And we felt that we should stay and show this guy and this

kind of America is still around, remains, is not defeated and is a constant enemy. That's really what we wanted to say.

INA MAE: *Getting back to* Hud, *I was wondering, when you were working with Newman, did you—because the whole time I was watching him, it's like, he was sympathetic. It's Newman. He's that way. The way he looks, his eyes, his hand, and your heart goes out to him, but he's a complete bastard and you hate him, but at the same token, all he has to do is throw that look at you and everyone goes, "What don't we really see? What is his inner turmoil? What are we missing?" And when you worked with him as an actor, did you feel that you were getting the heel? Or did you sometimes feel that you were . . .?*
MARTIN RITT: Most effective bastards are like that. Otherwise they're not very effective. He had to be very attractive and very charming. The things he had to do—you know a man finally by what he does, not by what he says or how blue his eyes are. So if Hud continues to do as he does through the film, he must wind up a heel, despite the fact that he's terribly attractive.

INA MAE: *That isn't what I was talking about. I mean, the looking at him of the character and I love Larry McMurtry and I was wondering, where was that shot?*
MARTIN RITT: Right outside of Amarillo.

INA MAE: *That was just curiosity, but like the scene when he has it out with his father and he comes in and he looks like he's crushed, but all the time, you think he doesn't give a damn.*
MARTIN RITT: I don't think he does give a damn.

INA MAE: *You don't think he does give a damn.*
MARTIN RITT: No.

INA MAE: *But I know myself, part of the time, I wondered, does he? Or is it just complete selfishness?*
MARTIN RITT: That's what he is. That's what we were trying to do. That's the kind of man we wanted to show. We wanted not to spit in the first reel. If you had, say, I don't know—I don't want to mention another actor. If you had an actor who had a lot of those really heavy brutish qualities, I don't think he'd get beyond the first reel in that character. Philosophically, the whole Marxian concept of the unity of opposites is very interesting theatri-

cally. And any actor that is at the same time very big and very graceful has something so theatrically available to a director at that point because of the opposite things that exist in him. Those things exist in Paul too. And we—the Ravetches and myself—really understood that very early in his career.

RICHARD ROSENTHAL: *I found that although it was obviously Newman's picture, it was really, for me, only Newman's picture by a hair. I wonder if you could talk about the focus in films on one character or on many characters.*
MARTIN RITT: It depends on what story you want to tell. We felt that it was the story of Hud. It was the story of a heel. Now he was into some—particularly Patricia Neal who is a super actress and had a marvelous part. Now that woman in the novel was a black woman. And again, we decided that we didn't think we could make it work at that place in time. My first film was a little film called *Edge of the City,* which dealt with the relationship between a black and white man, Poitier and Cassavetes. It opened to great notices and it cost four hundred and fifty thousand dollars and we have not gotten that money back yet. That's eighteen years ago. I thought I was digging myself an early grave. I managed to do that anyway, even trying to make commercial pictures. But it really was the story of Hud. We took a lot of things into consideration. We decided that what was original in that film was to tell the story of a heel. An American heel. A classic American heel. Because he's the most admired kind of man in that part of the world.

LEROY McDONALD: *Could I get you to talk a little bit about casting? I heard you talk about how important it is to you and rather than ask a leading question, could you just discuss casting as you cast a film?*
MARTIN RITT: Eighty percent of getting a really good performance is casting the right actor, I think. And casting is kind of an educated guess. It's a gut reaction again to actors. I really feel that the performance that Voight gives in *Conrack* is one of the most extraordinary performances that a young actor has given in American films because it's even a trifle away from the kind of realistic, solid, American performance that we've come to expect. It has antic qualities. It has a kind of joyousness. He has allowed himself to be possessed by the part in a certain way. That's just a guess. I felt that about him. I never knew that about him. I had never seen it in him any place. But I felt that about him and I was right. I have been wrong. But casting is always an educated guess.

LEROY McDONALD: *I asked you once what you look for when an actor that you haven't seen on the screen comes in to read for you, what do you look for in a new actor? And you talked a little bit about whether an actor can do more than one thing.*

MARTIN RITT: I have taught acting. Or have in the past, taught for many years. And I finally devised a series of exercises, which really finally told me how good an actor was, that is, separate from the charisma or the kind of personality that he has. If I say to an actor, "Sit down," he does that. Then I say, "Sit down and pour yourself a cup of coffee," he does that. If I say, "Sit down, pour yourself a cup of coffee, you know that you're going to have an affair with a girl who's in the next room and you're just kind of playing it cool until she comes out of the next room." That's three things. Then I pose the same dilemma and say at the same time, "Your wife is liable to come into the house in fifteen minutes." I can finally complicate the scene so that nobody in the world can play it. But when an actor can play five or six things at the same time, you have a fair shot as a director at any idea that you might ever get, because he's able to do it. There are many, many ways to train actors to do all kinds of things which are fascinating. You can give them exercises and you can do that even in a film. You can make it impossible for them to play a scene by posing certain problems in the scene and because you made it impossible, the first time around, the second time around, they'll play the scene brilliantly. You would simply set up the scene with, "The whole tendency of the scene is that, I want you to move your finger once every three minutes in the scene. You understand? I don't want it to move that way. And as you do that to him—" And the whole inner thing grows and the whole physical rhythm has been changed in some way, you can force—it's like those exercises that athletes do. There are emotional isometrics. The whole game is complication. The whole game is the various levels on which an actor or director or a writer can exist. And as I say, if you can get an actor or a director or a writer to exist on three or four levels, then you've got something very interesting, very complicated and very good. Texture, unless you're doing melodramas, if you're doing serious films, the texture of the people is the most important thing.

JOEL NORWOOD: *In your film,* The Molly Maguires, *I understand it wasn't a financial success.*

MARTIN RITT: That's the kindest remark of the evening.

JOEL NORWOOD: *Can you tell me what you think was wrong with the film?*
MARTIN RITT: I think that what I didn't do in the film was give the audience a simple enough person to root for. I don't think they knew whose side they should be on. I knew whose side I wanted them to be on, because it was a reflection of my experience during those lonely McCarthy days. And I knew that that man was a man I despised. But unlike the case of *Hud,* I think that's why it failed. I mean, I don't know why it failed. But I *think* that's why it failed, because the audience didn't understand the film and didn't know what they were supposed to feel.

LEROY McDONALD: *Are you saying then that you have to simplify those things?*
MARTIN RITT: I don't know. I really don't know. I love the film. I would say, it's one of my favorite films. And it was such a bad failure, I couldn't get onto the lot the next time. After that picture opened, I couldn't get back onto the Paramount lot. It lost everything. We didn't get back anything on that picture.

LEROY McDONALD: *Could you talk a little bit about preparation. I know it depends from one film to another, but as I said, I went through some of the preproduction stages of the film and could you talk a little bit about your approach?*
MARTIN RITT: I prepare every film very carefully. You know, with twenty to twenty-five, thirty thousand dollars a day, you better prepare. The most important preparation is the detailed preparation—for me, it varies with every director—of how I'm going to tell the story and what point I want to make. I don't really pre-stage anything except action sequences, because I don't want to ever inhibit the actors to the point where they feel they don't have enough freedom to move in the set or within the psychology of the scene. I just don't like it. Also, I try not to do those kind of scripts. Occasionally, there's quite a few things in this film that were improvised because of the fun we were having together. And some of the lines are Jon's. I mean, "Don't spit on the teacher" is Jon's line. Some of the lines in the gravity scene were his lines. They came out of the play. But I think every film has to be prepared very carefully. In terms of the style of the film, in terms of what you really want to do. If I do *First Blood* which it now begins to look like I

will, that is a big violent melodrama and it's going to have a whole different way of shooting. I don't impose a style on a film. I think style is a result of content and depending on the kind of film I do, I think the style of the film will vary. By preparation, I mean, you will know when you begin to direct a film that it's twenty-four hours a day. You just will not sleep. You go home at the end of the day and you know that you've done at least thirty or forty percent of the things wrong and you lay there and you make one long distance phone call to your family and then, you just lay there, until finally, you fall asleep from fatigue. You get up in the morning and you go back to work. It's not fun. I don't think it's fun. It's very painful, because you're terribly exposed and you're wrong as often as you're right. And everybody sees it. If you're writing a screenplay or a book or if you're directing a play, you have a chance to fix. Or maybe as Mr. Friedkin did on *The Exorcist*, reshoot, but ordinarily, those things don't exist. And you have to make a right guess that time. The minute you make that first decision, you're in trouble. You said, "Put it here." From then on in, you're in terrible trouble.

NEIL SENTURIA: *Do you storyboard? And when you say, "Put it here," do you map out your shots prior to your day's work?*
MARTIN RITT: Only in action sequences, where I have matching problems. Sometimes, I may use two or three cameras. No.

NEIL SENTURIA: *You say no to storyboarding also?*
MARTIN RITT: I never do. I did it once and I got my comeuppance and rightfully so, I feel.

Q: *How do you prepare with the actors?*
MARTIN RITT: I rehearse. And what I do is I try to rehearse for about two weeks, when I can, if the film makes it possible. Some films don't because they're so fragmented. But when a film makes it possible, I rehearse. But what rehearsal is for really is not to get them to play the scene because they're not going to play the scenes, in most cases, for three or four or six weeks. But just to put them in a kind of atmosphere where they can live and since they don't have that day by day rehearsal that one has in the theatre, they know from where they're going to where they're going. Now if I do *First Blood*, I don't have to shoot that film because of the nature of the film, for the first time in my life, happens absolutely in sequence, because there's an enormous chase and who the hell knows what he's going to look like when he falls through trees. Nobody's going to know. The main character is a Congressional Medal

of Honor winner, who is going through a small town in Oregon or California and he's picked up for vagrancy and they take him to the outskirts of town and he's told to keep moving and he comes back. He comes back three times. And the sheriff who's trying to control himself, finally is forced to arrest the kid. And they take the kid downstairs and they're going to give him a bath and cut his hair and shave his beard. And the minute they touch him, he explodes. And you realize you're dealing with—you don't realize it there; you do later on—almost an ace killer, trained by the Green Berets, *cum laude* graduate of violence, who is really trying to get some warmth and meet a girl and is not able to deal at all with what exists in this country. That's what the film is about. And an enormous chase starts in the middle of which is the man who trained him, the head of the Green Berets, because the kid kills everybody. They can't deal with him. He's in the same kind of country he was. He's dealing with small town cops—authoritarian fools—and one by one, he's picking them off.

TED LANGE: *I'd like to ask you a question about why you make films. You say it's not fun. Then why do you make films?*
MARTIN RITT: Because I have to express myself in some way. I stopped making speeches when I got my head kicked in a couple of times, so now I'm making films. I was an actor. Now I want to express myself. It's painful because it's difficult. It's very difficult to make a film. Particularly if it doesn't work. And I've been to that well.

LEROY McDONALD: *You say you stopped making speeches when you got your head kicked in. Would you talk about some of the kicks as a filmmaker?*
MARTIN RITT: I had my share. I've had my share of all of those along the line and I've had enough to pull my own weight in this room.

JEFF RUSH: *Can you speculate a little bit about the politics of* Conrack *again as to whether it might be either a script or an acting problem in that there's no point at all in which Jon Voight as an actor or the character in the script ever stops, which is traditionally the way a character comes to terms with his environment? Isn't that maybe part of what Ted is objecting to?*
MARTIN RITT: I know what Ted's objecting to. I'm not arguing with him because I think there is an element of truth in what he says and I was not unaware of it. I just felt the other thing is more important. And it finally

outweighed the other factor. And it will for some people and obviously, it will not for some others.

JEFF RUSH: *But when you dealt with the script, didn't you feel it needed a few moments where the character was ready to give up or he couldn't talk them into liking his things?*
MARTIN RITT: No, no. No, I felt he would try and try and try until they killed him, or fired him in this case.

TED LANGE: *I'd like to ask you a question about adapting plays to the screen. What are the problems and what are the—*
MARTIN RITT: —don't do it. They're really a different medium. A good play is written in the heat of the immediacy of time and place. Film's a totally different kind of experience and even, you know, you saw some very good plays in that series that Mr. Landau produced, but it's just very difficult. Actually, I like them better when they're done as plays, because if you try to open them up so-called, you tend to vitiate the impact and the force of a playwright and if he's a good one, you're ripping it apart. It doesn't really work. Excuse me, it doesn't work in today's market where everybody is so sophisticated about film.

Q: *What about Olivier's* Henry V?
MARTIN RITT: Well, Shakespeare is always an exception and Olivier is kind of an exception too. I was not really myself wild about the film, but I love Olivier.

NEIL SENTURIA: *We've been here over an hour but we neglected to mention* Sounder *which was probably the first major non-black exploitative film.*
MARTIN RITT: There were quite a few blacks that didn't like *Sounder*.

NEIL SENTURIA: *But it was a Hollywood—well, if you'd tell the story about it—*
MARTIN RITT: I had an actor—quite a good young black actor in New York—come to me, who said to me, "I don't want to know if my mother did any laundry." This was on the *Today* show. And I said, "Buddy, you win, go ahead." That was it. They didn't like it, because—they didn't like it partially and we had to face that too—because a black man didn't do it.

NEIL SENTURIA: *But it was a Hollywood movie, that was the first one that was different than the genre of* Black Belt Jones.
MARTIN RITT: Yes, on that level, many considered *Sounder* to be an exploitation movie because I was smart enough to do that kind of movie at that time. Who the hell knew—

NEIL SENTURIA: *—How did you come to get that financed and do it?*
MARTIN RITT: Very easily. I'll tell you that. I had just done *The Molly Maguires* and *The Great White Hope*. Both of them failed. And I didn't want to make another big picture. Radnitz called me one day and sent me this novel. He said, "I can't pay you anything." I took an eighty percent cut. I liked the book. It was written by a white man. I was very moved by the book. I had no notion that the picture would be a success at all, even when I saw it. We did the picture for nine hundred thousand dollars. I looked at the picture with my wife, when it was finished. I said, "It won't make a nickel. There's no sex; there's no violence in it." Sixty percent of that audience—and on this level, the blacks point with a certain finger—was white. Only forty percent of the audience that supported that film was black. In cities like Toronto and Minneapolis, where there are two or three percent blacks, the picture did enormous business. It was not really a black picture. Now a lot of blacks did support the picture. A lot of blacks will support *Conrack*. The entire middle class black population will support *Conrack*. They will like the film.

TED LANGE: *Let's wait. I'd rather say, let's wait.*
NEIL SENTURIA: But to go onward with *Sounder*, particularly Paul Winfield and Cicely Tyson. I mean, they had both been actors on the stage, but this was a major film break for them, wasn't it?
MARTIN RITT: It was. I had offered that part to another actress, who I shall not name. She turned it down. Cicely was going to play the schoolteacher. And she said, "I can play the other part." And I said, "Gee, you're too beautiful, Ciss." And so on and so forth. And she convinced me, so I gave her the part. Winfield came in and read for me and I just felt he was a first class actor. I had seen him play these small parts and both of them heavies. But I just felt there was something in him that was worth taking a shot and we took a shot. In both cases, we took a shot. I had seen Cicely in the Genet play, *The Blacks*, some years ago in New York and remembered her with admiration, but I had no notion she could play the kind of woman she played.

NEIL SENTURIA: *Do you direct first time actors differently than old pros like Paul Newman?*

MARTIN RITT: I don't direct them differently, except in the sense that when I'm working with Paul and I stop a scene, he says, "I know what you mean," because he's been there with me before. The reason for using actors and cameramen and art directors, again and again, is that it makes for a short cut possibility. And I don't—with Cicely, no. I had to discover a way to connect with Cicely and a way to connect with Paul and a way to connect with the gentleman who played the other character and did the score for the film, who had never acted before. The fellow with the guitar, Taj Mahal.

LEROY McDONALD: *Related to acting, there was an incident that happened in* Cunrack, *where an actor who had done a lot of stage acting and hardly any film was concerned about making the transition from stage to screen and you—*

MARTIN RITT: —there's no problem. There really is no problem. There was the myth around this town that stage actors did too much. If a stage actor does too much—by that I mean, he makes faces—he's no good in the theatre either. So it doesn't mean a thing. Any actor who is truthful will be good in either movies or theatre. It is more difficult very often because you have to be bigger, since the close-up doesn't exist in the theatre. An actor has to be bigger in his interior life to reach that big house and the second balcony. But if you have a guy like Hume Cronyn, who is really a very good actor, there's no problem with him to make—he can do anything. Anything. Anything at all. He's just a very good actor. But that's with Hume. As we sat and had dinner one night, we'd look at each other and say," It's a matter of longevity. You just hang around. The other guys die and finally, you get the good jobs."

RICHARD ROSENTHAL: *You mentioned that you try to make films up. Are there novels that you read that grab you emotionally that you just can't see any way to translate?*

MARTIN RITT: Yes. And also, there are some things that I read that I like, but it takes at least a year to make a film. And as you get older, years become more and more important. And so before you say, "Yes!" at a point in your life when you can't say, "Yes," and make a film happen, you sit down with your family and think it through. Is it going to be worth that year?

RICHARD ROSENTHAL: *Worth it, in what way? Do you try to evaluate whether the film will be commercially successful?*

MARTIN RITT: I don't really try to evaluate it, but I think somewhere in the back of my mind, I really try to evaluate what I like. I think I'm not the richest man in the world, but I think I can live without any problems. And I think I can work without any problems for the next seven or eight years that I have left to make pictures. So I really at this point, I will not do a thing that I don't really want to make. I mean, this picture, *First Blood,* is such a difficult film physically, that I almost don't want to make it because of that reason. I mean, it's so violent and physical. I've never made a picture like that and I tend to shy away from it because it's a lot of night shooting and there's very little tennis I can play on this picture. But there's something about it that's exciting and gripping. It's an exciting story and it's a melodrama and I've never really done a gung-ho melodrama.

RICHARD ROSENTHAL: *Could you talk about the material that you like that you just don't feel is cinematic?*
MARTIN RITT: I love Henry James. I just love it. I think Henry James is one of the greatest writers in the English language and I think he's possible to do on television, which is a headhunting medium, because he's so interior that it's possible. And early on in my career, I was working in live television. I did some Henry James and I tried. It's impossible for me to deal with it. I couldn't make a film with that material. I just think it's too difficult. I also don't think it's really my *metier,* except I like it. I will never do another play. Never. I think it's too difficult again, because I think to do one you're violating the other. If the other's good, it has been violated in some way.

LEROY McDONALD: *Could you talk a little bit about the problem of the young director, in terms of launching a career? And also, you mentioned once about making that first initial film and making that kind of impact.*
MARTIN RITT: The first film—take it from me—your most important film, from a career point of view. Because it's with that film that you set the tone about yourself. It's a very important decision. You should seek as much advice as you can on your first film. That is the choices of subject and everything else about it, Because you make a pretty good film, the first time out, you're going to win. You kind of make that imprint on the consciousness on the international scene and you become a director. It's very tough to beat that first impression if you do a very bad film. Of course, if you do the kind of film that's not seen, it really doesn't matter either. But I do think the first

film is very important, because the first film—first of all, you're all in absolute heat. Every one of you people here are in heat, creatively. So the first film is really going to be an expression, hopefully of that heat. And that's what's original. That's what I started the evening by saying. That heat is original. Get that imprint on the first film and you'll get to make a lot of other films. This town is much easier than it was. When I was a kid and I came to Hollywood, you couldn't come here and get a job directing unless you had a hit on Broadway. Very few people came up from the ranks, but it's possible to get together a little film and make it. I mean, *American Graffiti* was around this town two years looking to be done. If it hadn't been for Coppola putting his name on it, that film would not have been made. And obviously it was a quality piece of material and well made.

LEROY McDONALD: *What about some of the political repurcussions of dealing with some of the kinds of material that you have in the past?*
MARTIN RITT: Listen, I made a film about the McCarthy period with Woody Allen. And the McCarthy period is a period I know very well, because I lived through that time. Some of my friends didn't live through that time and when we made a deal at Columbia, I got final cut. They didn't care what I said. They didn't care what the film was about. It had Woody Allen and it had me. Now it's going to be as strong a film as we can make on that subject and still keep it a comedy. I think those barriers are down. I really do. I think if you can do anything good they couldn't care less. Look at the kind of material that's done today on every level.

LEROY McDONALD: *Why do you think you survived that period when some of your colleagues didn't?*
MARTIN RITT: Lucky. A little bit of luck. Good health. I don't know. I don't know. I had two friends who committed suicide. It's hard to say. As a matter of fact, we had forty pages of this script written and finally we sat down and I said, "Wait a minute." It wasn't fun and games. I had a friend of mine. I had dinner with him one night. We were sitting in a cafeteria in New York City. And he said, Good night, and checked into a hotel under an assumed name and took an overdose and that was the last I saw of him. There was a lot of wreckage in that time. Most of the people here are too young, too inexperienced to remember what happened. It was a bad time. I don't know. I really don't. It was a question of luck, I think, to some degree. Yes?

MARVIN KUPFER: *Could anyone make a serious film?*
MARTIN RITT: I tried twice, but I found I was getting hysterical and maybe a little self-serving, and I decided the form was the wrong way.

MARVIN KUPFER: *Would they finance a serious film?*
MARTIN RITT: I think so. I think this is going to be a serious film.

MARVIN KUPFER: *I mean, not the comedy-satire way.*
MARTIN RITT: Well, *The Way We Were* started off to be that kind of a film.

MARVIN KUPFER: The Way We Were *just scratched the surface.*
MARTIN RITT: Yes, obviously. I don't think there's any question about financing almost anything. Almost anything, except maybe *Ten Days That Shook the World*. I think they'll finance almost anything. Anything they think will work, will make money.

MARVIN KUPFER: *Has anybody actually tried to get a very serious effort out of the Fifties?*
MARTIN RITT: I don't think there's been a major piece of material around on that level. This is an original that I'm sitting with a writer and I'm working on.

MARVIN KUPFER: *Do you think if someone had a good piece of material—*
MARTIN RITT: —I think so absolutely. I'm also preparing a film on the Spanish Civil War. That's long been a subject that's not only been taboo. Now Spain is a fairly big market, like a million dollars and studios have already called me, two studios said, "Gee, Marty, you know—" I don't care. I really don't care. I'd like to make the film. If I lick the script, I'll get it made. But I will admit, at this point, I have a lot of muscle underneath some of this flab.

GREG McCARTY: *It seems to me what's important in the film is not to know about McCarthy, but about somebody.*
MARTIN RITT: That's right.

GREG McCARTY: *What's interesting is the relationships in the film.*

MARTIN RITT: This is a film about a front. A front was a guy who loaned his name to several writers. In this case, he became a writer of international importance and had trouble writing a letter home to his wife. That's the way we chose to attack the material. That's the name of the film. It's called *The Front*. And that's the part Woody Allen is going to play hopefully.

GREG McCARTY: *That leads me to something like* The Molly Maguires. *It failed for me because it wasn't enough about the relationship between those two men. That wasn't developed.*
MARTIN RITT: That probably is true.

GREG McCARTY: *You had the unions and the mines, but that isn't what makes a film.*
MARTIN RITT: No, it doesn't.

GREG McCARTY: *It's the relationship between the men.*
MARTIN RITT: That film had an incredible sense of ambiance and place, of all the elements, but it didn't work because the personal story obviously didn't work well enough.

GREG McCARTY: *You weren't in the heads of those two.*
MARTIN RITT: That's right. That must have been it. That's why I say, what moves you. And generally, what moves you is suddenly what you're into. You're into the heads and hearts of and gonads of. Once that happens with you, then you're into the right place. Then you should be doing that film.

MICHAEL JABLOW: *How close a rein do you ride on the film in post-production? How much do you concern yourself with the editor? How much do you concern yourself with the advertising of the film?*
MARTIN RITT: Well, with the editor, obviously, I edit my own films, as all directors do, so I'm there all the time. The advertising, I don't think I know a hell of a lot about it. I do have an opinion, a point of view, and I don't know how often I'm right. So I try, because I produce my own films, to maintain some of that control. It's hard to tell. I don't think in those areas—I hate to defer to the studios in those areas, but sometimes, I'm forced to, just by sheer weight of experience. I don't know enough about it. There's no way that I ever will know enough. And I don't really care that much.

INA MAE: *How closely did Larry McMurtry work on* Hud?
MARTIN RITT: Not at all.

INA MAE: *Not at all? That's interesting. What was his opinion of the film?*
MARTIN RITT: He liked the film very much. It's come back to me many times, from many people, and recently again, from a photographer. He may not have liked it so much the first time around, but since other films have been made from his material, he's grown to like *Hud* very much.

INA MAE: *I worked on* The Last Picture Show *and I was very interested in* Hud, *because I was saying, "I wonder if Peter Bogdanovich watched* Hud?" *Because the tone of* Hud *and* The Last Picture Show *were true and they both vary. And I love* Hud, *much more than* The Last Picture Show. *Because I think it's more true.*
MARTIN RITT: I think Larry thinks so too. But I think that whole feeling about west Texas is more indigenous to Mr. McMurtry than it is either to Mr. Bogdanovich or myself. What I did, I took it from McMurtry and so did Bogdanovich and it is McMurtry's. What was done on *Hud* in a serious literary way was in the screenplay really, an enormous job. And Larry recognized that finally. Because it really was the story of that young boy and his grandfather. Larry's story. It was about himself. And growing up on that ranch. And seeing his grandfather die and the sadness of that. It was sad and very touching and lyrical, essentially.

Q: *Was most of the dialogue written by McMurtry and you just excised the lines?*
MARTIN RITT: No. Most of the dialogue in—a good deal of the dialogue in *Cunrack* was written by Pat Conroy. A lot of the lines were just lifted out of his own biography.

Q: *I mean* Hud.
MARTIN RITT: Not on *Hud,* no.

NEIL SENTURIA: *Which brings us to the point of Harriet Frank and Irving Ravetch, who we've seen recently in* Conrack *and* Hud. *How do you work with writers? Those two in particular and anything else you might—*
MARTIN RITT: We go to make things together. I work with them very often. I've done five pictures with them. I did *The Long, Hot Summer, Hombre, Hud, The Sound and the Fury,* and *Conrack.*

NEIL SENTURIA: *In the editing process of the script, you say you work very well, fine. Do they come and finish scripts and then you take it apart scene by scene or do you all sit around a table or—*

MARTIN RITT: —we do both. Mostly, we read a piece of material and then we agree on the orientation of that material, how it's going to be developed. Then they go and write. I do a lot of editing and they've grown to trust that. I try to be as economical as I can always, in using language. They write very good language. They write as good talk as anybody in this town, I think. And I like them. I get along very well with them. And when you find somebody you get along with, you should marry them. I've done that seven or eight times unsuccessfully in my life.

NEIL SENTURIA: *Do you call them or talk to them during the production?*
MARTIN RITT: Yes, I talk with them. They're friends of mine.

NEIL SENTURIA: *Well, I meant more in—you need dialogue to cover something or you've got a scene that doesn't work. "What are we going to do?"*
MARTIN RITT: Yes, I do. As a matter of fact, in *Hud*, there is a young girl in the picture that was the girl friend of the young boy. And we had a terrible fight about it. I said, "It doesn't belong. Throw it out of the goddamn picture. We've got enough characters in this picture. Throw it out." They argued about the youth appeal, *et cetera*. And we've had a lot of that. But it's good. It's people who know each other and respect each other, creative people.

LEROY McDONALD: *Was there any reason why you—there was a scene in* Conrack *with a young girl who comes to visit Jon Voight, that wasn't in the picture.*
MARTIN RITT: I never wanted it in the picture and I fought with them and they said, "Please Marty, shoot it." We had a whole sequence where his girl friend came to the island and I never liked it. They are friends of mine and writers and very good writers and they said, "Please shoot it. We think it's marvelous." So I shot it and I cut it out of the picture immediately.

LEROY McDONALD: *I have a question: for a young director doing a period picture, what do you suggest? I mean, if a person is doing a film of the Thirties that wasn't in the era, how—*
MARTIN RITT: —I would just inundate myself in the material, the music, pictures, everything. Just inundate myself with it. I would really take a

month of my life and just do nothing, but do that. Listen to all the music. Read all the books. Look at all the clothes. So that the whole ambiance of the time becomes a part of your functioning daily psyche. So that if you see something that's wrong out of the corner of your eye, you'll know right away. Now obviously, any period film is murder, because you go one inch to the left or one inch to the right, you've got a '34 antenna, a television antenna you shot. So you must steep yourself so in that period that you, with your eye would see something that's wrong immediately. And also, try in some way to get into what was going on, at that time, with the people.

LEROY McDONALD: *What about going on location? What are some of the logistics involved and the problems? Could you talk a little bit about that?*
MARTIN RITT: I love locations because that's the way films should be made. Now sometimes, you get—I mean, this little McCarthy film I'm going to make is really part of the bedroom and bath. It's a talk film. And it can't be on location because there's no way to get New York, 1951, except in a couple of isolated places on the East Side or in Brooklyn Heights or something like that. It's very rough to get New York, 1951. We take a lot of shots at the networks in this picture. They were really the biggest villains and they behaved in an absolutely scurrilous manner, CBS, NBC, and ABC, the big three. But when you get into a period like that, 1951 or 1930 and you have to do it in New York City, you're dead. The art director and you have to comb the city and pick the few spots that can be either rebuilt or used as they are in total and the shot has to be very confined. It's very tough. Kubrick has been doing a Thackerey novel I think and I know he's had trouble with the film and it could very well be that part of the trouble is that it's not immediately discernible to his nature when everything's not right in terms of the behavior of the people. The *decor* is I'm sure impeccable because I'm sure he spent a lot of time and worked that out and he's got enough money to make that impeccable, but the psychology of the time, the behavior of the people, the movement of the people. You almost have to—it's very difficult. The film I admired very much this year that I saw was a film called *Mean Streets* and the night after I saw that film, I tracked down the director [Martin Scorcese] simply to tell him how much I liked the film.

INA MAE: *I want to ask you a couple of questions about* Hombre. *First of all, I was kind of fascinated that Paul Newman was playing this halfbreed, first of all, because he looked so Anglo to me and second of all, at the time it came out, it was a western and it deals with his whole inner thing with being happy. Currently, I've seen the film with a bunch of my Indian friends and they're outraged. Did you have political repercussions then or was it just totally into it because of Newman and what were your feelings about directing a white persona and how did that work, because it would seem to me to be very difficult?*

MARTIN RITT: It wasn't difficult at all, no. It was a good part and there are many halfbreeds that aren't Indian or black that are totally white. There are also Indians with blue eyes. And also, we could never get the picture off the ground. There was no way to make the picture without somebody like Paul.

INA MAE: *I was wondering: did you have much trouble from the studios or is that what you're saying about getting it off the ground?*

MARTIN RITT: We couldn't have gotten it—not much trouble—gotten it off the ground. Either we had a movie star or we couldn't have gotten the picture made. It wasn't my personal problem. For instance, at that time, if I had known a very gifted young Indian actor, I wouldn't have been able. If I had known one, there was no way I could make that film. That film cost three, three and a half million dollars. There's no way I could make that film.

INA MAE: *Was that idea based on a book?*

MARTIN RITT: Yes, that was a paperback. We were on a plane trip and we picked it up and we handed it one to the other. We liked it. We thought it was a good story. That's why we made it.

Q: *You say you only plan your action sequences. How loose are you on the set when you're actually shooting dialogue?*

MARTIN RITT: Very loose. Very loose.

Q: *And you rehearse the actors.*

MARTIN RITT: I rehearse and stage the scene. By that time, the camera movement is already very clear. Once the scene is staged, everybody around will know where I want to put the camera at that point. But in staging the scene, I allow the scene to happen. And I tell an actor where to move, but if he wants to move somewhere else, I let him move. And if I like it, I use it. If I don't like it, I don't use it. Every good idea that happens on the set, finally becomes the property of the director. And every bad idea is somebody else's fault. Yes, sir.

Q: *I watched you shoot* Adventures of a Young Man *in Wisconsin in 1961. Now this was Ernest Hemingway's story, but I don't think it was a financial success. What was the problem, do you know?*
MARTIN RITT: It wasn't a very good film. That was one of the reasons, probably the most important reason. Again, it was cut up. The various scenes by themselves were quite interesting, one or two of them were very good, but it just didn't add up. It didn't add up. It's beautiful to look at. That country is incredible. I kept some of that footage, a lot of footage that I shot from a 'copter. Oh, boy. But the film didn't really work. It was soft in the middle.

LEROY McDONALD: *You had a very easy relationship with John Alonzo. Your communication was almost sometimes not verbal. I would be standing there waiting to hear some words and I wasn't hearing words. You were saying, "Yes, hm-mmm, okay." And I was saying, "Wait a minute, talk." I'm wondering if you are that relaxed in dealing with other cinematographers that you haven't worked with before.*
MARTIN RITT: Yes. I'm going to have to have a new one, because he took a job. I couldn't give him a commitment. He's doing a Jacqueline Susann novel. It's got to be about sex, I guess. I don't know what it is. So I'm going to have to get a new cameraman. If I do *First Blood,* I'm going to have to get a new cameraman. And it will be like a new love affair. It takes time to make it work. It takes some time to understand what I mean, but I'll spend a lot of time with this guy. I'll take him on location with me for two weeks before the picture starts and go through every location and discuss why, where, how, when, and where we should put the cameraman and why or maybe we shouldn't or maybe we should do something else. Maybe he'll have an idea. And because the picture is so violent, I'm going to be shooting a lot of—I want lyric countryside. I want sunrises and dew. I want something poetic to be in the film. I mean, the film is incredibly violent, particularly for me, because I've never done anything like that and I don't really like it, but that's the story and I think it's a good story and a worthwhile story to tell. So I'm going to have to have a cameraman that has a real feeling for nature. That's why I want to go up to Oregon. I know I'm going to have fog. I know I'm going to have all kinds of interesting cloud formations and so much of it is a

chase. The whole middle part of it is a chase. Once the kid busts out of jail. He busts out balls naked and gets on a motorcycle and they're all after him. I don't know quite how we're going to do that. But we've already got copious notes from the board or whatever it is that writes you, "You can't do this."

JAMES POWERS: *Most of your films have some social comment and yet, several times today, you spoke of a lyric quality you like to have.*
MARTIN RITT: I don't think they're antipathetic. As a matter of fact, I think they help each other.

JAMES POWERS: *Is that a conscious thing on your part?*
MARTIN RITT: Yes. I keep looking in all cases for things that will complicate my own statements, for what I want to say in a film. I began in this business strangely enough as a hoofer. And so, I am rather a good dancer. And I was replaced by a now celebrated star called Gene Kelly in a musical in New York. So I go back a long time. He's a little better dancer than I was. And I am addicted to the unity of opposites. I am addicted to size and grace. I am addicted to beauty and violence. I am addicted to juxtaposing the most extreme elements that I can in any given situation. Charm and evil, whatever. There is a character in *First Blood,* who arrives in the middle of the picture, who was the man who trained this kid and who knows that they won't be able to catch him, who is the devil actually in some ways because he finally picks on the sheriff and sets the sheriff up as a patsy, as a target, knowing full well that that's the only thing that'll bring the kid back into town. And he sets up the confrontation so they will kill each other.

LEROY McDONALD: *Two more questions.*
BRUCE GEDDES: *You recommend that we seek. . . . I hate to bring up Paul Newman. In looking at his films, it seems as if you've played a considerable part in the films somehow or you have influenced his directorial point of view. Did you by any chance serve as consultant on his first film?*
MARTIN RITT: No, but Paul and I are close friends, in addition to everything else and we do talk to each other. I taught at the Actor's Studio for some time and the nice thing about, as I say, working with people, is you have a kind of shorthand of communication with people you have worked with. If I do another picture with Cicely, which I ought to do—I hope I find a part for her because I think she's really a first class actress—it'll be a lot

easier the second time. There will be less suspicion. There will be less ego clash. Most people who work with me know I have only one interest, which is to make the picture work. So it takes some time to learn that. It takes some time to trust that. If I did a picture with Paul Newman and Pat Neal was in the picture, Pat would have two or three weeks in which she would say, "Well, I and Paul are part of it." That's where the money is. And I would be foolish if I didn't know that existed in the actor. And I'd also be less of a director than I am if I couldn't deal with it. I did deal with it and it was quite clear that all I was interested in was getting the best out of all those scenes and never favored him. And of course, he's a kind of champ. If you ever work with him, you'll see that—I mean, he is totally related to what's best for the scene in the picture. I've worked with him for years. I have never heard the man say, "You're favoring her in the scene or the shot doesn't favor me." I've never seen him—in *Hombre*, we had him get off that damn stagecoach twenty times, just twenty times, because it never stopped on the mark. We had one of those highly trained stagecoach drivers. It never stopped on the goddamn mark and Paul would jump right out of the shot every time or he would be cut up here. Never opened his mouth. Did it. He got paid rather well, I might add, but still, he did it. And usually, when you get paid that well, you don't do it. And he got Redford that job in *Sundance*, over the objections of Twentieth Century Fox. And Redford is our new movie star. You ought to see the beautiful costumes and the great ambiance in *Gatsby*. That picture has twelve million dollars in advanced bookings already. For as ephemeral a writer as Mr. Fitzgerald, that's extraordinairy. I would never have believed it. I've seen two versions of that film. Neither one of them worked. This one, I hear, is very good. But six pages in *Newsweek*, I think, of costumes.

JAMES POWERS: *I guess that has to do with living long enough.*
MARTIN RITT: I guess so. It has.

Dialogue with Martin Ritt and Abraham Polonsky

ABRAHAM POLONSKY/1976

ABE: *I remember meeting Marty Ritt. And the first thing I saw, he was dancing. It was at the home of two friends of ours, one of whom was a producer of a television series. This was during the time of the blacklist and at that time Marty was more or less blacklisted and I was totally blacklisted. So he couldn't direct and he could act a little and I couldn't direct but I could write a lot if I could find someway to have someone put their name on what I was writing, as long as I didn't use my own name. And I came to this party which was being given by this producer of a television series and there was Marty Ritt dancing. And he is an elegant dancer, just as he is a very good athlete, and he's a wonderful actor. And so we thought of writing a television show in which Marty would be an actor. And now Marty should tell you a little bit about that television show cause it's just about his character.*
MARTY: Well, that's the show I did with Josh. It was a very good show and Abe and Walter Bernstein and a third gentleman called Arnold Manoff, who were then all living in New York and all blacklisted, and three of the best writers this industry has ever produced, ...

ABE: *We are the three writers, by the way, in* The Front,
MARTY: That's right, in *The Front*, they are the three writers in the restaurant, which was written by Walter Bernstein. They are also the three writers who almost exclusively wrote a very big and successful series called *You Are There*. which Mr. Walter Cronkite narrated. Abe saw me dancing. I got to

---

Reprinted by permission of Adele Ritt and Abraham Polonsky.

know Abe that night, and Abe wrote a very good script in which I played a convict who had escaped and I had a friend who was a comic who was a rat.

ABE: *And so I wrote a story about how he was betrayed which was exactly the story of our lives at the moment. And it was a very successful tv show. We needn't talk any more about that. So that leads to how we met. The next time that I met Marty Ritt he had reentered the motion picture industry. I had met him many times before that and we became friends, but the next time we became professionally related, I still was blacklisted, but he had come out of the blacklist and entered a kind of gray period in which he was not blacklisted but he was indeed partially blacklisted and he was doing a film for Paramount and he sent me a copy of the book called The Spy Who Came in From the Cold. But it turned out that Paramount Pictures still would not accept me as a writer.*

MARTY: From the time I came to Hollywood I tried consistently to hire people who I knew were gifted people who I had been associated with in my former life which was always part of my latter life cause I really haven't changed that much in any of my attitudes or feelings, and I brought Abe's name up at that point and there was a kibosh put on it. They wouldn't go, I pushed. They just said no absolutely. I was not able to get anybody hired till I did a film that didn't quite work when I hired Howard da Silva to play in a remake we did of *Rashomon*, which taught me never to remake any film much less a film of a master.

ABE: *It's better to be the master yourself.*

MARTY: Yes, it's always better. At any rate I got Howard da Silva hired at that point and I could sense that it was beginning to crack simply by saying to Metro at that point, which I had said previously to Paramount and they had paid it no mind. But to Metro, of course, I had just previously done *Hud*, which might have had a lot to do with it. And I said to Metro are you prepared to tell me that I can't hire him, can I let that out to the press? And they backed off. So I got Howard hired.

ABE: *That was precisely the way I got back into the industry, too. Because someone said well, I'm going to do it anyway, and they said all right. I mean this was much later on, this was during the 60s. During the 50s this was impossible.*

MARTY: Yes, it was impossible.

ABE: *All right, so we're joined together in the fact that we were blacklisted together, and we're joined together in another way which I'd like to hear Marty talk about.*

MARTY: Yes, I want to talk about it because when I met Abe, of course he had met me, he really met me for the first time when he saw me dance, and among my friends who are non-dancers, I might add, I was always considered an extraordinary dancer. Gene Kelly has other thoughts about that and he's voiced them to me at one or two times. I just manage not to listen.

ABE: *He wasn't blacklisted then.*

MARTY: That's right. At any rate, I had seen two films that Abe was deeply involved in that I greatly admired. I greatly admired, for many reasons—one is that they worked. They were good films. They told stories about people that affected me, and I consider myself an absolute barometer of quality and truth. When I see a film and I like it, I know it's good. I don't have to listen or read any critics or listen to any convoluted or involuted reasons as to why it's good or not good. I was affected and concerned and also deeply appreciative of the fact that I was watching the work of a man who cared very deeply about the human condition. And therefore I recognized immediately a kindred soul, because that is my main preoccupation. I've got many other things that I'm interested in, but fundamentally, if I had to evaluate myself, which is always a little embarrassing, I would say that I am concerned most with the human condition. Because I saw no other way in my lifetime except a social or political way, I became a social and political animal. If I'd found another way to alleviate or make better the human condition, I'm sure I would have chosen a less painful way than the way I chose, because it was painful. I did blow 6–7 years out of my career, that plus the 4½ years in the army. That's a legitimate 11½ years out of a man's life. That's at least 5 pictures.

ABE: *Yes, but that experience became in effect the content of your work.*
MARTY: Yes, no question about it. I'm not sure. . . .

ABE: *When you're beaten sufficiently, you're able to write about how people feel when they're beaten, and how they survive it.*
MARTY: Yeah, most of us are survivors.

ABE: *Well, we've lasted, I don't know whether you call that survival.*

MARTY: Yeah, we survived because . . . you know, it's very interesting to me. Of all the people I knew of that period, all the people I knew who behaved well, have come out well humanly. It didn't make anybody more talented because they were blacklisted. It didn't make them better directors or writers but humanly if they were able to survive that period, they came out as better human beings. The people who behaved badly, almost without exception, I don't know a single one who has emerged as a first class human being. None that I know. And I had some very good friends. I was really ripped by the McCarthy situation because I had some deeply, very close friends, deeply associated with me in many ways, who behaved badly, and it was a difficult thing for me to handle and to deal with, as we all did.

ABE: *But what does social responsibility mean to you. When you say you are a humanist, well that includes every dog in the street.*
MARTY: As it really does. I think any artist, actually Abe, I'm a political animal. I am a political animal. I don't think there's any question about that. Now there are many directors, many writers who are humanists who are not political animals. Any artist who is first class is going to touch on the human condition if he be the most reactionary person in the world. And he can be a first class artist. I mean one doesn't say that one has to be a political animal predisposed to what we believe.

ABE: *So, in a sense, what I'm trying to get at in this little brief discussion is that all works of art, one way or another, deal with aspects of what is human, whether in the abstract, or at the level of realism or any of the levels of the genre that we use, or the forms of art that we use. But what Marty is saying, and I agree with, is that what is submerged, what is hidden, what is suppressed, in the nature of humanity, by the society in which we live, those are the subjects we are interested in, and how they affect the emergence of what is human in people, and how that struggle goes on. Now this can be warm and grateful, as well as sad and beautiful as in* Sounder. *Or it can be rough and brutal and devastating as in* Force of Evil. *Or it can have the aspect of* Hud. *Or of the comedies that he does so well, you see. But what is important I think is that we are in touch, or try to be in touch, with what is hidden.*

Well, one way or another, as you remember, Marty, we survived the blacklist. And by the time the 60s came around, the middle of the 60s came around, I had been working with Harry Belafonte and I had made one film with him actually, which was . . . I had written a film that was directed by Bobby Wise, and the name of a friend of ours, a black novelist, was put on the film. It was called Odd Man Out. And it was about that time that Rosenberg, who was a producer at Universal Studios, was interested in making a film on the Office of Strategic Services, a series of films on that, and he knew that I had been in the OSS, and through it, had the great opportunity to visit France. And so he approached us and asked me whether I would do a pilot film on television for Universal based on what I knew or what I could find out about the OSS, which as you recall was a subversive branch of the American military service that has become the CIA. So I said no because after all, I was making enough money without writing for television films at that time. He said but I will put your name on it. So I immediately accepted the job without even asking what I would get for it. Because if I got my name on a film put out by a commercial studio appearing on television then the blacklist was broken because I was then still blacklisted and not doing anything under my name. And therefore, had no chance to direct because directors cannot appear anonymously, although my friend Joe Losey actually directed a film in France under a pseudonym. But that was an act of courage and outrage that I don't think anyone else has accomplished. So I came out to California then and I did this. And the pilots at least were shown on television. And about that time Rosenberg was doing Madigan. And he and the writer on Madigan, didn't get on very well. So Rosenberg asked me to rewrite it. I, of course, called the writer up first, who I knew, and said is this true? Because I was not about to take someone else's job. I never had done that. So he said I can't talk to him anymore. So I said in that case, I'll take the job, because this is my chance to get my name on a film as a writer. Well, I started to work on Madigan as you remember after I'd written about 45 pages of it I said the best director in town for this would be you. So I got in touch with you. You read the 45 pages and said I'll be happy to do it, and I'll get Paul Newman, too, to do this. And this of course, would have been a great boon to the picture and wonderful for the studio because both of you were then very important commercially, leave aside everything else about you. But Lew Wasserman, the head of the studio, refused to pay you the money you wanted, and therefore you wouldn't do it. Well, it ended up, of course, what was bad in one way turned out to be good in another way, because first it became a different kind of a film. A film I could make with you would be one kind of film and a film that I could make with someone else would be a different kind of film since in writing and working with a director it's better not to have a hostile relationship to content. You try to get the content you want but adjust it to the possibility nor the potentiality of the producer, the writer, and so on. And yet at the same time you try to win. And this difficult, ambiguous situation is one which writers in Hollywood always live, and directors live and everybody else lives in the commercial industry.

Well, what had happened is that Don Segal, who is a very brilliant director, had had a rotten career all during this period because he had been confined to television when he wanted to direct films. Through this and some other things that were going around Universal where I was, we got Don Segal into the picture so in a way he benefited from the fact that you and Lou Wasserman disagreed over $15,000. In fact, I called Lew Wasserman and went to see him and said I will pay the $15,000 for you so still you will lose no money. He said it's a question of principle. And so we didn't get you. But we got Don Segal and he's a marvelous director, he did very well. At that point in time I was approached by a producer who had purchased a true history of an Indian called Willie Boy and a book had been written about this true history and analyzed by a journalist. He asked me if I would be interested in it, and I said yes, and we can get Marty Ritt to direct it. Do you recall that?

MARTY: Yes, I do.

ABE: And so, Marty Ritt being an important director, everybody was interested in this. But then when Marty submitted my outline for this story to the studio he was working for . . . was it Columbia?

MARTY: Paramount.

ABE: Paramount didn't want to do the story. Then Marty tried to set it up on his own but found great difficulty with it at which point I decided I would direct it myself if I could get anybody to believe in me again. You must remember I hadn't directed a film for thirteen, fourteen, fifteen years, I don't remember how long it was. And I had only directed one film before that . . . Force of Evil. So I went to Jennings Lang and said I'd like to make a movie out of this. Jennings Lang said I can't get you on the payroll as a director of a movie, but I'm in control of television and if you will make it into a television show, a two or two hour and a half television show, we can pretend that we're preparing it for television, and then if it's very good, we'll turn it into a movie. Well, that's exactly how it happened. I wrote the screenplay for it and they decided to go with it as a film, but I was the director of the screenplay so they carried me on as the director of the film. And so by that series of incredible accidents in which your life is involved for some strange reason I don't know what it is. All our lives we've been trying to make a film together, we've never succeeded. But maybe now. That's how I got to do Willie Boy. And, of course, when I did Willie Boy, I had a terrible feeling having only directed only one film before that, that this would be my last film. It was just a sense of fate I had about it. So I said that I would only make a film that I wanted to make and make no film that anybody else wanted to make if they objected to it. I would rather lose the project. It wasn't worthwhile being separated so long from something I loved and not be able to do what I wanted to do. And in the peculiar circumstances in Universal at that time, with the role that Jennings Lang was playing; he was not in charge of all films, but he had a very important role, which later changed, of course, it changed in management. But at that particular moment, once he got Lew Wasserman to agree, I had an absolutely free hand in the film. The only problem I had was they gave me a list of 7 names and said I must get one of those stars or else I couldn't direct the film. Now there were very famous names on the list. The least famous name on that list was Robert Redford, but he was the youngest and closest to what my story needed. And I had seen some of his films, and he is an incredibly good actor. So, we got Robert. And, of course, I made the picture exactly the way I wanted to make it, with no interference from the studio, I hired Conrad Hall from the Pacific where he was on a ship shooting a film, and I hired him away from some other director who wanted him. First, I tried to get Haskell Wexler who was busy, so he suggested Conrad Hall. And then Conrad Hall and I made some experiments, well, he made the experiments, I sat around and watched him make them, and either approved or disapproved of the results of using saturated color in such a way that all the skies in the desert are always white and not blue except for one shot in the whole film. I tried to combine my aesthetic propensity with my social stupidity and I think I made a picture that expressed everything I felt during the years of the blacklist. That's how I got back into being a director.

Well, the film was relatively successful. It got relatively good reviews. It was very well received abroad and that seemed to be a death sentence on me as a director.

So I've reached the point now where I've done Willie Boy and have a good time going around the world with it and showing it in France and Sweden and so on, and everybody loves it and they're glad to see me back in the business. Bob Aldrich called me up on the telephone after he saw it and said you would think you were making films all those years. I said I was making films all those years but they weren't making them. I was thinking them. So, but right after that I started several projects. I got Universal to buy Childhood's End, the Arthur Clarke book. I made them buy a screenplay I had written for Harry Belafonte which we couldn't get made which deals with the south during the Civil War and previous to the Civil War. But by that time the management, the emphasis of the management at Universal had changed and they didn't make the film even though they had bought them. I went through more or less 17 or 18 different kinds of proposals of one kind or another, and suddenly I realized I was just as blacklisted even when they wanted to hire me as I was when they didn't want to hire me, so I had to assume that there is a kind of aesthetic and social blacklist which I create, which I carry around me, like a halo on my head, you know, and when they see that halo on my head, they say not him. So I finally was able to direct a film in Yugoslavia called Romance of a Horsethief, which is a very charming film I think. But nothing much came of that. And then I got very ill. And I haven't directed since. So, in a way, unless something strange happens, I probably won't direct anymore films. Although it can happen.

MARTY: Oh, I think it will happen.

ABE: *In any event, I will not direct any film I don't want to direct. I will not direct a film that doesn't mean something to me as a—not as a human being, but as a particular kind of person that I am, what I believe about society, what I believe about myself and what I believe about film, too. Because I'm interested in the aesthetic of film. Now, in telling this story about Willie Boy, which was a success, it led to the fact that I made no more films. Now I want you to tell me the story of* The Molly Maguires *which is one of my favorite films which led to the fact that no one wanted you to make any more films after that.*

MARTY: That's true.

ABE: *And I think you came out of that with* Sounder. *You tell about that.*

MARTY: All right. The Molly Maguires, the subject was first broached to me by Walter Bernstein, who you know, who was one of the three guys we spoke about earlier, and I found the material fascinating, and I had a deal at Paramount, and I convinced them they should let me make this film, and Walter and I worked on it.

ABE: *How did you convince them to let you make a film like* The Molly Maguires?

MARTY: Because I didn't tell them how much it was gonna cost. And then when the script was finally finished, I liked it very much, and when it came back from the first budget, they said we can't make the film, it is too expensive. And I said fine, ok. And I got a call from Bludorn. This always amuses me because when a film costs a lot of money and fails, the studio always absolves themselves from any responsibility. They had nothing to do with the making of the film, only you were responsible. So he said The Molly Maguires is going to cost $8 million. I said yes. He said well, we're not going to do it at that price. I said I understand that. He said well, what are you going to do with it? I said I'm going to get it made someplace else if I can. I'll break my ass to get it made. He said why? And I said because I like it and I believe in it. He said ok, we'll let you make it. Now Bludorn was a magnate, a colossus, a conglomerate all by himself, and a gambler, obviously. I made, I agree, one of the best pictures I've ever made, and it went right on its duff. It did nothing. It shows now only, I gather, once every two or three months in a little theatre in Paris and at universities and such but it didn't do any business.

ABE: *Why is that so?*
MARTY: I think we made a couple of commercial mistakes in the picture. That is, the picture was too gray and too sophisticated. I think that the audience didn't know really who to root for sufficiently. And they grew so fond of Richard Harris that they would not accept at the final curtain, the fact that he was evil. I think we made a mistake in that regard. Why, beyond that, I don't really know. I don't profess to know. I looked at *Sounder* with my wife and we turned to each other at the end of the screening and said well, it's lovely. It won't do 10¢. Now, I'm not talking about a script now, I'm talking about a finished picture. Well, we were right there, obviously. I looked at *Conrack* and I turned to her and I said our grandchildren will live off this picture. I was 100% right there, too. I have very rarely been right about which picture of mine was going to do business. I don't know. I think there is an inhibiting factor in subject matter with the kind of films that you and I are prone to make so that the studios are loathe unless you're coming off a big hit or something a big commercial hit, to make that kind of picture cause they feel that even if the picture is first class, like Columbia said to me *The Front* was first class, the picture got extraordinary press all through Europe, and the picture just about will come out. Well, that's a bad investment for us. Why don't you do this picture? So you argue and you fight. So I'm starting a picture on a strike situation, hopefully at Fox. I knew it going in. I went in with the writers, and I presented a deal from my own point of view and from the writers' point of view which I felt would be attractive to 20th Century Fox. I took half my salary and so did the writers. And it did help, no question about it. So they're going along with a script that is first class. I think I'm going to make a very good picture. How much money it will make I don't know. I think, unlike Abe, I have functioned much more as a profes-

sional director. I have taken more jobs that you have, because, I guess, I can't write and there's no other way for me to earn a living and to support my habits which are horses.

ABE: Well, my habit is to make revolutions and they're very expensive, too. But I haven't succeeded in making one.
MARTY: No. That's become a side habit of mine.

ABE: A side habit. No, but the thing is which is important here. You're talking about subject matter. It isn't just so much the subject matter, now for instance, it's the treatment of the subject matter. Now for instance, ever since I was ill, I was over in London, trying to do Mario and the Magician, talking to Albert Finney and starting to write a script.
MARTY: And a marvelous script it is. I've read the script. There's no reason in the world why that film should not be made.

ABE: I can't get any money for it, but leave that pass. So, lately I've been starting to write again for the movies. Now I find out that my role as a writer in the movies is directly related to their opinion of me as a director in the movies. That is to say, they bring all the impossible social subjects to me. For instance, aside from a little film which I just did for Mark Robeson which they're going to shoot I think in February, I was called up by Paramount Pictures. Billy Freidkin and Paula Weinstein. They want to do the Jablonsky murders. Now this is the biggest union story of the past ten years. It's the murder of a man running for president of the union by the then president of the union, people hired by him. These are . . . all these murderers have been convicted, yet these people are the heirs of John Lewis and the horror of what was created in the mineworkers is partly created by John L. Lewis although he is the man who in a sense also created the wonders of the American labor movement and the CIO and all the rest of that. But why did they call me?
MARTY: Because you understand it and they don't.

ABE: So they call me for the impossible picture, you see. So I'm working on that and I also have a friend Marty Ritt, he also has an impossible picture. If he has an idea for an impossible picture, if he has an idea for a subject that's impossible, he calls me on the telephone, like he says, I am sick and tired of making films which don't deal with the potential that's human nature. I'd like to make a picture about

someone who is as good as he can be and accomplishes his purpose in life against all odds. He says there's a play called Yellow Jack. *You tell me I've directed that play once or twice. I want to make a film that has to deal with that subject, but that film also involved the French trying to build the Panama Canal and having their efforts partially destroyed by yellow fever. And the fact that the Americans then take over the building of the Panama Canal, all because a group of scientists found a way and risked their lives to solve the problem of yellow fever in Cuba. And it involves the Spanish American War. I mean this is not all in the picture, we're talking about, but suddenly you come and you drop into my head an atom bomb. So once upon a time there was a great scientist and then suddenly I had the Spanish American War and the French trying to build the Panama Canal. I had malaria, yellow fever, I had the Panama Canal, and that's disaster.*
Q: That would be a remake, that film wouldn't it?
ABE: *Well, it would. I won't finish what I was talking about because it would take me forever. But, I'll have to ask you a question. You see all the films don't you?*
MARTY: I see most of the films.

ABE: *Most of the films. I don't as you know. Somehow I never got to see anything. I spent all my life on the verge of seeing movies. But you see all the films. What do you think of the modern films? The films, post-blacklist films?*
MARTY: Well, I tell you, I feel that there have been several very good developments and several developments that are a little distressing to me. The good developments, fundamentally is that with the relaxation of censorship, despite certain gross miscarriages of taste, I think that many more important subjects will become available to the American filmmaker and I think, more important American films will be made. The American filmmaker was always technically very proficient. He was always inhibited by the nature of what he could deal with. That has almost disappeared. And in its almost disappearing, there have been some childish excesses. I am only disturbed . . . therefore, I feel that everything is going to come up roses finally, because again, I'm an incurable optimist I guess finally, and I do believe that the young directors and the new ones coming up, the ones who are not yet discovered, will find a way to express themselves in a way that will make me feel happier than some of the films that I've seen, because I do feel mindless. A few of the films are really about not much. There's an incredible preoccupation with

the occult, which is not one of my favorite subjects, with the hereafter, which is less than my favorite subject, there is a kind of general religious tone, and I don't mean that, I mean religious in the fact that it's mindless, not that it's religious, "religious." And that bothers me. But I do think that will begin to fade, I do think that we've been in a generation much affected by McLuhanism, and I do think there's been an incredible preoccupation with form to the general failing of content, of human content and that is distressing, but as I say, I think it will be much better, and I think American films, I think in this country, we will develop some extraordinary filmmakers in the next decade or so.

ABE: *Well, I think you can say that about any period more or less. In the sense that under a period of restriction talented people find ways of operating one way or another, you know that. If you have to write, if they say you can only write poems that are 14 lines long, so they invent sonnets. If they say you can write epics, they write epics. If they say you can't write anything, then they write it themselves and they pass it around to each other. Now of course filming isn't quite like that because it's technological in a sense, and you need apparatus and that costs money. But in a sense it's part of our life now and they'll manage to do it. But what, for instance, what do you think is a very good film in the last 2 years. Not your own.*

MARTY: A very good film. An American film, you're talking about?

ABE: *Of course.*

MARTY: I'm trying to think now. As I get a little older, I'm not that sharp in remembering because I could turn around and ask you what won the Academy Award last year and I know you wouldn't know.

ABE: *I'd be happy to forget. I don't even remember what it was.*

MARTY: I'm trying to remember what was a very good film.

ABE: *Well, what did you like?*

MARTY: I'm trying to remember Abe, you know.

ABE: *All right. Pick any . . . the thing about it is that there's a reason why this thing doesn't come to mind because the film, whatever it is, the American film you're trying to talk about, didn't touch you and change you as works of art do. Every work of art changes the person who observes it, as well as the person who*

makes it. Now I saw a film recently, not too recently, which I thought was a genuine little masterpiece. It was called Outrageous. And it was made in Canada.
MARTY: I saw that film and I liked it very much.

ABE: *I liked it. It was a fabulous little film. It made no money at all.*
MARTY: I don't know that it's a masterpiece, but I liked it very much, I certainly enjoyed it.

ABE: *Well, you know small masters make small masterpieces. Large masters make large masterpieces.*
MARTY: Unfortunately, I hear those two young fellows sold the picture before they could reap all the commissions out of it.

ABE: *Oh no, how horrible.*
MARTY: That's too bad.

ABE: *What do you think of the critics? How do they affect you? You made films that they loved. For instance, you told me a marvelous story. Marty Ritt with me and perhaps a few other people, belong among the hated directors by Pauline Kael. She hates me because she thinks I'm unAmerican and she hates him because she thinks his films deal with human nature and social consciousness, occasionally. That's what I think. Anyway, after he made* Sounder, *Marty called me up and told me a funny story about Pauline Kael. Tell them the story.*
MARTY: She called me up to tell me how much she loved the film. She really adored the film. You know, Pauline Kael . . . for instance, I'll tell you another thing, Andrew Sarris in reviewing *The Front,* said I wonder what Mr. Ritt and Mr. Bernstein would do if they were writing a film about the Soviet Union. Period. He did not discuss the film. Now this is not to me because I certainly don't respect Mr. Sarris, but in many circles, he's a respected critic, you know.

ABE: *You see, that's the political context in which critics operate very well.*
MARTY: Pauline Kael said the same thing. She said Mr. Bernstein and Mr. Ritt were duped. Now I venture to say the political knowledge of both people is nil. Their political commitment is nil. They have suffered for their politics not one wit. There's not a political gut between the two of them. I don't know what the hell they're talking about. I don't know who the hell they are on that level to make such statements.

ABE: *I mean, politically speaking, that's one kind of criticism. And they make these statements because they feel that you cannot be socially responsive, not actually a radical, unless you first start out by saying that I despise the Soviet Union and I would like to attack it. Now I know you disagree with almost everything the Soviet Union does but that's no reason why you, before you make a film of what's wrong in America, should have to say first I hate the Soviet Union, which is what they are demanding. They are like the . . . , each one elects himself to become part of the McCarthy committee that says you come in here and first prove you're not a radical by hating the Soviet Union. Then you can criticize the United States. Otherwise, you're a dupe, you're a fool, you are this, you are that and another thing. So I was very happy when she called you up and said she loved* Sounder.
MARTY: Well, she loved that picture.

ABE: *She welcomed you back to the human race. Weren't you happy?*
MARTY: I tell you, the only value critics have, and they have value really only in New York, is that they do affect business of certain kinds of films, the kind of films that we are involved in making. A critic's opinion, after all, is the opinion of one individual. If I were writing film criticism, I would be a critic. I do think that the critics have very strong opinions; some of them are more intelligent than others, some of them are less. Some of them are available, some are not available. I don't think that a critic is any different than any other movie goer despite the fact that they've studied film history and have taken certain classes and have certain kinds of knowledge. I find that I agree with very few of their opinions and some of the more respected ones, even less.

ABE: *I have a simpler rule than you.*
MARTY: Yes, and what is that?

ABE: *I adore film critics who adore me. I despise film critics who hate me.*
MARTY: I think that's a fair estimate. I think finally if I were forced to come down to the nitty gritty, I would take the same position.

ABE: *But have you ever been illuminated by a critic?*
MARTY: No.

ABE: *But that's their role.*

MARTY: But that's not their role.

ABE: *Aside from selling pictures.*
MARTY: And selling themselves.

ABE: *And selling themselves, yes.*
MARTY: Because I know that many of them do sell themselves.

ABE: *I respect film criticism though.*
MARTY: And many of them do proselytize.

ABE: *And I respect literary criticism and so on. But of course that depends on your intellectual enjoyment in life. You play tennis. I read the critics, you see.*
MARTY: I have more fun.

ABE: *You're healthier than I am. That's all that means, but I am an intellectual and therefore I enjoy the manipulation of ideas and minds and opinions by people just the way you enjoy chess games. I even enjoy the truth when I occasionally read it elsewhere.*
MARTY: Well, I remember I got a call from Paul Newman the day after *Sundance* opened in New York. Canby didn't like the picture and he was very upset and I said Paul we saw that picture together. We know it is an entertaining picture. So Canby doesn't like it. He's only Canby. It is the *New York Times*. Mind you, he changed his mind 40 times after that on that same film.

ABE: *One of my interesting experiences when I directed my first film was that I had never directed anything when I did* Force of Evil. *I had never been to a summer camp, I had never directed a little play, I had never acted in a little play, and here I was about to direct a movie that consisted of some very fine actors including possibly a very high class one like Garfield and so on. And I had never directed any of them. And yet I found a way of doing it. Now the way I used was intuitive. First of all I realized that the soul of making a movie, feature film, is not the camera, although I made a very original looking film,* Force of Evil. *It is not the aesthetic although I tried an aesthetic experiment in the film, but that the soul of directing a film is your relationship to actors. Because that's the way a story-telling film tells stories. So I applied the cult of personality. I tried to understand the personality of the actor as a human being. I tried to let them tell me what the picture meant to them, and then in all kinds of secret, subtle ways I tried to convince them when I disagreed with them that my way of looking at it was really their way of looking at it. And so it turned out to be a very well-acted film, I thought. But I had no technical experience as an actor. Or with actors. In words, I applied the same rules to them as I would apply to organizing in a labor union or to attending a radical meeting or a parent-teachers meeting or trying to convince someone I love that they should love me. But fundamentally, all I could do was intuitive. And in a way, although I'm an intellectual, my relationship to actors was intuitive. But you are remarkable to me, anyhow, and I think to the industry, as someone who is exceptionally close to the actor and gets exceptionally interesting performances out of them. What do you do?*

MARTY: Well, the single most important thing, Abe, I think in getting a genuinely good performance, is casting.

ABE: *That's what Tyrone Guthrie said. He said 90% of every play is casting.*
MARTY: He's right. And it's more important in films because you're in closer. I also agree with you that the peculiar content that a genuine actor gives you in an extension of the moment in the film can be more original than anything else in the film. Even today, even in the theatre, I only remember what actors did, I very rarely remember what they say. That's a difficult thing to say to a writer. But when I have to remember something, I remember what the actor did. I remember the shriek of Olivier in Oedipus.

ABE: *I remember what you told me which fits right into that. You said I never listen to their voices, I only watch their faces.*
MARTY: That's right. I never listen to an actor, I only watch the actor. I never listen. I have a script person. If the actor says the wrong lines and I respect the script and I always do, because I shoot scripts, then I will redo it if I feel he has mutilated it, but I'm watching him. I'm watching for that moment of life and that moment of incandescence which comes to really good actors every once in a while when something happens, which is an accident of intuition. Now most of casting is intuition in the genuine sense. You sense that in the circumstances which exist in your film that that actor when pushed to that is going to give you that incandescent moment, at that time, which is an extension of what you and the writer meant. And that's what you look for. You look for those extraordinary moments which are extensions of what the director and writer intended.

ABE: *All right, but how about the role of accident in this.*
MARTY: And you set up accidents.

ABE: *Now that's the point I wanted to talk about.*
MARTY: You set up accidents as much as you can and only with certain kinds of actors. Some actors . . . I mean . . . there's no one way to act. When Stanislavsky wrote his books on acting he said I didn't make any of these things up. I went to see the best actors in the world and I decided that's what they were doing so I wrote it down. Now that became a way of life for a lot of actors in the world. But the actors from whom he copied never heard of Stanislavsky and they were great actors in their own right. So, if you do a film with a lot of actors that have been trained at the Royal Academy and a few actors who have been trained at the Actor's Studio, you're going to have 2 different kinds of actor, both parts equally as good. You have to find a way to have the same extraordinary thing happen to both of them that will tax you and you have to set up circumstances.

ABE: *You set up circumstances. I feel, that you just are alert to accident. You see, I can think of making a film in which there's no script. And I think Altman often encourages this relationship in his films. An improvisation is wonderful but in general actors, when they improvise, are improvising from remembering what they read in plays and acted in other pictures, unless something upsets them. That's the thing.*
MARTY: Now how do you do that? I've done it several ways. I've occasionally lowered a light bulb on a set, and I knew the actor would bump into it on the next take, and he did or she did, and something happened and I did not let them stop, or I changed the position of some of the furniture just a shade. Or I've done something in that nature which would tend to change the scene without changing the meaning of the scene for some kind of an accident to happen. Now I would only do that with certain kinds of actors. If you do that to other kinds of actors the scene stops, and they say wait a minute, wait a minute, what are you doing, I mean, that seems all wrong and you have to cut. But with actors who are trained to go on, something extraordinary can happen. So you have to make a judgment about who you are working with and how best to deal with them. Also, certain actors you can only trick once because you trick them more than once the next time they're not going to trust you. So you really don't trick actors in the theatre, but you can in movies. You only need it once and after that you may not

ever see that actor again thank God, so it's possible, in many ways, again, knowing the people, one of the reasons it's best to use actors you've used before. The more you know about an actor the easier it is to dig into him and to find things which are unusual and original. The only thing that is original in each one of us sitting around this pool at this moment is the subjective, and if you can find a way to get to the subjective of each individual, you'll get something original. Now actors have much easier access to this subjective, artists generally do, than other people. Most people have no access to that except in moments they get drunk or they smoke a joint or they take cocaine and they get a release on the subjective which is part of the reason they take all those drugs. Artists don't need, hopefully, that kind of excitement to get a release on the subjective because the subjective in each person is truly original.

ABE: *I heartily agree with that, biologically speaking you're correct.*
MARTY: Yes.

ABE: *But the reason they are able to understand this is that we're more alike than different or else there would be no communication at all.*
MARTY: Yes, the problem is how to get there and that will vary in each case with the actor.

ABE: *Let me tell you, if we have time, an experience I had at the end of* Willie Boy. *The end of the picture as I had it was that Robert Redford and Susan Clark were together while the burning of the body of Willie Boy was going on and that scene had to be shot at that moment of the day, the magic moment when for an hour of so you have the light of the sun just disappearing, and everything is just beautiful. So I had set aside two such magic moments to complete this scene and in the first magic moment I had them together and right in the middle of the scene as we're shooting, Robert Redford starts to walk away. So I nudged Connie Hall and Hall just followed him and Redford walks on and on and on and on, still walking, and I then nudged Connie Hall again to bring his camera back and put it on Susan Clark's face as close as possible as he can do changing focus and she is absolutely astonished. She doesn't know what to make of the situation because Robert Redford is walking off from her. After this is over I call Redford over and say what are you doing here? That's not in the script. He said I felt that moment that I should be walking away and that the picture should end with me walking away into the desert. I disagreed with him but we had one more night to shoot. So I said very well, but why don't you tell me in advance, and we'll shoot that scene so the next night we arranged it, but I now knew the picture was going to end on the burning and the expression of loss and strange surprise on Susan Clark's face which didn't have to do with the content of the picture but had to do with the fact that Redford was walking out of the scene without having told her. Now I shot the scene with Redford and dumped it, of course, the next day, and ended the picture that way. And when Redford saw it, he never called me on the phone again.*

Norma Rae's Big Daddy

BRUCE COOK/1980

SOME FILMMAKERS get taken for granted. At a time when remarkably young directors establish themselves as powers in the industry on the basis of three pictures, or two, or maybe even one, there remain a few old hands who have managed to amass lists of credits that seem to go on forever and that include some of Hollywood's best work.

Martin Ritt is one of these.

This rough-edged New York-born director has been plying his craft unobtrusively for more than two decades. And although lacking the superstar status of some of the younger directors, he is certainly one of the most respected. Ritt is an "actor's director," and he has drawn from such performers as Paul Newman, Patricia Neal, Richard Burton, and Melvyn Douglas some of their finest acting. Screenwriters know him as a filmmaker who really understands the power of the word. And the men who run the industry point to his films when they want to justify movies as a moral force in American life.

Since 1957, when Martin Ritt emerged from a brush with the blacklist, he has directed *Hud, The Spy Who Came in From the Cold, The Great White Hope, Sounder, Conrack, The Front,* and, most recently, *Norma Rae.* But he has also made more than a dozen other films, all of them representing solid moviemaking, not one a truly bad movie.

"Never made a bad picture? You bet I have—*Five Branded Women*, the only

---

Originally published in *American Film* (April 1980): 50–56, 58. Reprinted by permission of the American Film Institute.

one I'm ashamed of. Maybe you missed that one. It was hardly released in this country, and I keep it off my list. I did it for Dino De Laurentiis, and it was just for the money. I found out then what I should have known before—that you can never work just for money and expect to do anything good." Martin Ritt, of course, being his own toughest critic.

Stocky and gray-haired, Ritt knocks around the Twentieth Century-Fox studios in jump suits of every color, stripe, and check, sometimes topped with a well-worn navy blue sweater. The first time I saw him, a few months ago, I thought he was a grip who had walked off one of the sound stages on his lunch break. The first time he opened his mouth, I caught the tough eloquence of a talkative New York taxi driver.

We happened to get together because I had written a book about Dalton Trumbo, the late screenwriter, novelist, and political gadfly. That was enough to get me invited to lunch. Ritt had known Trumbo since the late fifties, when Trumbo, still blacklisted for his leftist politics, was writing movies on the black market. "He was one of the funniest, wittiest, and most charming men I ever knew," said Ritt. "How anyone could think that he was anything but the greatest American is simply beyond me."

Ritt took me to the Fox commissary, probably the only restaurant in Hollywood where he feels comfortable. He ordered a Tab, lighted up a cigar, and talked about the picture business: "So maybe I have made one bad movie, but I've got a pretty good reputation in the business. I bring my pictures in on time and on budget. They may not be the biggest grossers, but they're good enough to have some play time, so the studio people know they'll get their money back. That keeps them happy and makes it possible for me to go on making pictures."

The most financially successful of them? *Sounder*, the one that some say may also be his most successful artistically. "Absolutely," he assured me. "But, you know, the first time I showed it to my wife from start to finish, I turned to her when it was over, and I said, 'It's a nice little picture, but it won't make a dime.' I was amazed at what it did. I have no sense of whether a picture will or won't make it commercially. The only thing is, I don't pretend to, and the people who do don't have any better idea about such things than I do."

Earlier, when he had heard that I had had some difficulty in finding his office at the Fox executive building, he had laughed and said (referring to the studio's then leaderless state) that evidently I wasn't the only one who was lost there. "They say there's a shortage of executive talent in the industry, and that's the big problem today. But as long as I've been in the business, I've yet to figure out what studio executives really have to do with the making of a picture."

When lunch came—the usual salad for him (he watches his weight and plays a lot of tennis)—Ritt said, "I don't have a contract with Twentieth, but I did my last picture here—*Norma Rae,* which they were pleased with—and I've been trying to get a picture off the ground with them. It's to be a biography of Joseph Stilwell, whom I consider to be the best sort of man produced by America. A conservative, but an honest, able man, and a real hero. I was completely won over by the Barbara Tuchman biography, and I also read on him in Teddy White's *Thunder Out of China.* Anyway, I'm convinced it would make a good picture, but a war biography like this one will *not* be a cheap picture, believe me."

A lot of the talk at that lunch was about movies he had seen lately. On *Luna* he was especially outspoken: "I loathed it, just hated it. I felt I ought to go because I liked one of Bertolucci's early films, *The Conformist,* and I really think he's very talented. But this *Luna* was so pretentious. The incest theme didn't offend me—but the way it was handled! And Jill Clayburgh was miscast, too. Frankly, I don't know who could have played it, though, the way it was written.

"I disliked it almost as much as I disliked the one that won the Academy Award last time—*The Deer Hunter.* That one was also pretentious and was terrible as storytelling. Parts of it, I admit, were good. The beginning, all the way through the wedding sequence, was just fine. He had me. I thought, Here's a movie I'm going to love. But then it got unbelievable—such coincidences, such jumps in the story. And this is another case when I think the director is really very talented. I liked Cimino's first picture, and I met him and liked him. It really bothers me when I can't like a movie."

On our way out of the commissary, Ritt was stopped by Ross Martin, the actor, who had comedian Don Adams in tow. In a moment the conversation was all horses and jockeys. Ritt is not just an avid bettor, he is also the owner of a string of horses, and he is accepted as a sort of sage among Hollywood horseplayers. Don Adams solicited his opinion. Martin Ritt expanded visibly as he lighted up another cigar and responded.

"There," he remarked as we left, "you see another aspect of my character. I *love* the horses. I guess it all goes back to the time I started spending out at the Jamaica track back when I was blacklisted. So much of my life seems to date from that period."

Getting blacklisted was all a matter of being in the right place at the wrong time. Martin Ritt grew up in New York City—in Manhattan and the Bronx—a kid crazy about sports who found his way to a denominational college down South, Elon College, on a football scholarship. One summer he worked at a camp in the Catskills as an athletic counselor and appeared in plays presented by the local acting company. He heard applause for the first time and found himself hooked on the theater. At the end of the summer he informed his parents, who had hoped he would be a lawyer, that he had decided to become an actor. To put it mildly, they disapproved.

Ritt went out looking for work and promptly got himself a part in a play directed by Elia Kazan. That led to a kind of back door entry into the Left-militant Group Theatre. Luther Adler, who was then preparing for Clifford Odets's *Golden Boy*, needed somebody to teach him how to work out on the light punching bag. Adler was anything but an athlete, and simply couldn't make the thing go. Ritt taught him and as his reward was accepted into the company, where he got a first-class grounding in the theater from people like Kazan, Harold Clurman, Lee J. Cobb, and Stella Adler. By the time World War II came along he was an established professional and was given the chance to continue with all-service productions such as *Winged Victory* and *Yellow Jack*. He directed the latter, brought it to Broadway, and by the time the war ended had made his name as a director.

Then he turned to television. The medium was in its infancy. Broadcasts were done live under primitive conditions, but it was an exciting time for everybody involved. "It was something brand-new, of course," Ritt recalls, "and it involved a lot of young writers who may not have been up to getting produced on Broadway at just that moment, but were very talented. They learned their craft writing for it. There's never been that kind of explosion of talent in television since then. It was just all those people coming together, the freedom and newness of it all. Once it became a real mass medium, and they began pitching to the lowest common denominator, there was a drop in quality. It was inevitable, I guess."

In all, Martin Ritt appeared in 150 television plays as an actor and directed a hundred. All this before his career was suddenly cut short in the early fifties by "that grocer up in Syracuse" who, in his AWARE, Inc., newsletter, labeled Ritt a Communist sympathizer on the basis of union shows Ritt had directed and of contributions made during the war to Russian War Relief. It was, of course, part of the same cold war hysteria that had trapped Dalton Trumbo before the House Committee on Un-American Activities as one of the Hollywood Ten and sent him off to jail for contempt.

Nothing quite like that happened to Martin Ritt, who regarded himself as a left-of-center progressive. Although he found himself suddenly and completely unemployable in television, he did manage to survive: "I taught school, my wife began selling space in the Yellow Pages, and we went deep into debt. That was when I started playing the horses. I actually made a little money that way."

The television blacklist was not really as "official" as the movie blacklist, which was maintained in loose collaboration with the House Committee on Un-American Activities. Right-wing vigilante groups such as AWARE, Inc., based their charges on the rankest sort of innuendo and guilt by association. Later, when that archconservative Spyros Skouras looked at the political record of his new Twentieth Century-Fox employee, he asked Ritt, "You were blacklisted for *that?*"

(Ritt's experiences during this dark period provided him with the inspiration for one of his strongest and most successful films, *The Front*—the only Hollywood feature to deal directly with the blacklist and its consequences. With the exception of Woody Allen in the title role, many of those involved in the production had suffered the same fate as Ritt. He recalls: "Walter Bernstein, who wrote the film, was blacklisted practically the same day I was.")

After a time on the blacklist, Ritt took up directing for the theater on and off Broadway, in and out of New York. One of the plays he did was *A Very Special Baby* by Robert Alan Aurthur. "It opened and closed in a week," Ritt says, "but I told Bob then that it would make the 1956 ten-best list, and it did." Aurthur, pleased with the production that Ritt had given the play, pushed for him to direct his screenplay *Edge of the City*, which David Susskind was producing independently in New York. Susskind took a chance—after all, the blacklist was still a reality when the picture was released in 1957—and Martin Ritt was suddenly established as a motion picture director.

For a director who, by his own admission, didn't know then which end of the camera to look in to compose a shot, Martin Ritt made an impressive debut with *Edge of the City*. Not only was the film, which starred Sidney Poitier and John Cassavetes in their first major roles, a fine piece of work in its own right, it also foreshadowed themes and concerns that would occur in Ritt's later pictures.

Critics, for instance, have remarked on the frequent appearance of an outsider figure in his films, a single person placed in what is often perilous opposition to the many. Introduced as the Cassavetes character in *Edge of the City*, Ritt's outsider has often reappeared—played by Paul Newman in such pictures as *The Long, Hot Summer*, *Hud*, and *Hombre;* or by Richard Burton in *The Spy Who Came in From the Cold;* or by Richard Harris in *The Molly Maguires;* or by James Earl Jones in *The Great White Hope*.

"Subject matter is the whole ball game with me," says Ritt, and the movies he has made bear this out. They may echo the racial theme he first sounded in *Edge of the City*, as do *Paris Blues*, *Hombre*, *The Great White Hope*, *Sounder*, and *Conrack*. Or they may repeat the betrayal motif of *Edge of the City*, as do *The Spy Who Came in From the Cold*, *The Molly Maguires*, and *The Front*.

The point is that Martin Ritt is one of the few American directors who treat such subjects consistently, and in whose work such deep thematic veins can be clearly traced. He has been nothing if not consistent. Significantly, too, that first feature was not a political film. "Human experience is sufficient if it's dug into deep enough," he says. "It doesn't have to be some kind of ideological statement. That's what they say about me, that I'm a political director, but of mine only *The Front* and maybe *The Molly Maguires* were overtly political films."

Yet talk of themes and subject matter does little to convey the true quality of his films. For one thing, they are dependably well written. And they have displayed the best work of some of our top film actors. Yet he has never been so absorbed by the dramatic values of his films that he has neglected their look. Working with such cinematographers as James Wong Howe, and recently with John Alonzo, he has always hit a high standard in visual style.

The movie in which all these qualities combine most effectively received mixed reviews when it was released in 1970 and died at the box office—*The Molly Maguires*. From its marvelous long opening shot, which graphically depicts the back-breaking nature of nineteenth-century coal mining, to the last sequence, in which the betrayer visits the man he betrayed in the latter's jail cell, the film tells a story that deals in remarkably subtle terms with violence and self-justification. Perhaps too subtle for some. A few critics and many patrons apparently assumed that because the betrayer was played by Richard Harris, he was meant to be the hero of the film.

The Molly Maguires seems to be Martin Ritt's personal favorite of his films, the orphan child of the lot. He finds it difficult to account for its failure with audiences. "It was a movie done in shades of gray, while one like *Norma Rae* was black-and-white, easy to come to terms with. I still don't understand its failure, though. I really don't."

Martin Ritt lives far up Sunset Boulevard on a Pacific Palisades side street. Although the street is situated only a short distance from the ocean, the surrounding canyons and thick woods give it something of a sheltered, inland, almost eastern feeling. Once inside the house, however, glimpsing the swimming pool in back and the Jacuzzi spa under construction, a visitor can have no doubt that this place is pure California.

Adele Ritt greets me and steers me as far as possible from the noise of the workmen excavating the spa. A former actress, she is the mother of their two children, twenty-two-year-old Tina and nineteen-year-old Mike. Before I know it, she has a cup of coffee and a warm bagel in front of me. Ritt soon enters, trailing clouds of shaving lotion, dressed in another jump suit. Pointing at the plate before me, he nods his approval. "The bagel," he says, "the greatest Jewish contribution to American culture."

Trying to sort out Ritt's qualities as a director, I ask him first what he thinks is essential to the job. Perplexed, he shakes his head. "Very hard to say. Very. A director can come from any place because it isn't one job, it's many. But let me tell you how I think about what I do. First of all, I'm not a technician, a guy who works on a wristwatch and turns out a good product. I care what a film of mine says. It has to represent me. I get the feeling with a lot of young directors today that this isn't the case. I'm not knocking them, but I hope that sooner or later they find out more about themselves and want to make pictures about the human condition. The films that have affected me—practically all of Renoir, the best of Chaplin—are all about the human condition, and that's why they move me just as they did when I first saw them. They were made with perception and feeling. Skill is something you can develop. Perception is more difficult."

What does he mean, directing isn't one job but many?

"Let me say in front that casting a production is the most important thing for a director. It determines completely what kind of film he's going to have. Not just actors. Casting the right screenwriter to do the script, the right cinematographer to shoot the film, and the right production designer, too. Getting the right people to do the job is more important than my input. Believe me."

Is that why he seems to work with the same people in film after film—with, for instance, screenwriters Irving Ravetch and Harriet Frank, Jr. (*Hud, Hombre, Conrack, Norma Rae*) and Walter Bernstein (*Paris Blues, The Molly Maguires, The Front*)?

"Well, I work very hard on a screenplay. Once I get it where I want it, I don't change it on the set. When you work with people you have worked with in the past, communication is easier. You also know that in certain moments of stress they're going to deliver what you want. With a writer, you have to sense what's underneath the surface, what his resources as a human being are—and then you tap those resources, you get him to release them. I've been right more often than I've been wrong about the best writer to do a job. And the proof of that is the fact that of the—what?—nineteen films I've made, there are only a couple where there's been more than one writing credit. I like to stick with a writer if I can."

And cinematographer?

"I've only used a few. For years it seemed like it was just James Wong Howe. I guess he made such an impression on me because he was such a great artist—and such a strong personality, too. He could be very irascible and was very impatient with incompetence, so that some crews just hated him. I loved him. Hew was a pure artist and a very original thinker as a cameraman. Painting on a lens with Vaseline or using filters, he could get any quality of light I might want. He could make the sky look like anything at all. And he would do anything for a shot. I remember him when we were shooting *Hombre*. At a pretty advanced age, he was climbing up a stiff mountain with a camera on his back just so we wouldn't lose the light for the next shot. And on *The Molly Maguires,* when we shot the burning of the company store, we had three cameras going inside when some gas caught and blew up. The three operators came running out when that happened, and Jimmie, who was outside, went running in. When his operators saw that, they went back and finished shooting the sequence as the place burned down around them."

And actors? Ritt is known, after all, as an actor's director.

"Well, it's true I do know a great deal about acting, and that helps some of them, I'm sure. But the best thing I did for them was to cast them in parts I knew they'd be marvelous in. I'm not an acting guru, because I know that if I had cast the wrong actor, he'd be dead in the role no matter how much I know. Ofttimes you're forced to take chances. Certain actors make a movie more viable commercially. Certain others may never have done anything remotely like the role you want them for. Paul Newman was not wanted by the studio for *The Long, Hot Summer*. I had to fight to get Pat Neal for *Hud*. She had been playing ladies, and that was how the studio saw her. The Ravetches saw her differently and got me on their side. She won an Academy Award for that one, you know.

"It doesn't always go smoothly, understand. Richard Burton and I had our differences on *The Spy Who Came in From the Cold*—in fact, he fought me all the way—but I think I got the best motion picture performance he's given." Ritt shakes his head, frowning. "That guy—he should have been another Olivier with his equipment."

Considering the many movies they made together, working with Paul Newman was obviously easier. "Our backgrounds are similar—Actors Studio and so on, so we think in the same terms. But that's only part of it. He's a lovely man and a fine actor. Our association goes back to *The Long, Hot Summer*, and, in fact, we had a company together for a while and have remained good friends since the last picture we made, *Hombre*, thirteen years ago. I'm trying to work up a picture with him now. I want him to do Stilwell with me. He has the right combination of qualities."

The telephone rings, and Ritt takes the call. From the repeated name, Sally, I take a guess he is talking with Sally Field, the star of *Norma Rae*. He is. "She's down South with her boyfriend now," Ritt says when he returns. "She's another example of somebody I had to fight the studio to get. She made them very nervous. They knew she was a good actress, but she'd never carried a picture before, and so they were reluctant. Now they've forgotten all about that, of course, and they feel just like I do—that she's going to be a very big star.

"She's funny. She's awful good. She can do almost anything. I want her for another picture, an original script by Gary DeVore, a character piece about a hooker and an ex-fighter. Southern background again, probably Atlanta. It's about the lumpen proletariat. That's a phrase you don't hear much any more."

I start to ask just how many projects Ritt has up in the air at any given time. Before I can finish, he provides the answer: "Right now I've got four different film projects going. That's not unusual. A producer will have many more. There's one that I've worked on a year, 'Monsignor,' with a script by Abraham Polonsky and Wendell Mayes, that has to do with the big-business dealings of the Vatican. That may fall through. If it does, it will be the first time that's ever happened to me—to put in that kind of work, then have it go down the drain. That's why you have to have other projects ready, though—the Stilwell movie, the one I'm talking to Sally Fields about, and there's another one about blacks in World War I that Frank Pierson is writing the script for."

Always having other projects ready is part of the survival game in Hollywood. "After those years on the blacklist, survival is not just a word with me," Ritt says. "Financially, I've been careful, so I haven't had to decide between doing what I really want to do and making another *Five Branded Women*. Survival is tough if you really make up your mind to do only what you want to do. This business is fifty percent talent and fifty percent being able to take care of yourself in a street fight. I've known genuinely gifted people who couldn't take care of themselves, or maybe made the wrong decisions somewhere along the line, and simply sank out of sight.

"But I don't worry too much about that personally right now, because in spite of some problems, I've felt very good about the work I did in the last eight or ten years. I've had a flow of pictures I like that reflect me. I've been fortunate to be able to work. Who knows? Maybe the iron curtain will close and I won't be able to get any more pictures off the ground. If that's the case, I'll be sorry because my ambitions are to keep working just as long as I can. On March second I'll be sixty-six, and I don't feel in any way old. I know I can be a lot of help to my co-workers, so I want to keep at it."

He looks at me suspiciously, as though he has noticed for the first time that I have been taking notes throughout our conversation. Then, gruffly, he shakes his cigar in my direction: "I hope none of that sounded pretentious. If it does, I'd like you to cut down the pretension when you write it."

Dialogue on Film: Martin Ritt

AMERICAN FILM INSTITUTE/1983

CROSS CREEK, Martin Ritt's new film, is in some ways a quintessential Ritt picture. Set in the South, the scene of a half dozen other Ritt titles, including *Sounder, The Long Hot Summer,* and *Norma Rae, Cross Creek* features strong performances by Mary Steenburgen (as author Marjorie Kinnan Rawlings), Rip Torn , and Peter Coyote. The list of memorable performances Ritt has drawn out through the years includes Paul Newman's in *Hud* and *Hombre,* James Earl Jones's in *The Great White Hope,* Richard Burton's in *The Spy Who Came in From the Cold,* Cicely Tyson's and Paul Winfield's in *Sounder,* and, most recently, Oscar winner Sally Field's in *Norma Rae.*

That Ritt works so well with actors is no surprise, given his background as a stage and television actor (he made his Broadway debut in 1937 in *Golden Boy*). He began directing plays shortly after serving in World War II, and then moved on to television, where he worked with many of the Actors Studio graduates he would use later in his films, including Paul Newman. Ritt broke into movies in 1957 with the acclaimed drama *Edge of the City,* starring John Cassavetes and Sidney Poitier, and his stature in Hollywood has been on the rise ever since. Even a rare Ritt failure like *The Molly Maguires* has acquired a cult following.

In the Dialogue, Martin Ritt examines the reasons he works so well with so many different kinds of actors; he also discusses the financial climate in

---

Originally published in *American Film* (November 1983): 19–20, 22. Reprinted by permission of the American Film Institute.

today's film scene that restricts filmmakers who want to deal with serious subject matter.

QUESTION: *I think you've been called an actor's director.*
MARTIN RITT: For lack of a better name, yes. The most important thing in getting a first-class performance is getting the right actor. Casting is eighty percent, if not more, of getting the proper performance. There's a special divinity about casting. It's always an educated guess. You never know for certain. When I met Sally Field, I knew she was the girl I wanted for *Norma Rae*. I was looking for a certain kind of lady. She came in and I spent a little time with her and I knew she was the girl. I knew she was fierce. I knew she was angry. I knew she was avid for life.

QUESTION: *Did you have the same experience in casting Mary Steenburgen in* Cross Creek?
RITT: Not exactly, because I had seen Mary and I wanted her for that part; I didn't necessarily want Sally before I met her. I knew when I spent some time with Mary that she was what I needed to make *Cross Creek* work in terms of performance. First of all, she's a Middle American, and all the things that are good about that she has, and she has somehow managed to sweep all the crap away from herself. She has none of the rigidity of prejudices, and yet she has a kind of strength, stubbornness, and graciousness. She's a lady, and I knew I needed a lady for this picture, much as I knew I needed a kind of mutt to play Norma Rae. When I met Mary and spent time with her, I knew that she had those qualities and that she'd be right.

With a picture like *Conrack,* the ebullience of Jon Voight was needed in that part. One of the nice things about today's stars is that most of them are pretty damn good actors. It's not like the old days, when the kids were under contract because of the way they looked. Almost every one of these kids can really act. And they didn't get there accidentally. Some of them behave poorly, but that has nothing to do with their ability.

QUESTION: *Isn't every actor different in his or her approach to a role? How do you deal with that?*
RITT: Some actors I've worked with come to their performances somewhat externally. Sally is a little bit like that. She's unafraid; she'll plunge in and just play the shit out of a scene. Now, it can be all wrong, but something has

happened to her in the doing of it. Most of the actors trained by the Group Theatre and the Actors Studio go to the other extreme: They sit there and they mumble, and they're groping and looking for what the truth of the scene is. You have to relate that to what you think the spine of the scene is, or the spine of the character, sort of give them a clue; otherwise, they drift around and may or may not finally come up with the correct thing. You have to do this without ever letting them know that you're doing it.

When I did *Hud*, I worked with Melvyn Douglas, one style of actor; Paul Newman, another style of actor; Patricia Neal, a third style of actor; and the kid, a fourth style of actor. And I had to make them all understand what I meant and still not violate their own feelings about where they came from. Sometimes an actor's back gets up when he understands where you're from and he's not from there and he feels that perhaps you don't have the respect for him that you should. The assurance that you've cast him is sometimes sufficient.

QUESTION: *How closely do you work with writers?*
RITT: I work very closely with writers; I also keep writers on the set, because I recognize the importance of the job and I don't want to be suddenly left by myself. All I've ever done with the rewriting of a scene is cut it—cut it down to the essentials of what I feel the scene is about. But if there's a quality of language that's needed that's highly personal, then it's suicidal not to have the writers there. I have one record that nobody could touch: I've done twenty-three films and I've never fired a screenwriter in my life. (Perhaps I should have.) The Ravetches [Irving Ravetch and Harriet Frank, Jr.], with whom I've done most of my films, are, as far as I'm concerned, as good as they come. They know how to write a picture. They know how to make it work, they have a great ear, they're professional.

I'd break people in this business down into the following categories: About one-tenth of one percent are enormously and genuinely gifted. About ten percent are professionals. The rest of them are up for grabs. And if in some way your work as an actor or a writer or a director does not reflect who you are, then you're not very good. It must reflect who you are, what you believe in, what you want out of life.

QUESTION: *Did you work with Larry McMurtry on* Hud?

RITT: No, because he was the novelist; we bought the book. As a matter of fact, the character Hud existed in the novel only in a minor way. He was just one of the hands in the bunkhouse. The Ravetches and I had discussed several times making the kind of picture that Clark Gable used to make all the time, where he was this terrible son of a bitch, and somehow Spencer Tracy converted him in the second half of the picture. We said, "Why don't we take that kind of American hero and show that he really is a jerk?" A guy committed to his appetite and only to his appetite and really not much of a man, American or otherwise. And so they wrote that character.

QUESTION: *So why did* Hud *take off the way it did with audiences?*
RITT: I do have an idea, and I'm very sorry to tell you about it. I got a lot of letters after that picture from kids saying Hud was right. The old man's a jerk and the kid's a schmuck, or a fag, or whatever they wanted to call him. And if I'd been near as smart as I thought I was, I would have seen that Haight-Ashbury was right around the corner. The kids were very cynical; they were committed to their own appetites, and that was it. That's why the film did the kind of business it did—the kids loved Hud. That son of a bitch that I hated they loved. So the audience makes a film their own—it depends what's going on at the time in the country.

QUESTION: *You began directing in the days of live television. How did you break into film in the late fifties?*
RITT: I was in New York, unemployed. A friend of mine had written a teleplay which was to be made into a film called "A Man Is Ten Feet Tall." That turned out to be my first film, *Edge of the City*. He insisted that I direct it. Metro was going through one of their innumerable proxy fights, so they didn't even know the film was being made. I made the film in twenty-eight days and I was so inexperienced that when I finished it and I was sitting with my editor, he said, "You're crazy. We didn't have anything left." I shot it like it was a live television show, with the assumption that everything I shot was pure gold. I've never done that since, to the consternation of many people. But that film I edited entirely in my head as I shot it. Fortunately, whatever was wrong with the film was not so enormous that I couldn't make it work.

Now, the film came out, and got extremely good press, but it never got its money back, because of the way they booked it. It cost $400,000, and at that time, Metro had also opened a big film called *The Iron Petticoat*, with Bob

Hope. They booked that picture and they billed our picture above it in New York, where we got good press. We got five dollars for a booking and the other film got all the rest of the money. That was an accounting deal that Metro did to get the maximum money back that they could for that film.

QUESTION: *To what extent does* The Front *reflect the blacklist era accurately and to what extent is it dramatized for a mass audience?*
RITT: Everything in that film happened. I was there in that delicatessen when that front said to one of the writers I knew, "This is not up to my usual standard. I'm not going to turn it in."

QUESTION: *That's a real line?*
RITT: That's a real line.

QUESTION: *What about the final scene? Is that based on fact?*
RITT: It's based on fact in the sense that several guys totally defied the committee. As a matter of fact, when Woody Allen and I decided to use that line, to tell the committee to go fuck themselves, Columbia said, "You can't do that. This is a PG film, or a G film." Finally, we got an OK on it on the basis that a film had opened just prior to ours which had gotten the proper rating because of its high intentions. And when the screening committee that rates films saw *The Front*, they decided to go along with that.

QUESTION: *Do you think you could get a movie like that made today?*
RITT: I doubt it. The atmosphere today in this country makes it even more difficult to do serious films. It is possible to survive making films that basically represent who you are and what you're about. But it ain't easy. Of course, nothing easy is really worthwhile. Even today, if I go in with a serious film, it's, "You made a film like *Norma Rae* that didn't do anywhere near the business that this other film did." What they're interested in today is a film that they can get a return of a hundred million dollars on. Well, almost no serious film can do that.

QUESTION: *Speaking of political films, what happened to* The Molly Maguires, *a film I heard you liked very much?*
RITT: It was a total failure. I mean at the box office. It's a film that keeps coming back, and every time I go to Europe, they talk to me about it. It was

a very sophisticated film, in fact, because the leading character, instead of being painted black or white, was painted gray, purposefully. For an audience—a movie audience—it was too complicated. They didn't know who the hero of the film was. And many of them didn't agree with what Sean Connery represented. I thought *he* was the hero of the film.

QUESTION: *Do the economics of filmmaking today work even harder against someone who wants to make political movies?*

RITT: There are two pictures that I made for a percentage of my usual salary. One I did for a tenth of my salary—*Sounder*. I wanted to make that picture. On *Norma Rae*, I worked for half my salary. I wanted to make that picture; I wouldn't have gotten it made if I'd insisted on full salary. There's nothing shameful about that. This town is corrupt in the sense that once you get a certain salary, your agents tell you . . . well, agents don't make pictures. I hate to tell you what they do make, but I don't know of a single person, certainly myself included, that ever expected to be rich in this business. That's totally an accident. If twenty years ago somebody had offered me $15,000 a year for life, I would have gotten to the pen and paper before anyone else had spoken. And that's why we're all in this business; we're all here because we want to express ourselves. Otherwise, we don't belong here. The rest of it is all a by-product. Some people make it big and it's ridiculous. I mean, it's totally ridiculous what happens. I think probably Spielberg and Lucas between them could engineer twelve banana-republic uprisings. They could do whatever they wanted to do. They're both very expert filmmakers, but the money finally becomes ridiculous.

QUESTION: *Was it easier when you came into the industry to break in than it is now?*

RITT: In a way—but, of course, there are many more independent films being made now, and subject matter is so much more wide open. I've seen pictures that would never have been made when I broke into the industry. Nobody would have been able to make a picture like *Risky Business*, but it was made, and I'm sure it was not a very expensive picture to make. I don't like a lot of the pictures I've seen, but I do think, because of the relaxing in terms of subject matter, you're going to see some great films made on the American scene in the next decade.

QUESTION: *So many of your films—Conrack, Sounder, Norma Rae, and now Cross Creek—are set in the South. That has to be more than a coincidence.*
RITT: I think it is. I went to school in the South, at a little college called Elon in North Carolina. And the southeast section of the United States has undergone more change than any other section of the country in recent years. It's an extraordinary part of the country in terms of the literature it's turned out.

What probably happens is that I'm attracted to a certain kind of material, and the South's where it takes place. It doesn't take place in the Northeast, where I grew up, or in California. It takes place in that section of the country.

QUESTION: *The scene in* Norma Rae *where Norma and the organizer go swimming is one of the sexiest things I've ever seen. How did that come about in writing the film?*
RITT: Well, it was a combination of things. Because there was no violence in the story, we were looking for tension. And we knew that the worst thing we could do was to bring those two together. He was a professional organizer. The worst thing a professional like that can do is come to a town and screw the lady and go on to the next town and screw the lady. She was a woman who was just beginning to find herself, and this could have been the kind of concession that she would never have gotten over. Therefore, by not bringing them together, we did create a certain kind of tension. Everybody who ever saw that film was sure they were going to wind up in the sack. We didn't do it, and we didn't do it for that reason. It was a combined effort.

QUESTION: *You filmed* Norma Rae *on location in the South. Did you encounter any problems in coming up with a mill to shoot in?*
RITT: When I went in looking for locations, the guys who owned the mills had been told, "If this guy comes in and makes this kind of film, you know what he's gonna say." So everybody turned us down. To their everlasting credit, two guys who owned mills sent letters saying, "We don't like to be told what we can do and what we can't do; if you haven't found what you're looking for, come look at our place." That taught me something about the independence of certain spirits in our country.

When we got this location, I went down and saw it, I liked it, and we made a deal with the guy. Then he came back one day and said he was the president of some textile organization, and he said, "They'll kill me." I think we had offered him $25,000 for the location. I went back over my budget with the art director, and we got together $100,000 which she felt we could save. We went to see him, and I said, "I'm going to offer you $100,000 for two and a half weeks' work in your mill." He said to me, "Mr. Ritt, I'm going to have to reexamine my scruples." And we got the mill.

"I Don't Ask Questions. If It Works, It Works!"

PHYLLIS R. KLOTMAN/1985

IN JANUARY (1985) I interviewed Martin Ritt in his office at Columbia Pictures in Burbank, California. He is a feisty, energetic septuagenarian and agreed to this interview in spite of the fact that he was leaving the next day to shoot his recently released film, *Murphy's Romance*. His calendar and his office are efficiently handled by his secretary Brooke Carlyle who graciously assisted me in making arrangements for and typing the taped interview.

Ritt chews gum like a reclaimed smoker and he answers questions without hesitation; he does not however elaborate unless something strikes him as particularly significant. I was impressed by his candor: he says what he believes and he doesn't care who's listening. He knew I was there as the Director of the Black Film Center/Archive of the Afro-American Studies Department, Indiana University, of which he is a sponsor, and that I would particularly want to hear him discuss the black experience films he has made.

PK: *Let me begin by thanking you for your time. I know that you're busy, and that you're leaving Monday to shoot a new film. Are you willing to say what that is?*
MR: It's called *Murphy's Romance* and it's a contemporary love story, with Sally Field and James Garner, and I like it very much. It's very charming.

PK: *I've seen the interview you did for* American Film, *but you know my focus is different. I want to talk about your films that have something to do with black*

Published by permission of the author.

experience. I thought we would focus on Sounder *since* Sounder *is one of those films that's been so highly acclaimed and there have been so few like it. Number one, you did not, as I understand it, produce that film?*
MR: No, I did not.

PK: *I know when you produce something, you get the person you want to do the screenplay.*
MR: I get them anyway.

PK: *That was my question. Were you contacted originally by a producer or did you choose that script yourself?*
MR: I was contacted by Robert Radnitz, and he gave me the book to read, and then after that we did everything in cooperation.

PK: *So, when you found Lonne Elder . . .*
MR: I didn't find him. We both agreed on Lonne Elder. First of all, we had no money. In that case, I made that adjustment. That film cost a million dollars. It was the last film made with a very small crew, when the union allowed one to make a film at that cost with a very small crew. We couldn't even afford to hire a very expensive writer, so we got Lonne who was a black writer, who had written a play that we liked.

PK: Ceremonies in Dark Old Men.
MR: Yes, and I worked with Lonne, and Bob worked with Lonne. It was a collaborative effort, and he finally came up with a very good screenplay.

PK: *Yes, very good. You look at a child's story, essentially about a dog, and you don't think it's going to be a terribly exciting film.*
MR: Well, of course, that had a lot to do with me and the actors. When you do a film in which the two leading actors are nominated for Academy Awards, something special has happened. And I wish I could say that Cicely was my first choice—she was not.

PK: *That was my next question. When you cast, do you use a casting director?*
MR: Yes, but you make all the decisions.

PK: *And who was your first choice?*

MR: I don't want to embarrass the lady—she turned me down.

PK: *And so Cicely Tyson was . . .*
MR: Cic [Sis] insisted that she could play the part, and I said, "I don't think so, Cic—you're a great beauty, you're a high fashion model," and she said something that I never forgot. She said, "No black in this country is more than one generation removed from that experience." I bought that, and I knew immediately at the start of rehearsal that she was going to be terrific. And she is a terrific actress, there's no question.

PK: *I wanted to say something about that in particular, but let me ask you a little bit about the other casting. Winfield?*
MR: Winfield I met and liked. He'd played only heavies up to that point. He read and he read extremely well. I liked him very much. The boy . . . we were stuck. We couldn't find a kid. This boy was the son of an actor.

PK: *Robert Hook's boy.*
MR: That's right, and a very nice kid. Casting is always an educated guess. You cast really to the big scenes. When you cast *Hamlet,* you better be sure the actor can play "Now I am alone. . . ." And when I finally got Cic, I realized she could play anything—she's a terrific actress. If she were white, she'd be a great big star.

PK: *That's one of the things I was going to ask you to talk about a little bit. I think—this is personal—that that's been her finest film performance.*
MR: Oh, no question of it.

PK: *It's so beautifully understated. I wanted to ask how you work with her. She is a dramatic actress; I mean, she came from the theatre. Is it different working with somebody like that?*
MR: Not really, no. The truth is the truth. In theatre, obviously you have to reach the second balcony, so you can afford to be. . . . It's easier, in a certain way, in the movies to be truthful—but at the same time it's easier to be caught in a lie because the camera's right there, and if it isn't the McCoy, the camera will see it.

PK: *But you had experience in the theatre.*

MR: Yes. Oh, I've done everything. But I knew soon that our two actors would be terrific. And the boy was just a natural. I remember when we shot the scene with his father on the tree limb—and he said, "I can't cry, Marty." And I said, "OK, don't cry." Well, we started the scene and there was a waterfall.

PK: *If you'd said cry, he would never have been able to do it.*
MR: Those kinds of mistakes I don't make.

PK: *Some people do talk about problems when they make the transition from the theatre to being in front of the camera. And I'm wondering if maybe the fact that you had that kind of experience made a difference in your relationship with Tyson.*
MR: No, I don't think there is any problem. Theatre actors are generally better trained and better equipped, but they're not necessarily better movie actors. Gary Cooper was a great movie actor. Ronald Colman was also in the theatre. Tracy was also.

PK: *Hepburn was also in the theatre.*
MR: They're all terrific. If you're really good, it doesn't matter. You may have to come down a little bit, and you will when the microphone is hanging over your head and the camera is right there. You're not going to be playing to the second balcony. It takes a certain amount of pressure off. And also, if you don't do it right, you've got somebody out front who knows what's going on and you can do it again. . . . which you can't do in the theatre. It's very difficult in the theatre to keep a play really fresh, eight times a week, and you're lucky if you get into a hit. After six months. . . .

PK: *It goes on forever.*
MR: It's terrible, especially if you're the director and you go to see it and you see the performance has totally changed. Well, that doesn't happen in a film. When you say "Print," you've got what you want. You don't even have to *talk* to them any more if you don't want to. Making movies is a big kick in that area.

PK: *(laughter)*
MR: Because I've done a picture with actors I *didn't* like. I got what I wanted and that was it—goodbye!

PK: *That's good if you got what you wanted. Well, let me ask you a touchy question. We know that so few blacks have been nominated for the Academy Award and so few have received it—do you think there is any racism involved?*
MR: First of all, there are no films written for them, even by black writers—the same as now, even in this very strong feminist age, when so many more women are involved, every script I pick up has 20 men to one woman.

PK: *Isn't that terrible?*
MR: It's terrible. And I don't think that there's racism in the overt sense. There may be in isolated cases. But you are talking on an industry level—I think there's racism in the fact that black pictures don't make money. Sounder is the only picture that involved blacks that's ever crossed over to a white audience.

PK: *That's the other thing I was going to ask you. Sounder was a film about the black experience. Films that I see now—I mean, what Eddie Murphy does and Richard Pryor does—those films seem to me to be, if not completely irrelevant, then certainly peripheral.*
MR: That's what they are. I'm surprised at Pryor, because he is of consequence.

PK: *And he is extraordinarily talented.*
MR: And very powerful, very big. He can do whatever he wants, much more so, say, that I can, because he makes the kind of money that. . . . And Murphy—I don't know anything about Murphy. He seems a street kid. He's gifted. I have seen his pictures. They are amusing—I wouldn't accuse them of any genuine quality. But this town doesn't care. The bottom line here is: Does the picture make money?

PK: *So you think that explains the paucity of such pictures?*
MR: Yes.

PK: *You know those two film critics in Chicago, Siskel and Ebert, did a program on the life and death of black movies. Came the 80s and it seems like. . . .*
MR: Well, you got Reagan. Did you read the ad that that committee turned out, the inaugural committee? They asked for 200 actors—"non-union,

clean-cut American types . . ." I mean, public-relationswise, it's got to be one of the stupidest moves.

PK: *Well, everybody knows what clean-cut American types are, and they don't include most of us, and they certainly don't include black people.*
MR: No, they certainly don't.

PK: *Well, I remember that the NAACP in '82, I think it was, was very concerned and was even considering a boycott; they mentioned 1980 as the worst year for black actors and actresses since the previous decade.*
MR: Well, it's very complicated. When I made *Conrack*, for instance, I got a lot of flak from the black community about a white Jesus. And I said, "Listen, fellows, get off my back. Make your own goddam picture. I have believed in integration all my life. I'm not going to change my mind to suit your political needs at this point. You guys are for black studies. You don't want to know about white people who are doing good work. Ok, don't bother me, that's what I'm going to do." And everytime I made a picture that has involved blacks I've gotten some kind of flak.

There was flak about *Sounder.* I had two or three people I know—blacks—who came to me and said, "We don't want to know about that. We're not like that anymore. We don't want to know about that experience. We're hardnosed and tough today."

I said, "Fine. So make that picture. That's not what I can make. I'm making what I can make, and that's it."

I got a lot of flak on *Conrack,* an awful lot. I got very pissed off, frankly. But I would do a picture tomorrow about blacks if I found one I liked. And I could get the money to make it. I probably could, because I'd make it cheaper—it's a lot easier. And the blacks who are trying to break into the industry are not writing serious work either. They want to get in and make money.

PK: *You mean what is considered megabucks now?*
MR: Horror films, action-adventure films. I'm making a really charming, I think, a lovely film, a small picture by Hollywood standards.

PK: *But nobody wants to make a small picture.*

MR: No, because they think it won't do big business.

PK: *So what happened to the small films, I mean films that people really enjoyed seeing, even though they're not . . .*
MR: There are fewer and fewer of them being made, that's all, and only the top people can make them because the studio won't put any money in them.

PK: *That was really what Siskel and Ebert were talking about. They said that* The Wiz, *which did not make big bucks, seemed to figure the demise of these films, that it was not the kind of cross-over film they expected it to be.*
MR: Well, anyway, the blacks are not writing for the black movies. Nobody's writing them. *A Soldier's Story* . . . it was a white director who saw the play in New York. Fortunately, he had enough muscle to get the movie made.

PK: *I don't know how that's done at the box office.*
MR: It's done well. It's good melodrama.

PK: *But there's no way it's going to make millions.*
MR: It won't make megabucks. But it'll do well.

PK: *Do you think Hollywood has an obligation to make films that somehow reflect the black experience?*
MR: Sure, they have an obligation, as far as I'm concerned.

PK: *Thirty percent of the audience is supposed to be black.*
MR: Yes, but even that audience doesn't want to see *Sounder,* they want to see *Superfly.* So the only people with any responsibility are the creative people. Nobody else is at all responsible. They'll do anything to make money, whatever it is—they don't care.

PK: *But you think there is some obligation, there ought to be . . .*
MR: There is an obligation of every artist to mirror the society in which he lives. Therefore, there is that obligation.

PK: *Another question about your personal sense. I know a number of your films—I have probably seen all of them. But a number of them deal with real concerns, of maybe small people, people who are not important in the universe, whether they are poor blacks or poor whites, or union people. Do they reflect your social commitment?*

MR: I have a very strong social commitment, always have had. And it doesn't change. I have been fortunate that I have been allowed to make films that represent me. A lot of guys can't. And also, they settle.

PK: *And you didn't.*
MR: And I didn't. I've made some films I wish I hadn't made, but it wasn't for any other reason than that I made a mistake in the material.

PK: *Everybody makes mistakes.*
MR: Sure, sure, everybody does.

PK: *I wanted to ask some specific questions about* Sounder. *I have been working and meeting with some independent black film critics and some of the independent filmmakers. And one of their strongest criticisms against the industry is—well, first of all, people are left out—but the way in which blacks are photographed. They think that most whites do not understand how to shoot black skin tones, you know, the nuances of black skin color. When you have, let's say, Alfre Woodard in* Cross Creek, *when you have blacks in a scene, does the cinematographer handle that problem. Do you direct him or her?*
MR: I'm not sure what the answer to that is. I have seen several films directed by black directors, and I haven't noticed that they photographed their black actors any differently.

PK: *Do you know any of these up-and-coming young independent filmmakers among the blacks?*
MR: The only one I know is Melvin Van Peebles, and when he photographed blacks they were no different than when anybody else photographs them.

PK: *There was a real problem in that film with lighting.*
MR: Well, he has a big problem—you have to pour in the light. You're in there with a blonde actor, and it's complicated to shoot. Maybe the blacks understand that better. But then I'd have to see proof of that.

PK: *I saw the film that Van Peebles did in Paris,* The Story of a Three-Day Pass,

but it was in black and white, and he learned a lot about using the camera there. It was a really interesting film.
MR: He's an interesting filmmaker, there's no question.

PK: *Did you use any blacks on the crews? Are there more now?*
MR: On *Sounder* we used blacks. We had an assistant director. They are part of my commitment. I've used them wherever I can.

PK: *I really would like to see Tyson do something like that role again.*
MR: First-class things don't happen that frequently.

PK: *I mean, look at* Bustin' Loose.
MR: I don't even know what that is.

PK: *That was the film she made with Richard Pryor.*
MR: She needed money, I'm sure.

PK: *(continuing) You know, she played the kind of non-stereotypical role she wanted to play, but . . .*
MR: He's directing his first film here, Pryor, and he's using my cinematographer. That's why I don't have him on this picture. Because Pryor wouldn't make the picture without him, and Columbia wanted that picture desperately, because of the kind of business that Pryor's films do.

PK: *And so Columbia has put quite a bit of money into Pryor.*
MR: Well, they've gotten it all back.

PK: *That may have something to do with who comes up #1 in the slot.*
MR: He's a very talented man—he's written the screenplay himself. I hope it's first-class.

PK: *He's shooting it now?*
MR: He's starting very soon.

PK: *Does he had a title yet?*
MR: I don't know. I know Alonzo is shooting it for him. Listen, I'd love to see a first-class black film.

PK: *Do you know some very good black cinematographers.*
MR: I don't know any.

PK: *How has the union been?*
MR: The union's no good. It's very tough to get in.

PK: *That's the complaint I hear mainly.*
MR: It's very tough, all unions are very tough. They are dying to get employment for their present personnel. They've done some terrible things. They have behaved badly in many, many ways, but they're desperate. The industry appears to be shrinking, and they've got a lot of members.

PK: *It's just a matter of survival now.*
MR: Everybody's just clawing to survive.

PK: *Let me ask you a question about when we use films for courses. We always use 16mm, and we always go through the educational distribution market. Sounder has been off that market for some years. Is there any reason why?*
MR: Radnitz sold it to an outfit called The Rainbow Group in New York. They'd have the answer to that question. I should think a 16mm print would have enormous value.

PK: *That's right. And I want you to know there is no way even to rent it. What we would like, of course, is to have a study print. Is there any possible way for us to have that for the Black Film Center/Archive?*
MR: I don't have a print. Fox was very bitter about the way the film was distributed. You might go to Fox. You know, on a PR level, they might give it to you.

PK: *Whom should I see?*
MR: I would write to Barry Diller, who's the new head of Fox. Tell him what organization you represent and what the film *means*—what having a print of that film would mean—to your organization. Radnitz sold it—they just distribute the film. There's a funny history to that film. After the film was finished, we showed it and we didn't have a distributor, nobody wanted it. Just Gordon Stulberg and 20th Century Fox. Now I'm not talking about a screenplay or anything else—I'm talking about a finished film. Nobody wanted it.

And I just won't even dare say what some of the people said who saw the film. "We don't want any nigger pictures." It got that kind of reaction. So that's the nature of this industry, and if you want to live in it, you have to fight it on that level.

PK: *That's a pretty low level.*
MR: It's a pretty low level. Commerce is the bottom line. David Lean, one of the greatest directors of all time, for 14 years he couldn't get that damn picture off the ground. So when you bump into a struggling filmmaker, you can tell him that for anybody else it is a battle every time, if Lean had to wait 14 years to do *A Passage to India.*

PK: *It seems incredible.*
MR: He could be using some of his own money in the picture. Sure, it's incredible. But they want size 12 dresses. You give them 16 or 18, they're lost.

PK: *Just a couple of questions about* The Great White Hope. *I saw James Earl Jones do it in New York. When did you decide to make that film, and did you also produce it?*
MR: No, I didn't. Larry Turman produced it and I was hired. I had just done a film at Paramount called *The Molly Maguires,* which was one of my favorite films. I made a lot of mistakes in that film. But the central performance was so extraordinary that it overcame a lot of my mistakes. But I will never do a play again anyway.

PK. *I was going to ask you. . . . Do you think that was basically the problem, that you get married to the play?*
MR: That was *one* of my problems, and I'll never do it again.

PK: *Who adapted it?*
MR: The playwright.

PK: *That could be another problem.*
MR: Yes, it was.

PK: *You did an early film with Sidney Poitier.*

MR: My first picture. I liked that picture very much.

PK: *I liked that. I liked that better than* The Great White Hope.
MR: So did I. I didn't like *The Great White Hope* very much except for the two actors.

PK: *Yes, when you think about the performances, you can't be too unhappy.*
MR: They were terrific.

PK: *But* The Edge of the City . . .
MR: I loved that picture. I just saw it recently. At U.S.C., they ran about 12 of my films. I hadn't seen it in years—it's terrific.

PK: *It really is, it's a very interesting film. And when you started on that one . . . was that one you learned on?*
MR: Yeah, I didn't know anything about making movies. We shot it in 28 days. Made it for $400,000—never got its money back. Couldn't get booking. No theatre in the South would take the film.

I had a great time making that picture. When I finished the film, the editor said to me, "We have nothing left. If you had made a single mistake. . . ." I had just come from television where I was used to cutting live. I cut the film in my head as we were making it, and I had nothing left. I have never done that since, obviously, but I didn't understand. And if I had made any mistakes, the film wouldn't have worked. But fortunately, I didn't make too many on that film. If you show up to work, you're going to make mistakes. You have to make 40 to 50 decisions every day, and they can't all be right. But they can be more or less right, and if you shoot a lot of other films, at least you can protect yourself. I've done films where I've shot very sparingly. When I get really in heat about a film, as I was with *Sounder*, as I was with *Norma Rae*—the ratio in *Norma Rae* was about three to one, that's all.

PK: *Do you work directly with the editor? Do you look at the rushes every day?*
MR: Yeah, either that or I let them accumulate for two or three days if I'm working too hard. Then I sit with the editor for about ten weeks and put the film together.

PK: *Did you learn from television? What do you think is the relationship between those two?*

MR: The relationship basically is that, at least, you're using a camera, that's all. After that, everything's different. But it doesn't matter what the form is—the director is the director. And if you're really good, you can direct in the theatre, you can direct in television. Now, some people, who are trained in films, cannot direct any place else. They're not used to dealing with people, they're used to dealing with film. But if you're good in the theatre, you can work with anybody, I think. I'm sure there are some disagreements about that, but it is my feeling that you can. And if you have added television to your experience—it's a lot different than film.

PK: *Would you rather work in film?*
MR: Oh yes. Of course, you have much more control. Television, being live, when I was working in television—you had to accept the performance. You couldn't go back and fix it, clean it up. And that could drive you crazy. But in film, I only print what I like.

PK: *You know, there are these people who are prognosticating the demise of film—everybody is going to make films for television.*
MR: Not everybody. A lot of people will. Money—that's it—commerce you're talking about now. Listen, the Super Bowl is going to be put on television at a time which guarantees them the maximum audience. It has nothing to do with the players or anything else. It has to do with the people who put up the money. That's the country we live in. That's the way the little ball rolls. I'm aware of that everytime I start a project. I know what the bottom line is and I try, within that limitation, to do what I want to do. I don't want to do what *they* want me to do. I will not do that, so it is a struggle each time, that's all.

PK: *Do you spend as much time in that struggle as you do . . .*
MR: Sometimes, sometimes . . .

PK: *Because that could be a great frustration.*
MR: It is a great frustration, and it takes up a lot of energy.

PK: *But you'd rather be doing something creative.*
MR: I'd rather be doing what I should be doing. But nobody said it was going to be easy.

PK: *Let me ask you one last question. I don't know whether you have a crystal ball for this, but back to our major issue here. Do you see anything down the road for black actors or black-experience films? Or blacks in the film industry, period?*

MR: Specifically, I don't. But I know it will be better. Because I know there will be a rising protest among the black intellectuals and artists themselves, supported by a segment of the white artists and intellectuals. There's so much money involved, that's the problem. You know, this little film I'm going to make—it's going to cost $11 million. *Norma Rae* cost four and a half. *Sounder* cost a million. *Hud* cost two and a half a million dollars. Now everything is astronomical. And it's not the actors—the studio will pay the actors, they don't care. You get Redford, you want six—give him six. You want Hoffman, you get Newman—they'll pay the actors. They don't want to pay anybody else. They don't want to pay the crews. They'll pay the directors too, and some screenwriters. But it's the below-the-line costs that they try to hold back on, except for the science-fiction pictures, which are totally below-the-line costs. There's nobody in it.

PK: *That's right. You use James Earl Jones's voice, and you put somebody in a suit, and nobody can tell whose . . .*

MR: He's a terrific actor. He should be a big star.

PK: *And we are still at the place where, in fact, only two Academy Awards . . . and there are some great . . .*

MR: Well, there are no parts now for them. You're not going to get an Academy Award . . . I was very surprised when Alfre was nominated. I was very pleased and very surprised. But she's very good.

PK: *This is the first time you worked with her?*
MR: Yes.

PK: *And how did you cast her?*
MR: She came up to the office and read, and I knew that was it. She was terrific. She's a terrific girl, a lovely girl.

PK: *Had she had any other film experience?*
MR: Not much. She's doing a television series now, I gather. What else is she going to do? She has to make a living.

PK: *Well, what you're saying is, until some real protest comes, there's not going to be a change. Nobody's just going to opt to do . . .*
MR: There never is change without protest. If you want good work, you're going to have to fight to do it. They're not going to want to do it. They will go along grudgingly at times. I mean, everybody's getting so rich doing shit television, why would anybody struggle to make a nice serious film? A beautiful film like *Tender Mercies* comes along and it's a failure. Well, the audience is somewhere for it. At least that film was made. Somebody put up the money to make the film. The audience didn't go. The audience's taste is charred, there's something wrong with it.

PK: *There ought to be more demand for better work.*
MR: No question of that. The critics have gone along with it. They've taken the line of least resistance too. They like schlock pictures—the picture does good business, they are loath to take a position against it.

PK: *They're just commenting on what is a phenomenon of pop culture.*
MR: That's all they're doing. So here I am at age 70, still fighting to get a film made, because nobody really wants to make the kind of films I like.

PK: *I'm glad you're still in there pitching.*
MR: I don't know how long I'll be able to do it. I've started acting again and I had some fun with that.

PK: *Did you really! What did you do?*
MR: I acted in a film that Neil Simon wrote. I play a baseball manager. I had some fun. I hope it's amusing. *Slugger's Wife.*

PK: *Just between us, why haven't you made any film on Jewish life?*
MR: I don't know. I've never been a religious man. But I've had some antipathy toward the state of Israel and their relationship to the Arab world. Being a Jew has been a very important part of my life. And an important part of my talent, I'm certain of that. I don't know why. I almost did *The Chosen*, which I liked. But I didn't do it. I saw it and it was well made, but I'm glad I didn't do it. That kind of sectarianism . . .

PK: *No, I wasn't thinking of that. I was thinking of a film that might have something to do with your own cultural past.*

MR: I would do *Awake and Sing*. It's not really film material, but anything that Clifford wrote was always about Jews. Or Miller, for that matter. Even though he sometimes tries to Anglicize, they're really about Jews. I don't know, I really don't. I grew up in New York, and I've made nothing but films about rural America. I don't know why. I don't ask any questions. It's been asked of me several times, particularly why I've done so many rural films. I fell in love with a woman 45 years ago, I married her, we're still married—I don't ask any questions. If it works, it works! If I had started consciously to do that kind of film, I think I might have come a cropper. This film is very rural, charming—I think it's charming, funny, and I'm happy to make it.

PK: *And you're going to have a good time doing it.*
MR: I think so. I think I'll have a very good time.

Working Class Hero: An Interview with Martin Ritt

LYN GOLDFARB AND ANATOLI ILYASHOV/1985

CINEASTE: *Which of your films do you think, were most successful?*
MARTIN RITT: That depends on how you define success. *Norma Rae* was obviously a popular success. It has a great central performance and eighty-five to ninety percent of a great performance is in casting. Any great artist—an actor, director, composer, designer, whatever—has a vein of gold and, if you strike that, you're going to get something extraordinary. I knew what the big scenes in that picture were, and I knew Sally *[Field—ed.]*, and that's why I fought to get it made.

CINEASTE: *What attracted you to the story?*
RITT: I read an article in *The New York Times* about this woman who sat down with her children to explain to them why she was going to be ostracized in town. I've known a lot of women in my life, most of them much more educated and sophisticated, who would not have had the balls that she had. *Norma Rae* is the story of a woman growing up and that's the kind of film I wanted to make. You decide to make a picture, fundamentally, because of a gut feeling about the material. Her story affected me in the same way that the role affected Sally.

I was attacked by a lot of people for romanticizing the central character—and she *was* somewhat romanticized—but I couldn't have made the film any other way. The fact is she slept around, and had a lot of affairs. I didn't allow

---

Originally published in *Cineaste* Vol. xviii, no. 4, (1992): 20–23. Reprinted by permission of *Cineaste*.

the organizer to have an affair with her, however, because he had to go on to another town, and, if the audience felt he was going from one town to another, screwing every dame he made connection with, the whole moral fiber of the film was in jeopardy. Maybe in a very sophisticated society it wouldn't have been, but in this society it was. I was trying to make a labor film with teeth, in Hollywood, where it has never been easy to make an affirmative statement about the working class.

CINEASTE: *What drew you to a labor theme?*
RITT: I happen to be a very liberal fellow. I've had my ups and downs in the labor movement in this country, which has not always behaved in an ethical way. But, fundamentally, I believe in people, and most people are working people, so I don't have very much choice. Given my tastes and my feelings, I can only relate to people I really like. I like working people. And the truth of the matter is that people who make films about working people have no choice. They make films about working people because that's what they know and like.

CINEASTE: *What was your experience with the labor movement after making a pro-union film like Norma Rae?*
RITT: The loved the film and courted me. What I agreed with, I did. What I didn't agree with, I didn't do. I couldn't do certain things because I am not in the labor business. I am in the film business. I generally support trade unions because I believe in them. I believe the workers have no protection outside of the trade union.

CINEASTE: *What's been your experience with film unions?*
RITT: They're tough to get into and they're scared because a lot of the membership is not working. My daughter finally got into the Directors Guild as an assistant director, even though she had already worked on ten films, and she only got in because she threatened to sue. They've made it as difficult as possible to get in because there are not that many jobs. Thank God for television because that's provided a lot of work.

I wouldn't want to be a young filmmaker today, especially a young, serious filmmaker. It's tough to get a picture made. Management changes every six months to a year, so somebody new is always in charge.

CINEASTE: Sounder *also deals with working people, specifically a black sharecropper family in the South during the Depression. How did that film come about?*
RITT: I read the novel which was given to me by Robert Radnitz, the producer. I knew they had no money, so I made *Sounder* for under a million dollars. I worked for one-eighth of my salary at that time. I took a big piece of the picture, however, so I've actually made more money from that film than any I've made. I was very moved by the story, and I'm not that easily moved, and I wanted to make it. And we got it made. They turned it down at Columbia, so we went to Fox. No studio has ever given me a picture to make. All the good pictures I made, with the exception of *The Spy Who Came in From the Cold,* I initiated myself.

I knew that the homecoming of the father was the central scene in the film, so I looked for a location where I could have that rise where he would be coming up from the valley. We found the location but there was nothing there. The cabin I wanted, which was ironically owned by a white sharecropper family, was about a mile down the road. We paid them $1,000, cut the legs off, and moved it to our location. What I'm saying is that if I'm moved by the material, I make a hell of a shot to get it made. There are some films, like *The Molly Maguires,* that I'd wanted to make all my life.

CINEASTE: *Was that also a difficult film to produce?*
RITT: We had a lot of trouble making that one. It cost a lot of money in those days—$11 million, which is equal to $25 million today—and it was a total failure at the box office, it didn't make twenty cents. After I made that picture I was afraid I wouldn't work again for a long time, and I almost didn't because it was a disaster. But it's a film that's in all the archives, and it keeps showing in France and England and wherever there are film buffs. It's got some of my best work in it. It was also about a subject very close to me—it was about an informer—and I became myself in that picture.

That picture was much too sophisticated in the sense that the audience in this country—a totally unsophisticated audience—really didn't know who the hero was. They weren't sure it wasn't Richard Harris, the informer. I should have made it simpler for them. They should have understood that Kehoe, the Sean Connery character, who was a murderer, was really the hero of the film, but they didn't, and I think that hurt me with the mass audience. I'm not sorry about it now, because the film is done, it's out there. I love it, and nobody can take it away. That's the great thing about working in film and not theatre.

CINEASTE: *The Molly Maguires is especially noteworthy for its historical content.*
RITT: Absolutely. I remember reading that story as a young history student and being very taken with it. These poor Irish immigrants came off the boat and never even saw New York. They were shunted onto trains and were shipped out to these coal mines. It's also interesting what happened afterwards to the real life informer. He went out to Denver were he worked again for the Pinkerton detective agency and he was killed by a worker. It came about ten years too late. It would have helped *The Molly Maguires!*

I can see now the mistakes that I made. The love story was too prominent and there were many problems with the central character. It really is great material, though. I still remember two things about that film. At one point, Kehoe says, "I made my sound." That's very important to me. Then there's the scene where the Richard Harris character visits Connery in jail, and Connery looks at him and says, "You've come to me for absolution. I'm not going to give it to you, buddy." That's very important to me, too, for a highly personal reason which is not a secret to anyone in this country.

CINEASTE: *What's the message you wanted the film to convey?*
RITT: I wanted to show that the villain in the film was the informer, a man who wormed his way into the graces of his fellow workers and then turned them in. To me, that's a villainous act. And in the American tradition, an informer is a villainous person, although those ethics have been somewhat undermined by the hysteria of the communist scare.

CINEASTE: The Front *was obviously another film with very personal meaning to you.*
RITT: I'd been working on that material for years, but I was sure I'd never have a chance to make *The Front*. When I finally made an agreement, I couldn't believe it. I don't know how in the hell I got that picture made. It was tough.

CINEASTE: *What made it particularly difficult?*

Kathleen Maguire, John Cassavetes, and Sidney Poitier, *Edge of the City*, 1957

Joanne Woodward and Paul Newman,
The Long, Hot Summer, 1958

Anthony Quinn and Sophia Loren, *The Black Orchid*, 1959

Joanne Woodward and Stuart Whitman, *The Sound and the Fury*, 1959

Silvana Mangano, Barbara Bel Geddes, Vera Miles, Carla Gravina, and Jeanne Moreau, *Five Branded Women*, 1960

Brandon de Wilde and Paul Newman, *Hud*, 1963

Richard Burton, *The Spy Who Came in from the Cold*, 1965

Val Avery and Paul Newman, *Hombre*, 1967

Art Lund, Anthony Zerbe, and Sean Connery, *The Molly Maguires*, 1970

James Earl Jones and Marlene Warfield, *The Great White Hope*, 1970

Eric Hooks, Paul Winfield, Cicely Tyson, Kevin Hooks, and Yvonne Jarrell, *Sounder*, 1972

Woody Allen and Andrea Marcovicci, *The Front*, 1976

Sally Field, *Norma Rae*, 1979

Richard Dreyfuss and Barbra Streisand, *Nuts*, 1987

Jane Fonda and Robert DeNiro, *Stanley & Iris*, 1990

RITT: It was hard for one reason. As we began to work, there was a wave of emotion through so many of the people who had lived through that period. It was painful in the case of Zero [Mostel—ed.] and many other people. It was difficult to make only on that level.

CINEASTE: *Do you feel McCarthyism had a negative impact on creative expression in Hollywood?*
RITT: Sure, it was terrible, because he frightened everybody. When you look at the old films today, you can't believe that anybody listened to him. He was obviously an hysteric . . . or a psychopath. And in all the time he was around, he never uncovered anything, not one single communist, and I'm sure there were plenty of them around. A lot of people in Hollywood were accused. Some of them may have been in the Communist Party at one time or another, but many of them were not. None of them were allowed to work and many of the most creative people had their voices stilled. It was a terrible, terrible time.

CINEASTE: *Can the impact of that still be seen today?*
RITT: To some degree, yes, particularly among the families of those people. I had several friends who died during that period. There are quite a few stories like that. Of course, you mainly hear stories about people in the film industry. HUAC also victimized doctors, teachers, and other professionals, but they couldn't get the publicity with those people that they could get with Hollywood people.

CINEASTE: *Do you think it could happen again?*
RITT: I think if they pursued this—such a blatant expression of the Cold War—they'd have more trouble today. I don't say it couldn't happen again. But there's a constituency that's much smarter and a lot of people would stand up and recognize it for what it is—thought control, plain and simple.

CINEASTE: *What happened to you personally?*
RITT: I was blacklisted. I was teaching an acting class and my wife was selling space for the Yellow Pages telephone book, when I was offered a job to direct an Authur Miller play for CBS. I felt dutybound to go in and ask what I had to do to get the job. They told me what I had to do, which was to name names. They said, "We don't care who you name. You can name people who

are dead." So, if I hadn't understood it up until that time, I understood it very clearly then. They were simply interested in breaking the will of anybody who didn't agree with them. Thought control was the issue.

CINEASTE: *Why does Hollywood make so few films that deal with social or political issues?*
RITT: They don't make money, so they don't want to make those pictures. It all goes back to Sam Goldwyn's famous line, "If you've got a message, send it Western Union." If I had made a picture like *Norma Rae*, but on a more popular subject, and made it as well, and it was as critically successful as *Norma Rae*, it would have made three times the money. I know that. This is a business and you've got to view it that way, although there are people caught up in it who are not really business people.

I don't pretend to be anything but a professional filmmaker who makes very difficult subjects in the commercial world. And I've managed to stay alive in this business a long time. I'm practical enough and knowledgeable enough to make any kind of picture, and to know that a studio has to make a program of pictures. I can get any picture made. I could make a film on Karl Marx if I work for ten percent of my salary. The studio heads figure I'd find some kind of audience for it somewhere and maybe, God forbid, it might even turn out to be good.

CINEASTE: *Do you feel that there's less content in Hollywood films today?*
RITT: Yes, absolutely. With few exceptions, there is no content. There seems to be more and more of the *Flashdance* kind of film—all form and no content—which cater to popular tastes. The philosophy is, "Let's make the least meaningful film we can, the most attractive way we can, with the best director and actors we can get, and make a lot of money." Now, *Norma Rae* didn't cost that much money—it cost about $4½ million. But the studios prefer to make pictures that, even if they're no good, still have a chance to be a big hit. There're a lot of those around because they're junk and the kids go, and some of them they see again and again.

CINEASTE: *Has there ever been a time when Hollywood was more supportive of serious films on social issues?*
RITT: Not since I've been here. I'm sure right after WWII, until the Cold War really set in, it was a much more liberal, progressive place. It's not now.

Most of the artists—I would say ninety to ninety-five percent, with rare exceptions—are liberals, but they don't control the industry. When they're looking for a new studio head, instead of going to a veteran director like Fred Zinnemann or Billy Wilder, or coming to a guy like me, they either go right to an agent, who has connections with stars, or to a businessman who views the world the same way they do.

CINEASTE: *Of the various studios you've worked with, are there any that have been more receptive to your projects?*
RITT: It's musical chairs, really. I got *The Molly Maguires* made at Paramount. I got *The Front* made at Columbia. Neither of them wanted to do *Norma Rae*, so I got that made at Fox. But *Norma Rae* made much more money than *The Front*, so they made a mistake.

You know, there's a lot of ego involved. people in management want to be associated with creative people. They like them and respect them. They know they have guts and talent, so sometimes you get films made because they don't want you to go someplace else. None of the studios have a policy about social issue films. They don't want to make serious films because they're much tougher to make and they appeal to a more limited audience. I understand that and, in those instances, I think the creative people have to pick up part of the tab and say, "OK, we'll make it a little cheaper." So, instead of the picture costing $15 million, it will cost $6 million. If you want to make a picture badly enough, you have to do that.

I didn't choose subject matter that I thought would be unpopular. I chose subject matter that affected me, although it may not be the most popular subject matter in the history of the motion picture industry. I have never had a runaway hit. I've had a lot of successful pictures—successful in that they paid a lot of bills, studios kept operating, some actors won Academy Awards, a lot of nice things happened. But I never had a picture that did $50–$60 million. I'd faint if that ever happened to me.

CINEASTE: *Do you think that casting a particular actor or actress can be important in selling a more political film to the public?*
RITT: A great piece of music is a different piece of music when it's totally realized than when it's not totally realized. That's also true of a script or a play or anything. It has to be fully realized and the best realization is with the best people. *Norma Rae* would not have been more political if I'd used,

say, Diane Keaton. But in order to realize the part, you have to use one of the best actresses available. When we made *Norma Rae,* Sally was at a transition in her career. I didn't pay her very much money and she became a big star. One of the reasons the picture didn't cost that much is that I didn't have to pay big salaries to her, myself, or the writers.

CINEASTE: *Does a good film require a central character who undergoes a personal transformation or who changes the lives of others?*
RITT: I think so. It's the same thing in real life. What I remember from college is an individual teacher who affected me. In a film you need someone that you love or hate and who can move people. An idea is not going to move them. An idea will move only intellectuals and they're a vanishing breed. The nature of art is on much more of a gut level, on what you feel. I wouldn't think of doing a film without a strong protagonist.

CINEASTE: *What kind of political impact do you think films can have?*
RITT: Films do not intellectually convert anybody. If you want to make a film about a woman's struggle, for example, you have to move the audience emotionally, to make them laugh or cry—preferably both—then you have a chance to reach them. If you try to bludgeon them over the head with a lecture on feminism, you're not likely to convince anyone, no matter how logical your arguments or how impressive your documentation, except those who already agree with you. Films can educate, but not in a didactic way, and you have a better chance if you can emotionally engage the audience first.

In this sense, *Norma Rae* is not about the working class. it is not about trade unions. It's about a woman who changed her life. She had a need for education and a need to fight for her children and for what she believed in. You have to make that kind of commitment—to your children, to your church, to your union, whatever—if you want to change things.

A lot of people who hated politics loved *Norma Rae,* they were very affected by the movie. People who you couldn't get to go to a union meeting or to vote in any liberal way, had a whole new attitude when they saw *Norma Rae.* That's the power of a good movie.

Martin Ritt: A Shaper of the Medium Is Now Its Critic

STAN BERKOWITZ/1985

MARTIN RITT is best known as the director of a score of feature films, among them *The Long Hot Summer, Hud, The Spy Who Came in From the Cold, The Molly Maguires, Sounder, The Front, Norma Rae, Cross Creek,* and the upcoming *Murphy's Romance.* Ritt's success in features has all but eclipsed his early years as one of TV's pioneer directors. Beginning in 1947 and ending only four years later, that period was a bittersweet one for Ritt: he loved the work, but it came to an abrupt, frustrating end during the blacklist period.

Ritt was born in New York in 1914. His parents were Jewish immigrants from eastern Europe. Though they happily embraced their adopted country's work ethic, their son grew up idolizing his uncle, a Gypsy dancer who played the Palace.

Despite an emotional commitment to show business, Ritt went through college and then enrolled at St. John's law school. He'd been acting on the side throughout college, but it wasn't until the first semester of law school that he had an opportunity best described as "golden": he was invited to come to Broadway to understudy John Garfield in Clifford Odet's *Golden Boy.* The year was 1937, and Ritt's career-choice dilemma paralleled that of the play's main character. Ritt never went back to law school.

Ritt's acting career eventually took him to the Adirondacks where, in 1940, he met actress Adele Cutler. They married in 1941. They now live in the Los Angeles community of Pacific Palisades.

Published in *Emmy Magazine* (July/August 1985): 40–42, 46, 48. Reprinted by permission of the author.

Ritt was drafter into the Army during World War II and sent to weather school. But the armed forces quickly realized that someone with Ritt's background might better serve a propaganda function. So he began to act in patriotic plays produced by the Army Air Force, both for civilian and military audiences.

It was in the service that Ritt expanded into directing. Looking back, he feels the decision was sensible; he just didn't have the look of a movie star. A play Ritt directed while in the service got good reviews, and by the end of the war, Ritt had established himself as a theatrical director.

Ritt continued on Broadway, directing and still acting. Within two years, however, television opened up and Ritt and others from Broadway helped shape the infant medium. He directed scores of half-hour shows during those early years. Most were based on the previously published short stories of prominent writers, but some were original works.

During the blacklist period, Ritt's liberal associations and radical friends were enough to make one of the blacklisting organizations list him as a potential threat to the country. Though Ritt was never accused of anything specific, that was nevertheless enough to make CBS refuse to renew his contract in 1951. (CBS disputes this, according to Ritt. See below.) Ritt's revenge came in 1976, when he directed Woody Allen in *The Front*, a searing yet funny look at how the McCarthy era affected television.

Out of television, Ritt survived for five years teaching acting in New York. Then, with the blacklist fading from memory, Ritt was given his first feature film assignment by producer David Susskind. The film was *Edge of the City*, which was released in 1957 and starred newcomers John Cassavetes and Sidney Poitier. Setting a pattern that would flow through most of Ritt's work, it dealt with controversial social issues from a liberal/humanist perspective.

Ritt's second film assignment brought him to Hollywood, where he has remained. He and Adele soon after adopted two children, one of whom, Tina, has worked as an assistant director for her father and others.

Now seventy-one, Ritt is awaiting the release of *Murphy's Romance*. Somewhat ironically, this new film's three leads, Sally Field, James Garner, and Brian Kerwin, all had their early training in TV. At the production site in Mesa, Arizona, Ritt took time out to reminisce about TV and offer some comment about the current state of the medium.

EMMY: *Was the golden age of television really golden? Or is it just a golden memory?*

RITT: It really was a golden age, because a lot of very gifted people came out of that period. A lot of extremely good work was done. It was done because the full economic ramifications of television had not yet taken over. And it was a place to function on a very creative level.

EMMY: *Were you at all intimidated by the new medium?*
RITT: Not really. I don't think there's that much difference in directing live television, film television, and movies. It's a matter of quality. A director is a director.

EMMY: *What was it like working in that environment?*
RITT: There was only one studio, above Grand Central Station in New York City. We had one camera to do every show, and we didn't even have a standby camera in case something went wrong. The shows never went any farther than the Ohio River at that point [1947].

The work was very exciting, all half-hour dramas. [Ritt worked for CBS.] There was no limitation on what you could do. You could do Willa Cather, Irwin Shaw, Saki. You could do all the great short stories you ever read in your life. Advertising agencies were not yet in the business. No artistic restrictions existed until the agencies came into the business. Then it became commercial.

Sidney Lumet was my assistant director. Robert Mulligan was an AD on the next stage, where they were doing *Suspense*. Sidney Lumet later directed me [as an actor] in a rather famous television show called *The Paper Box Kid*, in which I played the leading part.

EMMY: *How did you direct TV with just one camera?*
RITT: You finished the scene, you went to black, and you just stayed there until the camera got over to the other set. It had a master shot implicit in it, close-ups, everything. You just staged it that way. The camera moved around.

EMMY: *Television is made very quickly these days. How was it in your day?*
RITT: We did a lot of television. It was different. There was no postproduction. Everything had to happen right there. That was exciting, but the most exciting thing was the freedom to do any kind of material you wanted.

EMMY: *How much preparation was there. How much rehearsal?*

RITT: You had a lot of things in work, and you did the ones that were ready at the time you had to go into rehearsal. You rehearsed a week for a half-hour show, as I remember, and then you went on the air. You had to wing certain things. The audience forgave an occasional boom dropping into the shot, or something sloppy in the physical production, because the excitement of doing it the way we were doing it and the quality of the material overcame the mechanical lapses.

EMMY: *How long would it take to write a script?*
RITT: If you're doing Willa Cather and Saki and Hemingway and Updike and Cheever, you worry less about the time constraints than if you're doing pap, because there's something fundamentally exciting about the material you're doing. There's a whole different attitude about it.

EMMY: *In an active year, how many shows would you direct?*
RITT: Anywhere from twenty-five to fifty. It wasn't easy. I was young. I had a lot of energy, and I wanted to work. Now there are many, many people in television. At that time, there weren't. It was a new medium, and it afforded a lot of people an opportunity to break in. It was very tough to get a job directing on Broadway or in film, and here was a new medium; people with ability and energy had a chance to break in. And they did.

EMMY: *Do you watch the old kinescopes?*
RITT: The quality is so bad, it's not worth watching. The technical quality is terrible. You can't really make any judgment. You just have to remember what you saw and remember that you thought it was first class, in terms of itself, in terms of its own ability to hold you.

EMMY: *At the time, did TV get much respect?*
RITT: No. We took it very seriously, because we knew we were doing interesting work. The fact that we couldn't compete with Broadway and Lillian Hellman, Arthur Miller, Tennessee Williams, Robert Sherwood, Elmer Rice, Max Anderson, that didn't faze us, because we were in a different business.

EMMY: *When you saw something directed by, say, Arthur Penn, would you think, this is good, or, this is good for TV?*

RITT: I would think it was good. Good for TV was good enough for me. That's the business I was in. And I never tried to compare.

EMMY: *Was there a lot of dross back then.*
RITT: Yes, [but] you must judge an artist by his best work, unless you know that for one reason or another he no longer is capable of producing that work.

EMMY: *CBS refused to renew your contract in 1951. That was the beginning of a five-year blacklist period for you.*
RITT: It was the Cold War, a time when the Red Scare became totally dominant. Nobody had to prove anything. They just had to accuse you. The networks, being in the PR business, just capitulated totally, though they've stoutly denied it. My contract was not renewed. Nobody would dare admit it, because it was against the law to blacklist anybody. They didn't want any legal problems on their hands. To this day, they deny that anything like that existed.

EMMY: *Did you know why you were blacklisted?*
RITT: I knew why. I had been around liberal organizations all my youth. The Group Theater. I directed a show for a trade union, which was one of the things they listed against me. I had directed a show for Russian war relief, a big show in Madison Square Garden. But they were on our side at the time.

I had never been subpoenaed; I had never been named. And many of my friends had been. It was all guilt by association.

One of my friends went to one of the people involved in the reactionary section of the [director's] union and said, "What are you doing to Marty? For Chrissakes, he hasn't been named, hasn't been subpoenaed." The guy said, "Well, we know he's not on our side. And we [don't want him] to get a big influential] job. So we're not going to do anything unless he lets us know he's on our side."

Obviously, I'd never do that, so that was the end of that.

I was at that point already a highly paid television producer; I was about to sell my own show. Among the properties that were being written for me [to act in] was a little show called *Marty* by Paddy Chayefsky. Apparently about two or three years ago, Rod Steiger finally got on the air and said this show was written for Martin Ritt to act in.

When I appeared on a couple of shows, [the blacklisters] would have cards sent in from people in their organization saying, "This man's giving his money to Communist China" or "Communist Russia" or whatever.

I had a direct encounter with someone from the FBI. He said, "Why are you being so difficult? Everybody wants to hire you." I said, "I'm not being difficult. I haven't done anything. What do you want me to do?"

"Name people," he said. I couldn't have named anybody, and anyway I wasn't about to, because I understood that the real issue was thought control. Because they said, "Name him, he's dead." So they were not looking for information. They knew I had no information.

If you look at the old films of McCarthy today, you can't believe that anybody ever gave him credence. He was a hysteric, obviously a hysteric.

The fact that some people stood up and were counted in that period I think has helped establish a certain constituency which cannot be had as easily as the American people were had in 1950 on this issue. I think it's unlikely, but it could happen again.

One of the ugly things that Mr. [Richard[Schickel [recently] wrote was an article called "the Injustice Gatherers" for a film magazine. It was referring to Hollywood people. The indication was that with a few exceptions, [those who were blacklisted] were just gathering injustice and squawking about it for the rest of their careers. I found it a foul and evil thing to do. I don't have any respect for Mr. Schickel because of that.

EMMY: *Your film* The Front *looked back at the blacklist period. Instead of making a hero a writer or actor, you and screenwriter Walter Bernstein chose to make him a front, someone who submitted blacklisted writers' work under his own name. Why?*

RITT: We started to write a script about Hecky, the actor [Zero Mostell], and halfway through the script Bernstein and I looked at each other and said, "You know, if we're not careful, it's going to be maudlin and self-pitying. Let's get away from this." And then we came up—individually or collectively, I don't remember—with the idea. There were a lot of fronts around. Some of them are now in Hollywood. Fronts who established their early credits on someone else's writing.

EMMY: *In your current film,* Murphy's Romance, *the three leads, Sally Field,*

James Garner, and Brian Kerwin, all came from television. Are TV actors at all different from film actors?
RITT: If they're good, they're good. Most [TV actors] are very skilled technically. They know how to handle themselves in front of a camera. Sally and Jim Garner are both very skilled. They know their way around a camera, how to take care of themselves. Whatever they have to do.

EMMY: *Do actors lose anything by training in TV?*
RITT: The quality of the material, it's very inhibiting. What am I going to say to you? You can't play with shit without coming up smelling after a while. They're used to settling for less; they're used to taking shortcuts, some of them. Indicating to an audience what's going on, things they don't have to do.

EMMY: *Any resistance on the part of Columbia executives to your casting TV actors James Garner and Brian Kerwin?*
RITT: No, because the price was right. With Garner, there was some slight resistance, but it was very quickly overcome by me and Sally.

EMMY: *The resistance to Garner being that he was a TV face?*
RITT: Yeah, and the audience had been getting him for nothing . . . [but] those opinions are never strongly held.

EMMY: *Do you watch current TV?*
RITT: I watch usually when I'm about to cast a picture, hoping that I'll stumble across an actor I might see.

EMMY: *Have you even found one?*
RITT: No.

EMMY: *Do you watch for entertainment?*
RITT: I watch sporting events and news, and once in a while, I'll be hooked in and watch a show. I saw a couple of *Bill Cosby* segments that I thought were very nice, and I've watched and liked occasionally that cop show, *Hill Street Blues*. PBS does extraordinary work sometimes. Those English costume dramas have been extraordinary well done, as well done as any film I've ever seen.

PBS is miles ahead of commercial television. There's no contest because of what they choose to do: material of quality. Commercial television is pap, for the most part. Absolute, unmitigated, aggressive pap.

EMMY: *Everyone watches commercial television, and PBS is largely ignored.*
RITT: Shakespeare doesn't have a big audience in this country either. And more people listen to rock 'n' roll than any of the great composers. I don't know what the hell that proves. It just proves that one is more commercial than the other. That doesn't interest me at all.

EMMY: *You work in a mass medium, so you've got to attract a lot of those people who* don't *watch PBS.*
RITT: I do, and it's not easy. The audience is the audience. They're the people in this country. They're all kinds. I somehow feel that if you give them really good stuff, you will be able to get to them. Maybe not as consistently as a rock 'n' roller or a punker or something like that.

Anyway, people like me have no choice. You try to do the best you can. You don't even think about the other thing. I think there's something ordinary and plain enough in me so that if I really like something, ordinary people will like it. I hate to think of myself as any kind of elitist, which I'm not. When I'm damning television, I'm not damning it on that level. I just think it's lousy.

EMMY: *Any prescription to fix it?*
RITT: No, there's no prescription, because the whole system is no good.

EMMY: *Any way you could be lured back to TV?*
RITT: If they gave me a piece of material I liked. But it's bound to be an action-adventure or horror or soft porn or some sensational subject, which they think will attract viewers. Never in terms of examining the human condition on any very serious level. Just on a level of sensationalism. Because they feel that without that, they won't get an audience. They may be right. I mean, they're doing very well. I'm certainly in no position to criticize the economic judgments of people who are making millions of dollars. But I do criticize.

EMMY: *You're politically committed. I would think that someone with a message to convey would be attracted to TV because of the massive audience it can deliver. Maybe a project like* The Front?

RITT: They wouldn't have done it. The last thing they want to do is a drama of ideas. They'll do it about sex and psychology, sure, because they think that's commercial. Also, it's not life-threatening to them. When I did *The Front*, I wrote to CBS, asking for that old [broadcasting] equipment [as props], because where else would I get 1950s equipment? And they wrote back and said, "We choose not to associate ourselves with that period." They have denied that it ever existed.

So if my name comes up to do a television show, and they read [the script] and it's slightly political, they run to the f__ing hills. Yeah, if they let me do what I wanted to do, I would come back. You're very naive if you think they'll do anything that is threatening to them at all.

There is so much money involved now, the kind of material is circumscribed. No sponsor wants to go out on a limb. They do sometimes when they support public television or special projects, but generally the kind of pulp that television does—all these sitcoms, soap operas—they can't really be first class. It's impossible to work that quickly and do first-class work. Television suffers from a terrific rap. [Even] the worst films are made to sell entertainment; television is made to sell soap. How you overcome that artistically, I don't know. I don't think it's possible.

EMMY: *Why isn't there currently a pool of people as talented as those of the golden age?*

RITT: The quality of the material doesn't allow them to express it. I'm sure there is a pool, but most of television is action-adventure or horror or science fiction. In the so-called golden age, there was not that premium on what would sell, because it was not that big commercially yet. Once it became very big commercially, it was a whole different kettle of fish.

There are more people around who can do pap than there are people who can do something extraordinary. When you are in a projection room and there's an advertising guy there from the sponsor and he says, "I don't like the way my sponsor's stuff is lit," he doesn't want to hire a guy who's going to turn around and say go f__ yourself. He wants a guy who *needs* that job and will comply with anything the sponsor wants him to do. They are selling *that*, not entertainment. And that's the orientation from which they can never recover.

The good ones get out. Nobody wants to sit and direct junk television if he's any good. Or write it. It's just a way to make a living. The minute you feel you can do without it, you get out.

A lot of the same things exist in films. Most of the films that are made, are made on an exploitation level. But there's not that inhibition in terms of content. And you have time to prepare and really do it properly.

I'm sure there are a lot of gifted people working in TV who are just buried by it and see no way out. To make a living; they have families or whatever. For a lot of them, the talent begins to erode. There's nothing static in society. You can't keep doing that kind of junk without being affected. Finally, you begin to think it's pretty good.

I've met people in TV, very bright, sensitive people, and I've asked them, why are you doing this? The answer is, to make a living.

They get so rich, they're not reachable on any level. I'm sure some of the TV producers who have so many series out are, as far as they're concerned, beyond reproach. You going to argue with the Bank of America?

It's tough to say to a guy who's making forty, fifty thousand dollars a segment in television that he's doing less than his best work. If he's bright, he may understand and be cynical enough to say, "I don't give a shit." If he's not bright, he thinks you're crazy. Or jealous.

Ritt Large

PATRICK MCGILLIGAN/1985

PM: *How did growing up in the thirties affect your view of making movies?*
MR: Well, obviously it affected me a great deal. There was a great liberal surge in the country, emotionally and politically, and I was part of it. All the gifted people and all the excitement I knew around the theater were part of that sector of our intellectual thought. I was lucky enough to be working with an off-Broadway group, the Theatre of Action. I met Elia Kazan there. I was lucky enough to be around the Group Theatre, which was probably the single greatest group of theater intellectuals who ever existed together as a cohesive unit. When I look for material, I look in that area. That's where I feel most comfortable and now where I feel most needed, the times being so different today.

A liberal working in the mainstream is a very rare item today. Maybe a lot of liberals are working in the mainstream, but they don't make pictures about what they believe; they make other kinds of pictures. There's nothing wrong with that, but that's not my bag. I'm more of an activist about what I believe, which is the difference between a liberal and a left-liberal.

My generation was totally committed to humanism. Implicit in all of my films is a very strong and deep feeling for minorities, the disenfranchised, the dispossessed, be they blacks, Mexicans, Jews, or working people.

Originally published in *Film Comment* (February 1986): 38–46 and reprinted in *Tender Comrades* by Patrick McGilligan and Paul Buhle (New York: ST. Martin's, 1997), 558–70. Reprinted by permission of St. Martin's Press.

PM: *With widespread unemployment and labor inequity, racism, and threatening global war why do we count so few socially conscious filmmakers?*
MR: It's very hard to understand the kind of historical time we're in. It's obviously a very conservative time—and not only here but all over the world. Filmmakers are not as affected or moved as I might be by certain dilemmas. I'm a complete reflection of the time I grew up in, as most people are.

I must say, to the everlasting credit of this country, that nobody has been shut up nowadays. People like me have been allowed to speak, whereas, in some other countries, I can well imagine that if I had the kinds of differences I have with the establishment, I might well be in jail. That kind of intrinsic strength which exists in our way of life is not in any way to be looked down upon—it's terrific. It makes it possible for good work to continue.

But it's tough to be a liberal, to try to make films about what you believe in. Because, starting with the corny old remark ascribed to Warners, Hollywood believes that if you want to send a message, try Western Union. People shy away—and those pictures have not been doing the greatest of business. My present film [*Murphy's Romance*] is really a love story about a man [James Garner] who is kind of an idiosyncratic liberal and the lady [Sally Field] that he meets. Just in dealing with the human elements in the film, the film becomes, in my mind, a liberal film. Maybe I have a greater feeling about the broadness of what being a liberal means. It certainly doesn't mean only something is direct politically, certainly not from a creative person, not from an artist.

I'm considered by many to be a very political fellow. But my films are hardly political, outside of two, maybe three—maybe *Norma Rae* would be included. I'm not interested in polemics, really. I'm not interested in making films that I feel are cardboard statements about what I want to say.

PM: *Why are most movies so valueless?*
MR: The whole psyche of the world is turned on to fast foods and comic books and teenage excitement and instant gratification. The country is conditioned to accept predigested food and prefabricated houses; the networks believe action-adventure is the best way to attract an audience. The studios partly believe that—along with horror films and teenage films. They are looking to make a size-twelve dress that the country will buy, and the only crite-

rion they have is last year's hit, insufficiently realizing that a really good film is the individual impulse of some creative person.

I don't think most audiences have the patience to sit down to see a Satyajit Ray film. They want, "What's going on? What's happening!" Everything seems more hyped in this country because we're more developed and more organized.

PM: *It takes a superior artist to resist the dehumanization process, to resist the cops-and-robbers rut.*
MR: Absolutely. However, the good ones will finally find their way back to humanism, because there's nothing else. That's why the great directors are always dealing on some level with the human condition. It's the more difficult kind of film to make, which is another reason why the studios shy away from it. There's more room for failure. The films have to be better. You have to fit a film into a mold which commercial audiences are prepared to accept. Even if it's first-class, sometimes audiences won't quite accept it, and the film won't make the kind of money it should, and *that* will scare the studios. The other thing is so much more predictable.

The comic strip is the art form of this generation. Now the new generation is rejecting that for computers, listening to music, working at home, and isolating themselves, so the new corporate executives are having to find a different kind of drone to do their bidding.

Humanism is in eclipse, except in the very gifted of the young—because once you're gifted, it's going to appear in your work; it doesn't really matter what generation you are. When what is going on socially is a violation of our human instincts, the artist always emerges anyway, on a human level. If I had to entrust my life to anyone, I'd entrust it to artists before anyone else, before politicians. Artists are more related to the truth. They're less available to be bought. I believe that, I believe that deeply, and it has sustained me in times which looked very black to me.

PM: *Does a good movie have to be truthful?*
MR: I think so. A good one—not a successful one. I differentiate between the two, obviously. Yes, if it's really good, it has to have a true perception. It's naive to assume that any film is not political; they're all social at least. They're either selling escape or they're selling reality. Even the Disney films at one time were considered totally without message. That's childish. They

certainly weren't without message. They were selling a different parcel of food, which the American public and the world public was prepared to buy.

PM: *According to that line of argument, there must be some good and truthful MTV videos.*
MR: I guess there are. The really, really good ones, yes—there will be some perception in them that makes the whole MTV worthwhile even if it's only an extraordinary visual perception.

PM: *Does that hold true for video technology in general?*
MR: There's a whole new impulse in the industry that's very interesting, even if I don't totally like it.

PM: *What's the downside?*
MR: That it becomes an end in itself. That it becomes all style without substance. That it becomes so popular, so faddish, that that's what they come to expect from every film. Film can't possibly be as exciting as a three- or four-minute video. It's fast foods and comic books couched in more artistic terms.

PM: *Yet an occasional visual perception can be as truthful and as positive as a thematic message.*
MR: That's right. Because it's a perception by a creative person. That's where his talents lie; that's where his inclinations lie. The video artist is lucky because his work is in a form the marketplace is excited about.

The word "truthful" is kind of rabbinical. I don't want to sound that way, and I don't believe that way. I do like very few MTV videos. I don't remember a single one I really like. But I see things on MTV which I find very interesting and attractive from the point of view of form.

PM: *Why did it take you so long to come to Hollywood?*
MR: In the early fifties I don't think they were hiring anybody from TV, and the two plays I did in New York were sort of *succès d'estime* but not big, successful plays. Also, I was blacklisted, so in those years when some farsighted executive out here might have hired me at a cheap price, I was not hireable.

PM: *How did you find out you were blacklisted?*

MR: I was working at CBS, doing very well, when I got a call one day from Donald Davis (the son of the playwright Owen Davis), a very sweet man, a friend. I went up to see him on the fourteenth floor of old CBS on Fifty-fifth Street and Madison Avenue. He said, "I don't understand it, Marty, but you haven't been renewed." Well, of course, I understood what was going on; my antennae were out. I said, "This is it." He said, "Oh, Marty, not in this country." I said, "Okay, Donald, you'll see." I went home and I told my wife I was going to have to find some other way to make a living. Adele went out and got a job selling [ad] space for the New York telephone book.

I was hired, finally, to act in a show that Dan Petrie was directing, produced by a guy I had helped a lot in the earlier days of TV. Two days into the show I saw the executives come to Dan Petrie and start to chew his ear off. I said, "What's the problem, Dan?" He said, "They don't think you're right for the part." It was a thirty-five-year-old Italian truck driver. So I told Dan, who at this point was a kid just out of Chicago, what was happening, and he said, "What are you talking about?" Well, the show never appeared. They put on some old kinescope—and after that I didn't work for six years.

So I started to teach acting, professionally. And I really didn't work again until I was hired by Clifford Odets to be in *The Flowering Peach*, in which I played the small part of the oldest son. I went on to help him, because he needed time off to rewrite the play after we opened in Baltimore. I directed the play through the Boston opening.

PM: *Isn't it bizarre that Clifford Odets, who became an informer, would hire you as an actor?*
MR: The Clifford Odets thing is so bizarre that I really don't want to talk about it. Clifford and I had been close friends. We played in a weekly poker game that he often sat in on at CBS. Clifford came to the poker game after his session at the Committee—which was a very strange one, because he had screamed at the Committee and right after that started to give names. The poker game was an apolitical group if I ever knew one, and I didn't want to get involved in a conversation—but I hated what he did. He told us what had happened, and then he turned to me and said, "What's more, I have this play for you. There's a part in it for you. I'd like you to read it. Let's have dinner." It was bizarre as hell.

PM: *You became a movie director in 1957. That's relatively early in the history of the blacklist. Almost a fluke, wasn't it?*

MR: It was a fluke. Metro wanted me to make a picture, *Edge of the City*. They were in a proxy fight at that point. I was very cheap. I think I directed the picture for ten thousand dollars. The writer of it, a very good writer, Robert Alan Aurthur, was an old friend; he wanted me for the picture, so I got the job. But when Metro saw the picture, they hated it, in spite of the notices, which were terrific.

Fox offered me a job. I was broke, I was in debt, I hadn't worked from 1951 to 1957. I was happy to get a job in Hollywood. I came out here and immediately went into a long session of meetings with [Twentieth Century-Fox president Spyros] Skouras, who said I was being attacked for my politics and I would have to go before the Committee, and on and on. I said, "I'm not going to do any of that. I have nothing to hide, I've done nothing I'm ashamed of. I've worked here for three days; pay me for three days and I'll go home." He said, "Come to New York."

I went back to New York and went into nine or ten days of more meetings with Skouras, in which he waved the flag and told me what a great country this was. He had come here as a poor boy and he sold popcorn and became a multi-millionaire, et cetera, et cetera. I said, "All that is fine and well, and I don't bow to anybody in my feeling for my country, but I'm not going to do anything that I don't want to do, that I think is shameful." Suddenly, for no reason that I could discern, he said, "Okay, you're a good boy. You come to Hollywood and you make good pictures for Twentieth Century-Fox." That was it. I came back under contract, and it was clear sailing.

PM: *It's a historical irony that we now have a president* [Reagan] *by way of Hollywood who insists that there never was a blacklist—just people in this country who did not warm to the notion that many artists and performers were American Communists. Of course, recently it was revealed that what some people suspected all along was true. Ronald Reagan was an informer for the FBI at the same time as he was supposedly testifying impartially before the Committee.*

MR: I was called by CNN when that item broke [verifying that Reagan had been an informant for the FBI in the late forties and early fifties]. I was down at Del Mar and going to the races for the day. A camera crew interviewed me, and I said I was shocked to learn that he was an informant. He was then head of the union [the Screen Actors Guild]. The next day, [Ed] Meese came out with a statement that any red-blooded American would have done the same thing. My interview never ran. And the whole thing was quashed in one day—first you read that the president of the United States was an informant; two days later it is no longer in the papers.

It's part of the mentality that now says we won the Vietnam War. In other words, anything that Communists come off looking well for, in their behavior, is shuffled under the rug: "We don't want to know about it. We didn't do that. That's not true. That was the feeling of the American people." As you say, "That's what the president said."

The establishment will never admit to the blacklist because they would be liable. CBS, to this day, does not admit that there was a blacklist. I know why I was fired. They will not admit it, because they have no legal position—they could very well be sued. There was a blacklist, unquestionably. It was imposed by the networks and the studios. It was unfair, it was unjust, and people suffered. In two cases, two of my friends were deeply cut up and died early in life because of the injustice of the blacklist.

It didn't make the people who were blacklisted any better than they had been before, artistically. Some of them were pretty good, some of them were not so good, some of them were bad, some of them were very good. That more or less remained. But the injustice was a terrible one. And a lot of people who might have developed never had that chance. The few of us who survived it are really among the most fortunate people in this country.

PM: *It seems a mystery to people today that so many capitulated, while so few others stood up to buck the tide.*
MR: A lot of people did stand up, certainly as many as capitulated. The country owes an everlasting debt to the people who stood up and were prepared to be counted at that point. Because without that body of people and without that body of thought, perhaps McCarthy would have been able to go a lot farther than he did. And perhaps any Fascist or neo-Fascist would be able to do a lot more than they've been able to do.

Philosophically, I don't think the country quite understands—nor do many writers and critics—the significant thing that happened when that small body of professors, doctors, teachers, musicians, actors, writers, directors, people from all kinds of professions, stood up to be counted against the grave injustice that was being done. It was a very significant point in American history to me. If those people had not acted as they did at that time, I would have had no chance to have any kind of career.

PM: *Does the bitterness toward informers still linger thirty years later?*
MR: There's a lot of bitterness, though personally I never had that kind of bitterness. I don't feel that I have any personal scars, except for the close friendships and the people whom I love who have really been hurt. My wife, to this day, will not speak to certain people. I know several people who, if they saw certain people on the street, would spit in their faces.

PM: *You seem to have drawn strength from the experience.*
MR: Well, I felt they were wrong then, I know now they were wrong absolutely. I've been variously called a dope or fool myself, for certain things that I did. I feel those people who've called me those names were wrong. I'm not and have not been a dupe. I knew what I was doing all my life. I made certain mistakes, obviously. I indulged myself in certain excesses. But I don't feel I have anything to be ashamed of. Everything I say or do now represents me.

I must say I don't know a single person who behaved, in my view, properly, and who has been any less of a human being for the rest of his life. And I know a lot of guys who behaved badly, and who have not really realized themselves as artists or human beings since that time.

PM: *How do you account for that?*
MR: They made a wrong move. They violated themselves. For an artist, it is the most dangerous thing in the world you can do. You can't deny who you are or what you are. If, suddenly, you find you're not popular because everything has swung the other way, you've got to have enough class to pick up the marbles and say, "That's who I am, that's what I am, that's what I am going to do, and if you don't like it, fuck you."

PM: *Does that hold true for Elia Kazan?*
MR: I'd rather not talk about Gadge. He was once my friend, my teacher. I've never been able to look Gadge in the eye, nor he me. Because he knows that I know.

PM: *What about his work?*
MR: I think his work suffered. I don't think he ever realized his great talent. I think his films before the testimony were better than afterward.

PM: *The blacklist was really a form of censorship, wasn't it?*

MR: That's right.

PM: *When you started directing movies, in the late fifties, films were bland, smug, repressed.*
MR: Oh, the fifties were probably the worst decade in the century.

PM: *Was there a permanent effect, or did the sixties bring it all back?*
MR: The sixties brought it back. But the eighties are in the same area as the fifties. Probably the nineties will bring it back again. The strength of the country is incalculable. It survives everything.

PM: *Could a blacklist happen again?*
MR: Sure, it's possible, but it's less likely because there was that core of people who did the right thing at that time. It has nothing to do with politics; that has to be understood. It has to do with morality. I have never in my life confused ethics and politics. I know some very ethical people with whom I have no agreement politically, and some very unethical people with whom I have all kinds of agreement politically.

PM: *You once told me that* The Front *should never have been a comedy.*
MR: We started to write a more serious film—the film was originally about Hecky, the Zero Mostel character. Halfway through, Walter [screenwriter Walter Bernstein] and I decided it was going to be maudlin and sentimental, so together we came up with the notion of "the front"—we remembered the story because it really happened—and decided that's what the film should be. And that's what the film became. I would like to make another picture that deals more seriously with that time and that subject. It might have a chance to be a better film.

PM: *Which of your films is closest to the way you'd want them to be?*
MR: I'd have to say the three pictures which were nominated for Academy Awards—*Hud, Sounder,* and *Norma Rae.* But I'd also include *The Molly Maguires, Conrack, The Front, The Spy Who Came in From the Cold,* and a little picture called *Casey's Shadow.* I've made about twenty odd films. Two or three of them I really don't like. Most of them I do like, in varying degrees.

PM: *Norman Jewison directed* A Soldier's Story, *Robert Altman made* Streamers, *and now Steven Spielberg has directed* The Color Purple. *Very few white directors have shown an interest in racial subjects or themes. What are the problems in doing films like* Sounder *and* Conrack?

MR: That you're not black, so that you're not as close to the material as you would like to be. There's no way anyone can understand what it is to be black unless you're black. Some of us make a pretty good facsimile thereof, and I hope I am one of those. But I'm very aware that blacks don't really get a shot.

I had a lot of arguments with some of my black friends about *Conrack*, a film that I really like. They felt I was doing a film about a white Jesus. They were into black studies and such, and I've been into integration for fifty of my seventy years. I said to them, "Make your own picture. Get off my back. This is what I believe in, and I'm not violating anything I believe in; if it's violating something you believe in, I can't deal with that." And they did not support the film.

PM: *Why do you persist in making movies about blacks?*
MR: That's what I have to make movies about. Because I cannot make movies about things I don't feel about deeply. I feel deeply about the dilemma of black people. I always have.

Certainly the blacks in this country have been disenfranchised for most of their lives. I'll never forget—I didn't intend to cast Cicely [Tyson] in *Sounder*. I had asked another actress to play the part, and she turned me down. When Cis came to me, I said, "Cis, you're a high-fashion model, a great beauty. I need a working-class, peasant woman." And she said, "Marty, there are no blacks in this country more than one generation removed from that experience." That sold me, because I realized the truth of what she said. I said, "Okay, you have the part."

She reminded me of what I was trying to say: that no amount of seeming sophistication or movement into another class—an upper-middle class or an intellectual class—would remove the genuine problem that has always existed. That every black really knew about all the time. That scar tissue is there and *deep*. I'm aware of it and very sympathetic toward it and feel that it is one of the most grievous errors we have made in this country.

I would like to make another picture about black people, but it would have to be a picture done at a price.

PM: *Would it have to be a comedy to satisfy Hollywood?*

MR: It would not *have* to be anything. Yet so many of them do seem to end up being in the South. I've found, singularly enough, that I'm very related to rural America. Why, I don't know. Certainly I was a big-city boy; I grew up in New York City, and I wasn't out of the city until I was forty years old. Why I have a feeling for rural America, I'm not sure. But I've learned to accept things about myself that I don't totally understand, particularly if they're good. I'm not putting any boundaries on it. I would just like to make a serious film about the contemporary black experience, be it in Mississippi, or Detroit, or anyplace.

PM: *Obviously one of your other great thematic concerns has been labor. Why?*
MR: Same reason. The dispossessed. I think working people in this country have gotten a raw deal.

PM: *Have I missed any of your other concerns?*
MR: I did one picture where Paul Newman played an Indian, *Hombre*—again, a disenfranchised group. God knows, if I could find a picture on that subject that was first-class, I would jump at the chance to do it. Because Indians don't even have the strength that the Negro population has. Because the Negro population, by virtue of their extraordinary gifts in show business and athletics, has dominated a lot of our culture in the last decades. The American Indian has really been neglected. That's a terrible tragedy.

PM: *What about feminism? Beginning with* Norma Rae, *then* Cross Creek, *and now* Murphy's Romance, *you've made pictures that empower women.*
MR: That's accidental, partly because women are suddenly bankable in Hollywood and acting as their own producers, partly because of my friendship with Sally Field. She's a terrific actress. I like her very much. And I like to work with people I like. I'm not much of a feminist, unfortunately. In fact, I've been called the opposite—by my wife—though we have a happy marriage of many years' standing.

PM: *Do you still have a predilection for Faulkner?*
MR: That really happened because of the Ravetches [screenwriters Irving Ravetch and Harriet Frank, Jr.], because they are devoted to him. They think he is the greatest American writer, which he well may be.

The Long Hot Summer was a good, entertaining, commercial film. The other one, *The Sound and the Fury*, I didn't like. I made some mistakes on that. I shouldn't do Faulkner again. There's something in the language that's too rich. With great writers like that, it's very tough, because in a film you have to tell a story, and when the language becomes so much the star of the story, it's almost untranslatable.

Ironically, the one Faulkner film I have seen that I liked was *Intruder in the Dust*, directed by Clarence Brown and written by a man who turned out to be a friendly witness [Ben Maddow]. It was a much better film than either of mine.

PM: *What do you look for when you go about selecting story material?*
MR: I pick up something, I read it, and I'm affected. When I read that article about that woman in the *New York Times Magazine*, with her explaining to her two children how tough life was going to be because she was on the side of the union—out of which we made the film *Norma Rae*—I was very affected.

PM: *Do you feel inhibited because you don't write?*
MR: Somewhat. But every director writes, whether or not he really writes the written word. I've written two plays in my lifetime, and I've tried to write two or three screenplays. They're all serviceable. They're never really good. I've done seven films with the Ravetches. I know how good they are. I know the kind of talk they write, and I could never compete. I manage that talk sometimes in conversation but never when faced with the empty page. I feel that very often the performances in the films that I make illuminate the subject matter.

PM: *Why is it that you can achieve this, and another director can't?*
MR: It's partly having been an actor. I was trained as an actor at the Group Theatre, and I've taught acting at the Actors Studio and several other places. I love actors. I really love them. And as I see them begin to function, I can be very helpful. As an actor you look to complicate a part as much as you can. I think there's something very kindred between my training as an actor and the films I have made.

PM: *What's the value of complexity in a performance?*

MR: There is extraordinary value, because the mark of an artist, finally, is the complexity with which he deals with his subject. That facility, which some actors have to a very high degree, is of some importance, but it's not nearly as important as the ability to perceive things which make a character genuinely come to life.

PM: *How do you now categorize yourself politically, relative to Hollywood?*
MR: I would certainly think I am in the left of the Hollywood contingent, definitely. Also openly and admittedly. I'm not careful. I have not made a career out of being careful.

PM: *How do you categorize Hollywood politically, as compared to the rest of the nation?*
MR: Hollywood is probably more liberal than the rest of the country at this point—but not so it will hurt business.

Have you heard this joke? A guy walks into a bank and walks up to the girl behind the counter and says, "I want to make a fucking deposit." The girl says, "Whoa, wait a minute, sir." He says, "What do you mean, wait a minute? I want to make a fucking deposit." She says, "This is a bank, sir, you can't talk that way." He says, "I'll talk any way I want to, and I want to make a fucking deposit." She says, "Well, I'm going to have to call the bank manager." He says, "I don't give a shit who you call. Call him." She calls over the manager, who asks, "What's the problem?" "No problem," says the guy. "I want to make a fucking deposit, that's all." The manager says, "Wait a minute, this is a bank, sir." He says, "I don't give a shit what it is, I want to make a fucking deposit now. I just hit the lottery for two million dollars, and I want to make a fucking deposit." And the manager says, "And this cunt won't take your money?"

That's it—that's your short essay on capitalism.

PM: *What are the limitations for a progressive film artist in Hollywood? Altman ultimately became persona non grata here, while John Huston has to work outside the city limits. You are almost an anomaly.*
MR: Fundamentally, the studios don't want to make serious films. They just don't want to. They've come to the conclusion that they're not as good an investment as the other kinds of films. That will pass, too, as the horror films go by the wayside, as they have in the last year or so. Consequently, I think

it's maybe a little easier to get a serious film on, but it's never been easy to get a serious film on. Never!

PM: *But in the heyday of the studios, the moguls put out four or five serious movies a year, either as a matter of ego, or for award purposes, or for their own personal aggrandizement.*
MR: And for the PR value.

PM: *Darryl Zanuck may have produced his share of fatuous musicals, but he also insisted on an occasional important picture.*
MR: Just think back. The five pictures that were nominated for Best Picture Oscars last year [1984] were all turned down by major studios—every single one of them. That has to tell you something about what the major studios are prepared to subsidize at this point. Any guy who is going to give them a picture that can't be channeled into some mold is going to make them nervous. They're nervous because business has fallen off. There were some mistakes made about the immediacy of cassettes. Cassettes are beginning to bury motion pictures in terms of economics.

It's even hard to criticize the studios, because it's just a business to them. They would like to make good pictures, but no picture is a good one to an exhibitor unless it makes money. By definition, that's a good picture—a film that makes money. Of course, we know that isn't true, and we've seen a lot of schlock in the last few years make bundles of money.

If I happen to find a picture I want to make that's too political for this gang, I'll find another way to make it. I may be able to sell them even a political picture by bringing it in at such a price that they can't resist it. No money up front. I'll get stars and I'll make the film. If I really found something—and I'm always looking—I'd find a way to get it on. For the films I've wanted to make I never charged the kind of money that I did for the others.

PM: *Can you even find stories where the writer pushes the limits of political acceptability?*
MR: It's very tough to find that kind of material. most of it exists in the past. I haven't found anything on the level that I'm prepared to go to bat for. Now, this will probably bring me a rash of the worst goddamned scripts anyone could possibly read—crazy political scripts that are just godawful

because it's all politics and they've forgotten everything else. They're cardboard. Agitprop.

First and foremost, a movie has to be entertaining, because if it isn't entertaining, you're not going to affect anybody. Any film that is fundamentally cerebral will play to only a small segment of society, since the greater part of society is immediately inhibited. I feel I'm plain enough in my tastes that if I really like something, I will be able to get it across to most people. Because I feel I'm more or less like most people, maybe a little more sophisticated, a little fatter, a little more gullible, according to some of my critics, but I figure I'm pretty close to a lot of American joes.

PM: *Where are the great political screenwriters of today to help you solve the problem?*
MR: [Laughs.] I don't think there are a lot of them around, because they were developed at the same time that I was developed. Nowadays writers think, more or less, in terms of straight entertainment.

PM: *If you can't be political in Hollywood, at least you can be iconoclastic.*
MR: It's a safe philosophic form for political differences with the establishment. It's not political in the sense that it's against the establishment. It's artistic. Most true artists are iconoclastic.

PM: *Do you ever wonder whether you would have made more overtly political films if, as a result of the blacklist, you had been forced to work abroad?*
MR: Perhaps. I think making political films is a problem for leftist filmmakers all over the world. It's not really their time. They have to find some way to keep alive during this time, until the time comes back, and it will come back, because it always has.

PM: *Let's say you were invited to host a Martin Ritt weekend at some college and asked to show five great leftist films—great cinematically and as political statements. What would you show?*
MR: I know what I would show. I would show *The Battle of Algiers* first, and maybe second or third, because I love that film.

PM: *And if you had to add a few Hollywood films to your list?*

MR: I wouldn't be faring too well.

PM: *I've heard you express your admiration for John Ford's version of John Steinbeck's* The Grapes of Wrath.
MR: A great film. A great liberal film. I love the film. I love the director. The director is maybe the greatest director we've turned out.

PM: *And an interesting case—since Ford was a conservative artist, or at least a traditional man who created liberal, progressive films.*
MR: Because he was a great artist, and a great artist will always tell as much of the truth as he can. And it's my deep feeling that the greatest truth is in the liberal tradition.

PM: *It's unfortunate, and somehow indicative, that so many of the great directors of the forties and the promising directors of the fifties are no longer working steadily—Billy Wilder and Robert Wise, or even Don Siegel and Stanley Kramer. What happened to that generation?*
MR: Partly it's attrition. Partly it's the kinds of pictures that are being made. In some cases their work went bad, which I can't quite understand. I don't really know. I feel fortunate that I'm able to work.

PM: *Is it difficult for people of that generation to relate to the kids who run Hollywood today?*
MR: Do you want to hear a story? They swear it's true, but I can't believe it. It's too absurd. Fred Zinnemann "takes a meeting" with one of the young executives at Tri-Star. Introductions are made; there are handshakes across the table. The Tri-Star fellow turns to Zinnemann and says, "Well, Mr. Zinnemann, before we start, tell me a little bit about yourself. What have you done?" And Zinnemann looks at him and says, "You first."

It can't be true. It's too perfect!

Martin Ritt and the Group Theatre

STEWART STERN/1986

v: *Maybe we should start in a kind of very general way and then hone in. What would you think ought to be the point of a program about the Group Theatre as you—let's start with that very general observation and you can zero in.*
MR: The Group Theatre was the single most important force philosophically in the American theatre. It had great artists within it. But more important than the artists that came out of the Group Theatre is the influence that the Group Theatre has had in directors, writers, actors, as through the Group Theatre into the Actors Studio. Actually it has helped shape my life. Very much so. I have lived by many of the principles that were basic to the artistic integrity of the Group Theatre. And so I've had an inordinate respect for artists all my life. Prefer them to anybody else in the world. They are the people I grew to respect early in life and my respect for those people has continued. I think the single most important voice in the Group Theatre was Harold Clurman, who was an extraordinary intellectual and an important artist. I stress the intellectuality of it because I believe that finally the heritage of the Group Theatre will be in the fact that what they believed and what they tried to do was the proper way, not the only way, but the best way. I say not the only way because obviously there were great artists before the Group Theatre came into being, and there have been great artists who considered themselves lucky not to be sullied by the Group Theatre. But from my point of view, the philosophic impact of the Group Theatre has been the most extraordinary of any artistic experience in the theatre. I don't know much

---

Published by permission of Paul Newman.

about the dance—I don't know nearly as much about dance or music, but in the theatre it's unquestioned in my opinion that they've made an incredible contribution, and will through the ages. No question of it because there are still many very capable practitioners of what it was all about.

INT: *What was it all about, Marty?*
MR: It was the deepest humanistic impulse on the American scene. It tried to codify, sometimes very well and sometimes not so well, the nature of what it meant to be an actor, director or writer. But more important was the pervasive humanism that it poured on the American scene in terms of the plays they did, in terms of the personalities they directed, they graduated, they sent into the world as emissaries.

INT: *Can you describe, can you live out for me a man whom I never knew and have only heard about very, very briefly, and that's Harold Clurman—what his color was, what his passion was, what he was like? Even in actors' terms. How he sounded.*
MR: Harold was the greatest talker I ever heard in my life. I mean, he was incredible. He was a deeply passionate man, committed to humanism, committed to America, committed to the importance of the artist, and I loved him. I got to know him when I was very young, and I knew him very casually because obviously I was just a kid around there. I was not in the inner circle of the leadership. But I was there at the first—I'll never forget this—the first rehearsal of *Golden Boy*. I had met Gadge [Elia Kazan] working in a little off-Broadway theatre, and he helped me get this job punching a bag backstage, because I think I was the only ex-jock around the Group Theatre. And I was an assistant stage manager. And I punched the bag and I had two lines. At any rate, I went to this first rehearsal of this play, and I never really understood why [John] Garfield had not been cast instead of Luther [Adler]. Gadge soon explained that to me and I saw it in the rehearsal of course, that the play was really about a musician and not a fighter. And Harold got up, I don't remember the year the Group Theatre started.

V: '31.
MR: '31. Then that was '37. He said this is the sixth year of the Group Theatre, the greatest acting company in the world. And by my nature that would embarrass me a little bit, so I looked around to see if anybody was smiling.

And nobody was. So I figured he meant it. And then I watched that play which still is the best acted play I've ever seen, come in to shape. We rehearsed upstairs at the old Belasco Theatre, where I'm sure the old man had chased a lot of ladies. And it was—I mean, I had never met such people. I'd just been in New York—though I was born in New York, I'd been down South in a little college, played football. And I came into this extraordinary group of intellectuals and artists. And I mean, they were extraordinary. That was some cast. The three new actors who all had small parts were Karl Malden, Harry Bratsburg and myself. And I had the smallest of the three. And history has proven that it was the right way to cast me.

But I mean the cast was incredible. The performance—as I saw it grow day by day, it was extraordinary to watch. And Harold, in the first two weeks of rehearsal, may well have been the greatest director in the world.

INT: *Can you describe that?*

V: *How the hell did he actually work?*
MR: Well, he was—Harold was so passionate. He was so committed to what he believed that it was impossible not to be affected by it. And if he talked to you about a part and started working with you on a part it was impossible, almost impossible first of all not to agree with him which really was impossible. But even then to fire you up and excite you in a way—I'm not even talking craftwise now, I'm talking personawise. Craftwise was another matter. By that time most of the actors in the Group Theatre had a pretty good hold on their craft, you know, outside of the new people coming in. And they knew where to go and what to do to get what they wanted. And if they were not all the greatest actors in the world—and they were not—they were all gentlemen with extraordinary perception and ladies with extraordinary perception. So the purity of that gut excitement, the purity of that commitment, the purity of the belief which is almost religious was overwhelming. And you were caught up in it willy-nilly.

V: *So it wasn't essentially a technical thing that he did, particular procedures or anything like that?*
MR: No. But the technical thing of course was there. The craft was there. And actually I think the proof of the pudding was that Harold's work the first two or three weeks of rehearsal were always better than his work once

he began to have to do the ordinary things that directors do—put a play on its feet and so on, he lost some of his interest. I mean, he was still highly skilled and highly professional, but it never had the excitement of discovery that he brought to the material that he fell in love with. And that was always extraordinary. So it was always terrific to be around whether he was discussing Chekhov, Ibsen, or later on Odets, a playwright with whom he fell in love. And I guess Clifford owed his first productions to Harold, because as you probably know, Lee was not that enamored of *Awake and Sing!* And they were two diametrically opposed gentlemen. I got to know Harold better because it was easier to get to know Harold. Harold would commit himself. He was a perfect artist. It's inartistic not to commit yourself. And Harold committed himself totally on every issue. And I knew the level of commitment was very high with Lee too, but because of the different personality it was more difficult to get to know Lee.

V: *Marty, that's a tough word for me to visualize, what that commitment looks like in action. Can you be more specific about it in terms of the specific moments that you can use as examples of his commitment?*

MR: Well, when the Group began to make it, so-called, Harold didn't leave. I mean, there were all kinds of opportunities for them to leave. They were the revolutionary artists of that time. They didn't have too much commercial success, but they had enough. And they had developed a major American playwright, several major American directors and actors. And with a funnel for all that was new and exciting going on the American scene at the time. Harold must have had, as many of them did, and some of the actors came out here, Julie came out here and Franchot came out here . . . and those guys I only knew in a very shallow way because they were there before me. But right to the very end, there was a party given for Harold at the Bistro here at which I gave him a rather tongue-tied introduction—right to the very end there was that kind of excitement about Harold. Still, to the very end—to the end, Harold remained in my opinion the purest of the lot. I mean I would easily say he was the most important single influence in my life and in my career. And I was not that close to him either. It's just that I admired him greatly and I just felt that his commitment was a pure one. And that it would take something extraordinary to shake him. And that's why actually nothing ever did shake him. To the very end I believe Harold would have died to make another Group Theatre.

v: *When he would walk into that first rehearsal, what happened? Can you describe that scene?*

MR: Well, with much complicated feeling they all adored him. With much reservation and some jealousy, they all adored him. He was the boss. He and Lee were the bosses. And Gadge was sitting right below at this shoulder because I think Gadge was Harold's protegee. And they all loved the play. And they all wanted to act. They all had to make a living, which was a very shaky—I mean, a very shaky profession at a very shaky time. And so the rehearsal was very exciting. Just the atmosphere of rehearsal was exciting as hell. Everybody was waiting for things to happen, actors to explode, scenes to be realized, a play to open. The opening night of *Golden Boy* is still the most memorable night in my life. And I had nothing to do with it—it's not like some of the pictures I had where I was involved and my reputation and everything else was on the line—they were never as exciting to me as that time. And these people were bound together by a common belief. It was not a political belief. It was a human and social belief. Obviously there were political differences in the Group Theatre. We know historically those things eventuated into some great bitternesses. But the Group Theatre was not a political organization, not at all. To the dismay of some and I'm sure to the happiness of others. But the kind of commitment, theatrically, that goes into behavior of priests in Central America or the Philippine Islands, that existed in the Group Theatre. You'd die, you'd fight for the Group Theatre. You'd fight for what it was about. Only later as I grew older did I realize that they weren't right all the time, that they did make serious mistakes. But that's in the nature of things.

v: *Could you talk a little bit about some of those, because I think you're articulating so movingly the very religious sort of spirit. I think one wants to use religious terms. I'm going to call my book* The Chosen Ones *because one feels in reading Harold and having heard Harold, and all of them, that wonderful spirit. But also one knows and you have said several times, reservations, complications, they weren't always right. And it's hard to get at that quality. Even in relation to the women, for example. There was Frances Farmer, and her life—If you could suggest any of that to us—one knows about it a little bit and it's hard to put it down.*

MR: Well, with Frances Farmer it's very hard to say. One has private opinions that are not substantiated by known fact. She was a marvelous woman. But I think she was in over her head. And her husband was in over his head.

I think Frances was rushed too quickly. I don't think she was ready. Emotionally. She was really more ready as an actress than she was emotionally to deal with what she had to deal with at that time. She was a good actress and she was a great beauty.

I remember driving into an Equity meeting with Clifford one night. He told me he had written a play with a part for me. And the play was *Night Music* and the part was Marty, and again I had two lines. And I got so pissed off when I heard about it—but he was a good friend. We were very close. At the end I saw a lot of him out here when he was ill. Obviously he wouldn't face that. And he had changed a great deal. This is a tough town for a writer. And for Clifford it was always an uneasy marriage. Whatever work he did on film was an uneasy marriage. Because what was original to him the film tended to pacify in some way. I don't really remember what question I'm answering at this point.

V: *You started talking about Frances Farmer. I have a little paper about the women in the Group Theatre because I've done a book about them for the American Theatre. It's a very dominant male presence. You can hardly see the image of the women and yet of course there were very interesting women.*
MR: They were very interesting, but they were never quite on the level with the men.

V: *They never had the opportunity either.*
MR: That's probably true. I'm sure that's true. Stella was the closest. Stella was as dominant a personality as any man in the Group Theatre. And has been a great teacher. I've had occasion to be around her, and she's terrific. I personally enjoyed Bobby the most as a teacher because he made the work enjoyable. Too often, with some of the other people it was painful. It was squeezing it out. Knowing better than that because one knows that that cannot be done. You cannot will the emotion. And the squeezing it out really means that you're willing emotion. You've seen that with actors, with directors, with writers.

V: *Marty, can you describe the differences between the way Stella taught, Lee taught, Bobby taught, and Sandy taught? Characterize each of them as teachers?*
MR: Well, I didn't see enough of Stella really and not enough of Sandy, though I did spend time with both of them. Bobby, as I just got through

telling you, made things a lot of fun. He was very perceptive, very good, and managed to make it entertaining, managed to allow the actor to fly. With Lee one was very often inhibited and one was afraid of this—Lee was very good for highly developed actors, because Lee was very shrewd and very perceptive and probably knew as much if not more than any of them. But he was difficult with beginning actors and he was disapproving and therefore the atmosphere sometimes in his class was not really conducive to the flowering of the actor. And that never happened with Bobby. It never happened with Gadge. Gadge was terrific because he was clear and strong, like he was as a director. And he would go right to the heart of the matter and be able to help. Sandy, I can always tell you everybody I know loved Sandy and loved working with him. I loved him too. I didn't get to know him as well as I did a couple of others because we were separated for all the years that I've been in Hollywood. And we were not too close there either, though I've always had high regard for him. But I can tell the graduates that he's turned out, and some of the people that he's turned out that have become teachers themselves. Sandy was first-class. As a matter of fact, they were all first-class as teachers. One of the big problems out here is there weren't any—there wasn't anybody like that. That's why when Bobby and Stella came out I knew they would be engulfed. Stella is very bright, very funny too. Very incisive. She was as close as they had to a female star. She was a star. And she's still a star. She's still a terrific actress. If you got the right part for her she would be terrific.

V: *It's hard for me to even think of her in that context, because from little hints that people have given, it's as though there was this enormously dramatic presence who really had nothing to do with the other actors in that group, who was so far ahead of them in terms of her own success and viewed her role in the theatre in a way quite separate from what was happening there in terms of the ensemble. And I keep wondering what it looked like—Stella Adler and summers in the Group. Who was she connected with? What did she do? How were she and Harold with each other during that time?*

MR: All I know is he was nuts about her. And I wasn't in any—I came to the Group after those early tempestuous summers where her sexuality dominated the summer proceedings. I've only heard about that. So Harold was so nuts about her and so dominated on that level that—but from the little that I've observed, because I came around later, was that she would have been dominant on any level. She's just an extraordinary woman. That's all. And she probably didn't need the Group Theatre and they all did. She probably didn't need that special philosophic point of view about life and art. And they all did. She didn't need that for sustenance and they all did, as I did, as most of the young people around need—that's one of the reasons I'm teaching at UCLA this spring. I finally decided to do it just so I could say some of the things I feel about life. Not only what I feel about making movies, because to hell with that. It's not that important. But what I feel about life and what I feel about what's going on in this country, as that reflects itself in my work and in anybody else's work—the kids should know that there are some people who are not only committed to making money in this business. I don't know how much that will affect them because it's a very strange generation, living in a country which is related only to winning and has a fast food appetite for success. For artists, these are so debilitating, these concepts, that somebody should say no. That's why I'm going to work. I've agreed to take six scripts that I like best, and produce twenty minute pictures with these kids. Let them direct their own films. And I'll help them with the script, help them cast it, and help them put it together. And then try to get some other guys like George Roy Hill or a couple of other guys to come in so that it's not just a one semester thing. Many of those guys don't agree with me about anything outside of film. But still most of the guys I would talk to are serious guys and I know would be dealing seriously at least. And it's been a big departure for UCLA because they're in a position where a lot of the academics who have tenure are getting on. And they've been looking to try to do this for some time. They've brought in three or four professors, and I think it's going to help the arts and sciences—the fine arts school—a great deal.

But I mean, you look at this picture. This is a funny picture because the remark that you both made about how serious everybody—everybody does have (LAUGHS) it's terrific. My God, look at the intensity in Odets and in Harold. God! Have you talked to Morris [Carnovsky]? There's a lot of bitterness in him, I'm sure, particularly about Gadge.

v: *When I tried to make this reunion I talked to a number of people and I did talk to Gadge too, but I knew I could not have both him and Morris on the same stage.*
MR: I got an invitation from Whitehead last spring about something that was going to be held for Gadge at Williams College where he went to school,

and Paul's name was on there. So I called Paul and said, I don't have that strong feeling about Gadge, but I have some friends who would be destroyed if I would go. And I felt that therefore I shouldn't go. My wife would also be destroyed. She's not forgiven him. A lot of people haven't forgiven him. And he shouldn't be forgiven. I believe that. But I was very close to him for a short time. We were very close. And I've not totally gotten over that because he was a great influence in my life. And Gadge was the smartest of all of them. He not only had talent, he had an even more important element for success—he had incredible judgment. If you look at all the Tennessee Williams plays he did, they were all hits. The other ones didn't work. I mean, it's a little frightening to be that smart. But he was. I've met Gadge I don't know how many times over the past twenty years, and if one could photograph what was unspoken, one would have a very interesting piece of film. Because what was spoken was hi, when are you going to make another movie? Have you read my latest book? I consider him one of the great tragedies of the McCarthy period, because he was easily the most talented director of my time. And he's produced nothing since then.

v: *Marty, I just want to say in relation to your work at UCLA, I've been teaching at USC, and the thing that appalls me is that the world to most of these kids seems to have started—their memory seems to have started—with* ET *and* Close Encounters, *and their whole referrent, instead of being the referrent of life, even their own lives as kids, as anything, is the movies they've seen and I cannot find anywhere even an idea of social connection, social responsibility, social impact, social concern. It's as though what's happening in the world—they don't even know. They know what's happening in Westwood. But as far as the world is concerned, they simply don't know. And when you talk about the pain . . . I talked to Norman Lloyd about why it was that almost none of the people—Morris, Phoebe, Kazan I can understand—I mean, he keeps saying well, I'm saving that for my book so he didn't really reveal very much—but I talked to Lloyd about that sort of benign surface that people had had in their interviews, and he said that when Jean Renoir was in his final illness he used to go over and see him everyday. And before Renoir died—he had always had a limp, as you know—suddenly the wound that he had received in World War I opened again. And he died with the wound open. And he said that he thinks that that may be why, that the pain was so enormous and there's so much unresolved about it that people aren't being as forthcoming as they might about what happened, about what the temperature was, the political temperature, the cross-over between people's experience in the Depression and what seemed like Hope out there—how the Moscow Art came from somewhere, and how people felt that if that could be the flower that could be headed toward them, then the ideal that created it or at least fostered it or allowed it to survive, was also something to go toward. One could understand in the context of the time and I certainly could, walking in the parades that I did when I went to Ethical Culture School—it was everywhere. I mean, we all wanted something to believe in. It was an optimistic time, in spite of all that.*

MR: Very optimistic time.

V: *And I think people don't understand what created quote communist activists who were also actors. How the communist influence came to be felt within the Group. What its aims were. What did they want? I mean, if those four or five committed people who were motivated by their ideals, who apparently were manipulated from the outside, at least so it seems because in the case of Kazan and Clifford they left the Party within eight or nine months when some new information or feeling must have gotten to them, that was in the way, what their real purpose was. But had the Party been successful in taking over, if that was their aim, the Group, what would they have done? I mean, what was their aim? How would the Group have been different? Was there resistance to it? Were there people within the Group who were politically not that way? Aware of what was happening? How did they resist it or did they during that time?*

MR: I was there too late for that, Stewart, see. I have a point of view about it.

V: *That really had ended by the time you came in.*

MR: By the time—1937—it had ended. Of course McCarthyism had not reared its ugly head at that point, so the rift—but with Clifford and with Gadge and with the others, the few who were politically committed, if the communist party had overtaken the Group Theatre it would have destroyed the Group immediately. Nothing could have flowered in that atmosphere. That's patently obvious to anybody who knows what goes on in the creative community. The communist party never overtook the Moscow Art Theatre. The Moscow Art Theatre was an entity by itself in a communist country. Stanislavski had come upon this fundamental point of view from watching all the great actors in the world and from being a major intellectual himself; he had codified a way of work. And the communists had nothing to do with that at its inception, nothing to do with it at any time in its history, had enough sense to let them alone. As far as the Group Theatre was concerned, there were a few people in the Group Theatre obviously that were very left-oriented. Most of them were not. I came too late to really know if there were any real struggles in the interior of the Group Theatre. But when you ask me why Kazan and Odets behaved the way they did, I would say it had nothing to do with politics. It had to do with appetite. Neither one of them were prepared to give up success. I mean, if Gadge had not taken that full page ad in the *New York Times,* he wouldn't be able to work in Hollywood for a couple of years. He was the king of Broadway, he could have worked anyplace else in the world. It comes down to appetite. Everybody had the same opportunities. And Gadge was the most successful. In my opinion they couldn't have done a thing to him. He might have had a little less money—very dear to him. But appetite, that's the basis. Everybody had the same opportunity. The story they tell about Clifford and Z is a little frightening when he was doing *Rhinoceros* here.

V: *Zero Mostel?*
MR: Yeah. And Clifford saw the show, went back to see him. And as he walked in—this is the story, I don't know if it's true, I was not there—Zero said well, how are you doing, Loose Lips? And you know Z—Z was brutal. Kept calling him Loose Lips all through the conversation. Then finally he said, don't call me. I'll call you. Now that can be a fabricated story based upon legitimate feelings they both had, obviously. And to this day I think if Morris would see Gadge on the street he'd spit in his face. I don't know. I haven't seen Morris since I came to Hollywood. I haven't seen Morris. I love Morris. Morris is a great man, an extraordinary man. And one hell of an actor. And I'm more surprised about Morris's politics than anybody else. I had no notion that he felt as deeply as he did.

V: *Why?*
MR: Because it was never discussed. We didn't discuss politics. Not at all.

V: *Did you know about the Actors Committee?*
MR: No. That was before me. That was all before me.

V: *There weren't still reverberations?*

MR: But the day after Kazan took the full page ad in the *Times*, I had a hemorrhoid attack and went to the hospital. I couldn't understand that. See, I know that that's all a lie. Because what he said was turn these people in. They're dangerous. I mean, that's silly. I mean, I know he didn't believe that. He couldn't believe that. But that was the deal he had to make. I know that out here suddenly the private access to Zanuck's office had been cut off to him. I had it for a short while after I did *The Long Hot Summer* with Buddy Adler. I know the entrance to the office. But that bitter political thing which split the Group Theatre apart, finally, really happened before I got there. I know only one absolute. Nobody who behaved well in that period is any more talented than he was before that time. But nobody who behaved well has been much less of a human being. Nobody who behaved badly has gotten away with it, humanly. They just haven't. Clifford never got away with it. Gadge certainly has not gotten away with it.

V: *Marty, you said that it tore the Group apart. And even though you weren't there, what do you know about it? What have you heard about it, about the way that happened?*
MR: Well, it didn't tear it apart until the McCarthy period because that's when it came to a head.

V: *And that was after?*
MR: Yeah. I mean, they may have had internal arguments. That was early in the 50s.

V: *It's very hard to get a sense of how many people were aware that there was a little core of people. One senses that they didn't, that there wasn't an awareness, although they obviously carry out certain actions.*
MR: I'm very left-oriented, and I had no awareness. I mean, nobody came to me and nobody approached me and said there's a caucus of us here. And I never gave it a thought. And I didn't think it had any meaning at all.

V: *One thing I would like to ask you and I don't know whether you want to get into it—I don't know how directly related it is, but it comes out of the work with students. The kids don't know what the blacklist was, they don't know how it operated. They don't know what its toll was on people. They don't know what it was like not to be able to work. What happened to Joe Bromberg, what happened*

to Bud Bohnen. They don't know. And if you would be willing to talk about that, even briefly, it would be I think a very important part of this.
MR: Okay. I knew they didn't know because when I made *The Front* and I went to show the film in several colleges, a couple of the kids said to me, you made that up. They didn't believe . . .

V: *This is how I've pieced it together for myself, though I'm just sitting here listening because you're offering me insights that are extremely valuable. There was a struggle in the Group Theatre between the directorship and the members. I mean, you know this was a group effort and there were leaders, as you said. The leaders were in a sense the bosses of this sort of quasi-democratic humanistic organization. So they were arguing for more say-so, more input by the members in the decision-making process, about what plays they were going to do, which had both an aesthetic and a political implication.*
MR: Yeah.

V: *And yet that doesn't seem like a communistic plot when you put it in those terms. What I was wondering was if they had succeeded within that actors' company, if Cheryl and Lee had not left because of all of that, and they had succeeded, how would things have changed? What plays would they have done instead of Odets? How would the results have changed?*
MR: Lee was the one who didn't want to do Odets. The actors and Harold finally forced the production of *Awake and Sing!* But nothing would have changed. Every impulse was totally a humanistic impulse. It happened to have the trappings at that point in history of the communist party. Period. But every impulse was a humanistic one. But that has nothing to do with the actual position of informing on one's friends. It's not a political thing anymore. It's an ethical thing.

V: *Would you be willing to talk about your experience about what blacklist was to you and what happened and what happened to friends of yours?*
MR: Yeah. I was working at CBS at the time. And I got a call from Donald Davis, the son of the playwright, who was the head of production at CBS, and he asked me to come in and see him. CBS was then on the 14th floor at Madison Avenue and 54th Street or 53rd. I went up that day to see him. I already knew because I knew what was in the air. I knew what was going on in the country. I walked down the 14th floor, which was the executive offices.

And I saw a guy that I had—I was sort of a trouble shooter at CBS at the time. I was an actor/director and producer. I saw this guy that I'd helped on a television show recently who had been in trouble. And as he saw me he ducked into a little room that was off the hallway. So if I didn't know what was going to happen before, that certainly solidified it. I walked into Donald Davis's office who was a very nice, decent guy. And he said I don't know what's happened, Marty. You haven't been renewed. So I said I'll tell you what's happened, Donald. I've been attacked. And he said oh come on, Marty. This is America and so on. And I said okay. That was it. Now at that time the sponsor of the program that I was doing—a program called *Danger* which was a successful TV series—was the Block Drug Company. And they didn't want to let me go. CBS insisted because of the PR nature of what was going on, with the kind of mail they'd been getting which obviously was all organized. And that was it. Nothing else was said. I was not renewed. And I got a job acting—I had done a Mark Hellinger short story which had been a very big critical success called "The Paper Box Kid" that Walter Bernstein wrote and that Sidney Lumet directed. And I got a job playing a 35-year-old cab driver or truck driver—I don't remember—Olive Deering was playing my wife. Dan Petry had come to New York and this was his first television show. After about two or three days of rehearsal one day the producer of the show walked in, he grabbed Dan, took Dan aside, started to jaw at him. Naturally I knew what was going on. And this guy left and then I said Dan, what is it? He said well, you're not right for the part. I said a 35-year-old cab driver, New York cab driver, and I'm not right for the part? So I said the same thing to Dan. I said this is what's going on Dan. He said come on, Marty. He was fresh out of Chicago. Very sweet, very nice guy and a good director. And just before air time the show was canceled. And I knew then that the die had been cast. Somebody had made a mistake putting me into the show as an actor. And they'd caught up with that and I was persona non grata as a director and producer. And I had a few friends in New York, writers—Polansky, Bernstein, Manoff—who were the hottest writers in town because they were working cheap. One must never forget the element of greed involved here. When I did *Edge of the City*, my first film, I got $10,000 to direct the film. I was happy to get it, of course, but still it places everything in some kind of perspective. These three guys wrote 95% of the shows, scripts of a very successful series called *You Are There* which Lumet directed. It's impossible to believe that all those people didn't know what was going on at the time, impossible. But success coupled with greed overtook the proceedings, and a lot of my friends were blacklisted. I'm one of the few who were lucky enough to beat the rap. And even when the career—well the careers were always brutalized by what was going on, plus the family lives, plus kids who couldn't understand, who just are not equipped to understand—the famous Brecht play about a Germany family where the kids were informing on their parents. Part of the Nazi/Hitler youth. And a kid coming back from school and reading in the papers that his old man was blacklisted. You know that the whole drug scene has been so related to peer pressure. You can imagine what was going on in families of people who had been accused. Nothing had to be proved in that time. I mean, I think McCarthy never turned up anything. He finally was so frustrated that he had to turn on Marshall and Eisenhower. There's nothing to turn up. I daresay that the left wing members of the Group Theatre were a microcosm of most of the left movement in the United States, on a humanitarian basis based on what was best for ordinary Joe's and what was right and humane. I daresay that—I don't know this to be a fact—outside of a few hardened left wing professionals, most of the people were there for the same reasons that there was that kind of movement in the Group Theatre. So it was a terrible, terrible time. I remember I came out here to work. *Edge of the City* had opened here in New York and had gotten very good notices, and Metro was not interested—I'd gotten the job because Metro was in a proxy fight at the time. I don't think they even knew the film was being made and it only cost $400,000.

And I came out here and I was called immediately into meetings with Spyros Skouras who started to yell at me, why you don't like this country. I come here a poor boy and I sell popcorn. Now I'm rich. You know, waving the American flag. I mean, it was embarrassing. This went on for eighteen days. Finally I said, Mr. Skouras, I have nothing to say. I have nothing to be ashamed of. I worked here for three or four days. Just pay me and let me go home. They didn't want to let me go because they thought I might make some money. And called me to New York. I went there. I took Jay Kanter who was then a young agent at MCA, and I was in eight days—I can never forgive them for the one luncheon I had with my mother who didn't understand what was going on. And finally her son after much privation is going to Hollywood, is going to make money, is going to be rich, famous man . . . and she said what have you done? I said Mom, I've done nothing, nothing, absolutely nothing. And I wouldn't go to the Committee. And then after eight days for whatever whim, Skouras finally said okay, you're a good boy. And that was the end of it. And the two reigning queens of Hollywood smut at the time just never—my name was never again in one of their columns. And life went on. Just a certain amount of luck. And the fact that they thought I could make some money for them. They were very wrong about that of course, because of the kind of pictures I wanted to make. But that was it. And as I say, I'm one of the lucky ones. I had never been named, of course, and I had never been subpoenaed. It was all a matter of guilt by association.

v: *Was it the association with the Group primarily?*
MR: With the Group.

v: *Can you put that in a statement?*
MR: I remember one day going to CBS, there was somebody there at CBS—there was a kind of clearing house. And he said to me, they want to hire you. You're going to get a very good job if you just behave properly. Adele was then working selling space in the Red Book in New York. And I said well, what do I have to do? And I was told that I could name anybody I wanted to that was dead, didn't matter. So if it had not been clear to me before that they were not interested in any information, that they were just interested in breaking the will of the American people to resist this kind of behavior, I knew it then. You know, mention Joe Bromberg, mention Julie Garfield, things they already knew. And as I was leaving—I was getting ready to direct *A View from the Bridge*—he said and by the way, we think you'd be better off without that, the Arthur Miller play. So I mean, I never had any doubts about what I was going to do. The choice was very clear. And because the banality of it was incredible, just incredible, absolutely unbelievable what people were doing to each other. A lot of it was jobs, getting jobs that other people would have had. A lot of it was money. Because the politics, as a substantial factor, never really existed. Who gave a damn—what the hell—I certainly didn't care about the Party. Never. I was as interested in anybody else in getting ahead and getting something I wanted to do, and getting a good part or a good play to direct and hopefully a movie to direct. I didn't think about anything else.

The thought control was the issue of the day, like it is beginning to be again. The way the President is now attacking the whole Central American issue is obviously an attempt at thought control. If you take this position you're aiding and abetting the communists.

v: *Can you make a statement for those who don't know, those who are too young to remember or too ignorant to have bothered to find out, what the blacklist was, what* Red Channels *was?*
MR: *Red Channels* was a book that was published which included all—fundamentally all the people they didn't agree with. People who had jobs they wanted, who had supported liberal organizations. One of the charges against me was that I directed a show for a trade union. That's how idiotic it finally became. *Red Channels* was a document which the networks for a short time lived by. And if your name was in *Red Channels* you just didn't work.

v: *Who provided* Red Channels? *Who wrote it?*
MR: I don't remember who published it. But there was one guy whose name I don't remember at this point, who was very instrumental in getting together all the names that they included. And I had a friend who went to see one of the guys because he was one of the actors who was on the leadership of the right wing of the union. And he said, what are you guys doing to Marty? I mean, he's never been named. He's never been subpoenaed. And the guy said to him, we know he's going to get a very big job. And unless he's on our side we're not going to do anything to help him. It was as plain as that. If we don't have this cloud over him, he's going to be hired and be hired in a very important job, and we want to be able to control him. That's what it all came down to.

Once it got down to that level it was as minor and misely and as meanspirited as that.

v: *Did they want you to go and testify and name the names of the dead?*
MR: Yeah.

v: *But you weren't actually subpoenaed?*
MR: I didn't even know anything about these people politically. Even what I would be testifying to would be hearsay. I didn't know what Bromberg or Garfield did or anybody else. It would all be hearsay. But they were trying to make it easier, they were trying to represent it as making it easier for you when actually what they were doing was trying to break your will to resist.

That I understood. Because why would that be okay? I mean, it's not going to—it was just shocking to me.

v: *Did you—this is way off the subject—did anybody describe to you in detail the conflict between Stella and Lee after she came back from seeing Stanislavski?*
MR: No, no. That was a theoretical disagreement which had to do with egos, too, I'm sure.

v: *Was any of it percolating around in any of the rehearsals? You said that when you were in* Golden Boy *that the major actors had already mastered their technique.*
MR: Yes. You could see that. You could see how they began to include what they had to include, how they were able to use themselves.

v: *How about the younger people coming in? Did you work at all with them?*
MR: Well, there was a Group Theatre Studio at that time. That's where I began to get trained.

v: *And that was with Bobby?*
MR: That was with Bobby, with Gadge. And then of course the Actors Studio later on in which Gadge and I taught the first class of beginners.

v: *How did Bobby's studio within the group work? Was that an official activity of the group or was it a spontaneous thing? Were other people teaching that way?*
MR: No. Bobby was original in the sense that he—we went along with most of what Stanislavski had to say. His expression was much more theatrical, and because he was singular in that regard he drew that element among those people who were really interested in that. And that's why he got to direct a play like *My Heart's in the Highlands,* the Saroyan play which was a beautiful challenge. Bobby was a much more theatrical entity. The rest of us related to a certain kind of reality, not necessarily naturalism, but a certain kind of reality. And Bobby was different. And Bobby is different.

v: *Did he charge for those classes at the Belasco or did that just—*
MR: I don't remember. No, I don't think anybody charged. I don't think anybody charged. Nobody had any money to pay. I mean, in 1937 I was an assistant stage manager and I had two lines and I got $25 a week, and I lived

in a little apartment with Curt Conway and we had two rooms. So it was—nobody had any money. Nobody had any money. Money, when that began to come in, that was terribly corrupting. That's why Hollywood began, and who could say it was wrong? It wasn't wrong. I mean, that's the nature of life. But it was corrupting.

V: *Which leads me to a question I'm always fascinated about, the whole relationship of the Group to the Depression era. Could it have become a reality as this marvelous inspirational organization if it had not been the Depression years?*
MR: Probably not, because you can't separate any group of people from the time in which they live. And the affirmation of the Depression, the Roosevelt spirit of the Depression was part of the birth of the Group Theatre. I mean, you look at a film like *The Grapes of Wrath* from a great director, a great conservative, even reactionary, not in his work, because an artist somehow always manages to tell the truth, even though he doesn't necessarily agree with it. Politically you separate the issues. I mean, I'm sure if you sat down and talked with John Ford about those Okies, it wouldn't be a pleasant conversation. But when he makes a film, it's a whole different matter. I mean, that's happened historically with Balzac certainly. It's happened with great writers. The great ones tell the truth, despite where their appetites take them. The whole story of that period was a story of appetite. People behaved if they could control their appetites, and they behaved badly if they couldn't. So that's an acting lesson. It's also a political lesson. That's what stimulates every artist and every politician. I hate to reduce it to that, but I think that's the truth.

V: *And it was the willingness to forego some of the appetite that made the Group possible?*
MR: That's right, and made people behave well in that time, in that bad political time.

V: *I found a wonderful quotation when I was working on just this aspect of the relationship—I'm interested in the social history dimension of the Group, and about the fact that because there wasn't so much possibility then to get ahead, to get big jobs and so on in the early days of the Depression, people thought we might as well do what we want to do.*

MR: That's right.

V: *I found a quotation in Burns Mantle, believe it or not, in which he said—something along this—it may be because theatres are closing and people are losing jobs, it may just be that the theatre is finding its soul in this great Depression. And I wept with joy because in a sense that—from a conservative guy—captured it.*
MR: That's right, absolutely right. When we were going to talk about Paul [Newman], one of the nice things, one of the very nice things, one of the good things that has happened in his life—I've said it and I've been quoted before on this, that talent is a genetic accident. You have nothing to do with it. You have it or you don't. The ability to run 100 yards in under ten seconds. Somebody is graced with that. That's why prejudice about color or anything else is ridiculous because nobody had anything to say going in. What a man or a woman does with the equipment that is given to them is finally the mark of a man or a woman. And Paul has gotten to be a better and better actor all through the—I don't think he looks down on himself. He used to. He disparaged the shit out of himself, and that's one of the nicest things about Paul Newman. And one of the things I have such high regard for him for. He's gotten better and better. But he's made it happen for himself. And because I love him I'm very pleased about that.

V: *I remember him telling me way back in the beginning, in 1954 taking a walk and people had come up and asked him for Brando's autograph. They thought he was Brando. And he said Jesus, I would give anything to be Brando, Jimmy Dean, to have what they have. He said if I get anywhere it's just going to be through sheer hard work.*
MR: And he was right. Well he still had that extraordinary physical equipment. Those baby blues are not visited upon ordinary mortals.

V: *Marty, I have some questions that I wrote that I'd like to ask.*
MR: Okay.

V: *Before you joined the Group did you see* Waiting for Lefty *or* Awake and Sing? *Did you see any of their productions? And can you describe your reactions if you did.*
MR: I saw *Waiting for Lefty*, and I was actually transported into heaven when I saw it. I thought it was the greatest evening I'd ever seen in my life, and

still is one of the greatest evenings I've ever seen in my life. I mean, there was an explosion that included the audience. I had never seen that before. When I was twelve years old my mother took me to the theatre, and I saw a play called *Jarnegan* with Richard Bennett. I was so excited that we got into the theatre, and I threw up immediately. I went into the john. And then I cleaned up and I watched this play. And I knew I was in the presence of a great actor. That's all.

When I saw *Waiting for Lefty* I was in the presence of a way of life, which changed my life. Something happened on that stage which was extraordinary, absolutely extraordinary.

v: **Were there specific moments that you remember?**
MR: I knew that I was in the presence of something original. I knew that I was in the presence of genuine artists and I remember the flush of that excitement.

v: *Why didn't Odets say that Awake and Sing was his best play? Why did he scream at you when you thought it was?*
MR: Well, I was in a play of his at that time. We were in Baltimore with the play he wrote on Noah.

v: The Flowering Peach
MR: And we were going out to dinner. And he was about to leave—he knew he had some work to do on the play. And he had asked me to take over. And you know, most artists think that their last work is their best. And the first half of *The Flowering Peach* is absolutely stunningly brilliant, funny, original, marvelous, but I criticized the second half of the play. I cut out about eight or ten minutes of the second half of the play, which when he came back to the play in Boston, he immediately put back in. I just grew angry. I left the dinner with him that night as a matter of fact because I was going to ask him to let Harold take over because I was in the play. Already an actor resented the fact that I was taking over. And he was at that time on the outs with Harold. So I didn't even get to say Harold Clurman. I got to say Harold. And he started to scream and they threw us out of the restaurant. Whitehead had come to me and asked me to speak about Harold, because he knew that Clifford and I were good friends. But Clifford was bananas at that point. That was a funny production because Menasha Skulnik, a brilliant actor, was a

monumental pain in the ass. And we had some trouble technically opening night in Wilmington. I think it was Wilmington or someplace, maybe it was Baltimore. And he managed to find the only light that existed on the goddamn stage and stayed there. And everybody else was kind of improvising around him. And at the end of the act Clifford stormed down the aisle and came backstage. He was looking to yell at Menasha and he says you're worse than Joe Ferrer and Menasha, who had locked himself in the toilet at this point, yelled that's bad? (LAUGHS) Menasha hated the play. He said to me at one point, he said you like this play, Marty? I said I think it's a terrific play. He said this is a piece of shit. He says *The Fifth Season*—that was a good play. That was a kind of sit-com he was in on Broadway. And he always carried his notices with him, all the notices of the play. And we got very mixed notices out of town. And he was one time in an argument with Clifford, he took out the notices. He said here it says I'm a genius. You're a fucking bum. I thought Clifford was going to kill him. But they were all afraid of him because they knew that if he left the play we'd have no play. Whitehead produced that play. That was a funny experience.

V: *I loved that show.*
MR: Oh, it was so funny.

V: *Marty, if you had one thing to say to the kids today, to young people today, about what the Group was, and how they might be able to use something like that in their lives, if you had some message to them out of your own experience of that time in your own youth, what would you say to them?*
MR: I think the nature of what Harold and Lee and Cheryl were trying to do at that time was to make the artist discover himself to the fullest. Knowing full well philosophically that the only thing that's really original in any artist is for that artist to get a release on his or her subconscious. Anything that's really very fundamentally cerebral you've got from a magazine or a newspaper or a play or ballet or whatever that you've seen. But if you can get a release on what is truly personal to you, in each individual, that's original. It's always original in each individual. And if you get a release on that you then have a chance of becoming a major artist. And I think fundamentally what the Group was about was the ability of first understanding that it was important that one know himself and know where to go in himself for the most private of moments which nobody else need know. And to be then able

to express it. All of us who have come into the arts have come there because we have a need to express ourselves. The most original need is the most subjective need. The trick is how to get it released. An artist is able to do that. Everybody has that same highly complicated interior, but very few people get a release on it. So one never sees it. The artist manages to get a release on it.

The Group was trying to teach everybody who wanted to be an artist to do that, to get that release. I mean, reduced to its simplest statement, I think that's what it was all about. And you see that in the best work of those people. They understood it. They were not necessarily better than anybody else, but they understood what had to be done. That gave them a little bit of an edge.

V: *Now that brings me to one other thing which might be my final question. You have taken your very particular background and worked with it very very successfully, with people from entirely different backgrounds, from Orson Welles to Paul to Joanne to Jon Voight, Sally Field. And what you said now gives me a hint, which is the release. How do you achieve that with people who speak a different theatrical language and come from a different theatrical training? And if you could talk about them specifically in terms of their names and moments that you've been able to get to them or free them up for themselves, it would be very valuable.*

MR: All casting is an educated guess. You never really know what's going to happen. But if you're smart, you cast for what you think the biggest scenes in the picture are. There's no sense in trying to get an actor to play Hamlet who cannot play Now I am alone. Once he can play Now I am alone, you have the right to assume that he can play everything else in the play because that is such a complicated moment and such a decision-making moment for him, that if he can realize that he'll be able to realize everything. So when you cast actors you guess. You guess—you know what you think is the most important scene in the picture. The reason I didn't want to give *Sounder* to Cicely Tyson at the beginning was that I knew that the homecoming scene was the most important scene in the picture. And this girl was such a great beauty and a high fashion model, and I said, you know, I don't think she'll get there. And then one day she said to me, Marty, I don't care how much of a high fashion model I am; no Black in this country is more than one generation removed from that experience. I knew she was a good actress. And so I decided to take a shot. And I was right. But she helped me. She helped me because she said something to me that was so irrevocably true that I knew about myself. People have asked me, why do you make so many films about rural America? I don't know. I don't know. But I obviously have some affinity for it and I'm smart enough when I can do something well not to ask too many questions. I don't want it to leave me.

In the case of *The Long Hot Summer* with Orson, I, above all, I knew a better actor to play that part. Lee Cobb. But I wanted that incredible persona, which Lee didn't have. Nobody had. The Welles persona. So I took a lot of crap from him because I knew that that extraordinary figure would be there on the screen, and if he wasn't the greatest actor in the world it was not the greatest picture in the world. I wanted that. And when I met Sally I met this feisty little girl who was attractive enough without being a great beauty and had a fierceness about her children. I knew I needed those elements in the picture. So I went to Jay at Fox and I said she'll be terrific. I didn't know. I was guessing. But I've guessed right more often than I've guessed wrong. And that's why I keep working.

With Paul it's a different matter all the time. I knew that he—at the beginning—he was tight and embarrassed and very angry about the way he looked really. I knew that those things could transmit themselves into—with *Hud*, with *Hombre* he played outsiders, which are very close. I knew that psychologically about Paul. I knew he'd be comfortable. Even though it was an Indian with blue eyes, which I subsequently found out a lot of them had. But I knew emotionally what was going on. I knew he didn't have at that point the skill or the craft that Joanne had. But she was tougher to cast because she was just a very good actress. Paul had this extraordinary outsider feel about him. And that, complicated by the way he looked, made him a genuine theatrical entity. The nicest thing I got out of all the readings of Marx was the whole philosophic notion of the unity of opposites. That if I'm playing a scene with you this way and I say to the actor now I want that same level of anger, but I don't want the rhythm to be hitting like the other rhythm like I just indicated. I want it to be even slower. That's already complicating the quality of the anger. Paul had that in his persona. I never have said this to Paul. I wouldn't have gotten *Hud* out without Paul. But I knew this about him. And that's true of every actor I've used. I knew in *Murphy's* what kind of a picture I was going to make. I knew it was going to be my fifth film of the decade. But I knew that this man Garner, with that ease and that charm, still had a lot of country in him. And he is really incredibly sweet and shy, and even more disparaging of himself than Paul was. He's lovely and he's sweet, and I did get a script about six weeks ago which was very pleasing to me. They said we'll take Nicholson, Newman, or Garner. So . . .

Casting comes down to that essentially. What I've just said about Paul, what I said about Orson, what I said about Sally, any of the actors I've worked with—for instance, a very interesting case in point was when I did *The Spy Who Came in from the Cold*. I wanted Burton. I didn't know why I wanted him. Because when I heard him speak I said to him on the first day of rehearsal, I said Richard, the key to this character is anonymity. The key to any spy is anonymity. And that voice of yours will bury us. And that was like taking a sweater away from Lana Turner. You took it all away. And I had a terrible time with that picture. And it started that time when I started to take the voice away. And yet it was one of his best, if not his best, screen performance. We fought about it all the time. He's the reverse of Paul. He had the equivalent of Marlon and he really pissed on himself. He should have been at least Olivier. Appetite ruined him totally. Booze, women, you know . . . money . . . I don't think any of this can be discussed without mentioning appetite. It's the basis of almost all human behavior. And only people with strong feelings can control their appetites. The other people don't and then they have to pay. We all have to pay finally. But one of the big tragedies is Gadge. He should've by now done enormous work.

V: *Marty, that is about as moving and original a description of a director casting actors. I mean, that—and relating it to appetite, relating it to the whole Group experience that way—is extraordinary. Why don't you write for God's sake?*
MR: The politics are too painful. I really don't want to write.

V: *I don't mean about that—I mean, your art. Your way of honing in so precisely on this complex dynamic that makes your films so exciting.*
MR: Well, maybe after I teach and I get a sense of what's going on. I'm teaching because I was disturbed by the kids. That's why I'm teaching. Somebody's got to say to them, that's not true. And that's not all there is in the world. Hank and Irving understood that about Paul, too. And that's why they wrote so well for him.

V: *I should talk to them, shouldn't I?*

MR: I think so. I think so.

V: *You know, his favorite story is Tony Kroger. Do you know that story?*
MR: No.

V: *Maybe before we talk about him I'll send it to you. It's very important, very important key. A key and a mystery at the same time.*
MR: Well, now you know why I've cast Paul that way, and why those films—

V: *The one thing that I want to know about that—I mean, the casting is wizard-like. How did you get the release at specific moments when you needed that?*
MR: Well, that depends a lot on the actor. You have to know when an actor's ready to play. I kept stalling for instance, with Cicely until I felt she was ready to play the homecoming scene. And then I scheduled it for the next day. And I wired her so I knew I would never have to loop any of those sounds that came out of her. And I never use long lenses in pictures. But I had to to get that shot. We used 1000 mm lens on her. And when Alonso came away from the lens, he looked at me; he was crying. He said you'll never get a better shot than that in your life. It is the single best shot I've ever had in a movie. And you have to sense that. When I did *Cross Creek* I met Alfrie Woodard. She came in and read. And I hired her immediately. I wouldn't let her rehearse because I didn't want to blow the performance. I knew—I just didn't have to rehearse with her. So we'd get to her scenes and I'd say okay, go out and have a cup of coffee and I wouldn't rehearse. She's terrific. She's terrific. And she was so well cast.

V: *What did you have to tell Cicely before she did that scene?*
MR: I didn't. It was all—I'll tell you a perfect example. In that picture Kevin Hooks played the boy. And the night before we shot the scene where he sits with his father on the log, he came to me and he said, Marty, I can't cry. I said, what do you mean? He said, I have to cry in that scene. I read the scene a lot of times. I can't cry. I said, don't cry. No big deal. Next day we started to shoot. I say action. Niagara Falls. And I knew it would. The minute he got into the situation. And with his kind of sensitivity to the entire father/son relationship, I knew that was going to happen. And after that we couldn't

stop him from crying. He cried and cried the whole day, every set up. But I knew that was going to happen because the actor was right. When the conditions are right, the whole trick really in directing is to get people on the track that's going to open them up. And you maneuver, you lie, you tease, you cajole, you flirt. You do any number of things to precipitate . . .

A Conversation with Martin Ritt

RONALD DAVIS / 1987

THE FOLLOWING IS AN INTERVIEW with director Martin Ritt, taped in his office in Beverly Hills, California on July 13, 1987.

D: *As a boy growing up in New York City, was theater always an important part of your life?*
R: No. I was taken to the theater by my mother, and it made a big impression on me, but there was no way that I could get involved in theater. We were lower middle-class people, not people of any means. It just evolved in my life. I went to school and came back and started to go to law school. It was obviously a big part of my need, and I was lucky to be around at a time when that kind of excitement and ferment existed in American theater life.

D: *When you went to Elon College, what kind of a career did you envision for yourself?*
R: Coaching football and teaching English. I fully expected to be a schoolteacher. I realized before I was finished that that was not really what I wanted, that my appetite was totally different, and never thought I'd get a shot. I wanted to be an actor, and I was the most commonplace-looking sort of fellow. Even as an athlete, where I was fairly gifted—certainly not extraordinarily gifted—I would not have been able to play at, say, SMU, even before the scandals. (Both laugh.) But I came to New York and did start law school

---

Oral History Collection [A80.154 Martin Ritt]. Published by permission of Adele Ritt, Ronald Davis, and the DeGolyer Library, Southern Methodist University, Dallas, Texas.

and I found this off-Broadway group at which a fellow named Kazan was teaching.

D: *I wondered if meeting Elia Kazan had a great impact on your life.*
R: It had a great impact on my life. He made a great impact on my life because he was a great director. I haven't met many like that in my life, certainly not at that impressionable age.

D: *How would you describe his approach to direction?*
R: Gadge had a great appetite, extraordinary appetite, for everything: women, theater, whatever. And he was great with actors; he was a very good actor himself, actually. The first play that I was in, he played Fuselli in *Golden Boy*, and he was terrific, really terrific. But he had this inordinate appetite for life and the theater, and a lot of the good work came from that. A lot of the bad problems came from that, too. He was very impressive at that point. The Group Theatre was there. I mean, you've got to be lucky that something exists which, in some way, mirrors what you want to be about. If the Group Theatre hadn't been there, I might have evolved into what I have, but it probably would have taken longer and I would not have had as firm a base.

D: *As a novice coming into theater, what special vibrancy did you find at the Group Theatre?*
R: A commitment, a genuine commitment to doing first-class work, which is really the most important thing for any artist. They had it, and they had it in spades. They were always broke. The economics of Broadway were ridiculous at that time, you could do a play for $25,000, and yet, they couldn't raise money. All of the plays were socially oriented, they were not a political group, though I'm sure there were isolated members there who were much more political than some other members. But it was a time of great ferment, and New York was the most exciting place in the world at that time. I felt, and I still feel, that a lot of it, in that sense, was luck that it was there; you are born at a certain time in the history of the world. If you're born when those things don't exist, I mean, if a young man is born today and President Reagan controls the artistic life of the country to some degree, it's going to be a lot tougher. And you'll find that the creative work tends to be more concerned with form than content. It's a different game, a totally different game. All of us are creatures of our own time.

D: *Did you feel, at the Group Theatre, that there was any conflict between art and social conscience?*

R: I never felt that. They were not interested (as, generally, I am not interested) in making films that are not about anything. They were definitely not a political group. I mean, I could tell that because I was fairly political; I could tell immediately that they were not, and that being political was not going to be of any help on any level, except in terms of my own conscience or whatever. But they were totally committed to doing American work, American plays. They didn't want to do revivals, they didn't want to do classics. They were in some ways not equipped to do some of those things. Finally, some of them did want to. But it was in the true tradition of what they conceived to be a democratic America, and what they conceived to be serious work, creative work. And not all the plays they did were any good, a few of them were fairly good, two or three of them were very good, but it's tough to find good plays. That is the single toughest commodity in all the entertainment world, to find a good play. It's so rare that today there's no Broadway theater, there are only a few serious plays. Whatever is being done that's any good at all is in the regional theater, and maybe it gets a chance to come up to Broadway—*maybe*. The economics are so horrendous. Here's a picture, I look at it: "Attached is a preliminary estimate for the project, which totals ten million, eight-hundred-forty-three thousand, nine-hundred-twenty-two dollars—without cast, cast travel and living expenses, or cast fringe benefits." It means the picture has to cost twenty million dollars if I use a couple of stars, which is my intention. So. . . . (Chuckles.) I can understand from management's point of view that it is a tough investment, but they don't lose any money. They don't make as much as they'd like to, but that's true about everybody in the world.

D: *In the Group Theatre, of course, they were very innovative in terms of content. Were they also innovative in terms of staging, sets, design, that sort of thing?*

R: Well, that differed with the directors. Kazan was the best director they had developed. The others—[Harold] Clurman, [Lee] Strasberg, to some degree . . . although I don't think he directed too much when I was there. Gadge was the most inventive. Gadge also had the best judgment. All of us who have been around this business as long as I have realize that judgment is just as important as talent. If you look at the history of Tennessee Williams, you'll see that Gadge only did his good plays, the other ones he didn't do.

So you have to give him credit for extraordinary judgment, which did desert him at a certain point in his life. I think that's probably the history of any art. But I think he was far and away the best director they turned out. What they did mostly was affect American theatrical life on the philosophical level. The Actors Studio (which came after the Group Theatre) and the Group Theatre were the only two aspects of the theater in this country that tried to formulate a way of work. And the formulation of the way of work was totally in concert with the kind of plays they chose to do. The kind of plays they chose to do benefitted mostly from what they were trying to do with their work. If you tried the same thing with *Boy Meets Girl*, *Three Men on a Horse*, or the great comedies in the period, it would never really work as well, different things were required. But you couldn't teach anything about that. I taught one semester at UCLA, a graduate group, and I had problems with the kids. First of all, they had read nothing, they had grown up with the idiot tube, and images consumed them from morning until evening. The fact that the images were very often empty didn't seem to bother them. Their favorite directors and such were all image-makers. I shook them up somewhat, because I got very rough finally. I realized that they were consumed by the need for money, consumed by the need for immediate success, would not believe I was seventy-three years old, didn't believe a frame of *The Front*. They said, "It would never happen, not in this country." I must say, I was very rough—as I can be—and I shook them up a great deal. The only reason, really, I went there to teach was that I had some sense of what I was going to encounter, and I felt there were very few guys around with my background and my point of view. If that point of view is not articulated to anybody, it may never exist except in an occasional film. While I am convinced that films are highly artistic, I am not convinced that films are an art form. I think we should all have the grace to wait some thirty or forty years before any judgments are made on that level. Again, it is in the need of those who have proclaimed it an art form almost from the word go, since that was their baby and that was their commitment and they wanted that commitment in their lifetime. I have never trusted the furor about films, I have never trusted it at all, for that reason. I believe it was created by people who *needed* that kind of thing to somehow complete their lives. And they may be right, they may be dead right, I'm not saying they're wrong. But I really would like to wait before I measure a film I've made with *War and Peace*, or a film *anybody's* made with *War and Peace* or any of the great painters or composers. I think we should all be a little graceful and wait. The value of critics is difficult to discuss, but the industry is in the hands of those people. They've all become kind of semi-clowns and semi-personalities. The two kids from Chicago are the most successful. It's a funny business, it really is a funny business. One never expects, when one works in a business like this, to make the kind of money that one can make—very few can make it, but some can. At the Guild meeting the other might, Gil Cates, who's the president of the Guild, announced that 75% of the Directors Guild makes under $17,000 a year. Now most of those are A.D.'s, but, whatever, it's not a living wage. And I had no idea that that was the truth. Everybody who directs, of course, makes a hell of a lot more than that. But a large section of that Guild (my daughter is one of them) are assistant directors. It's a funny business.

D: *You mentioned* Golden Boy *as your first play. I'm sure, at that age, you must have found this a tremendously exciting experience.*
R: Oh, boy! We rehearsed upstairs at Belasco Theatre, I'll never forget. I'll never forget anything about it. That's where I met Karl Malden. It was fifty years ago, and we worked together, finally, after fifty years, in *Nuts*, I hired him in *Nuts*. We both sat there one afternoon and talked about . . . Clurman was really at his best. That was really the best-acted play I've ever seen in my life. Clurman was brilliant. He was always brilliant in the early part of rehearsal, because he was learned, articulate, passionate. At that point, I didn't understand why he had cast Luther Adler and not John Garfield to play the lead. I found out very soon, in rehearsal, why. I learned a big lesson in just that one play. It was a terribly exciting time. That was some cast, my God! It's hard to believe that all those people existed in one play—not a great play, but a good play. It was not Clifford's best, by a long shot, but a big hit. That opening night was tremendous, oh, boy! We all started to cry, and the audience. A large part of it was the general group audience, obviously adoring whatever they did. But there were all kinds of intellectuals and artists, critics, who didn't care too much about the Group one way or the other, but they were caught up by that evening.

D: *I guess that's Odets's most successful day.*
R: I think it is, commercially, yes.

D: *Do I understand correctly that you taught Luther Adler to box?*

R: Yes. Well, I was an athlete, and I could punch a bag—which nobody else there could do. And the offstage effects . . . that's how I got my job. When Kazan got me the job he said, "This kid can do something we can't do." And I took Luther to the gym. There was an old gym in New York, the Pioneer Club, which you could smell for two or three blocks away. (Chuckles.) I got Luther in there, he looked around. He really didn't have to do any boxing in the play. He was well built at that point; he got very heavy in the latter part of his life. I just had one of those miraculous times. A lot of that is luck.

D: *In addition to your own part, weren't you also understudying John Garfield?*
R: I was. But when he left they didn't give me the job. They gave it to a fellow (who's now dead) who became kind of a national figure in that PBS show about the kids . . . I forget the name of it, it was a big hit. Will Lee played it. I played it subsequently, on the road. Marvelous part.

D: *What kind of a fellow did you find Jules Garfield?*
R: He was a very sweet man, a terrifically gifted actor, charismatic as hell, sexual as hell (which is what made him a movie star). The whole political thing was ridiculous, absolutely ridiculous.

D: *Did you get to know Frances Farmer well?*
R: I got to know her and like her very much. She was very sweet, very nice. There was Henry Morgan (Bratsburg), Karl Malden, and myself; we were the three new young people in the company. She was very sweet, close to our age, and very nice to us. I liked her very much. She was, I thought, pretty good in the play. But I didn't follow her after that and I don't know just how she began to fall apart, which, obviously, she did. It was a very heady atmosphere, because you were in with the leading theater intellectuals in the United States, if not the world. And also I didn't suffer from being a beautiful lady, which is a big cross to bear. That's the tragic part of that experience. Whenever I think of it, or whenever it comes up in conversation, it does give me pause. She was the only wreckage out of that. All the other wreckage that came through the political and the McCarthy period, people brought on themselves, except for those who were blacklisted. There was nothing they could do about that. It was a bad time in the history of the country. But the country had so much vigor that it rebounded from that. That's one of the great things about being in America: the country does have extraordinary

vigor. Even though sometimes it seems so stupid that you can't believe they would be taken in by what's going on. The whole evangelical thing, for years, I would just look at the television and want to kick it in. It finally came a cropper, the way it should have a long time ago. The thing with [Oliver] North will come a cropper, too, because he has lied, he has cheated. They'll find out he is a profiteer to some degree, like all the rest of them were. He did bring up (which I think is a mistake) the fact that he and Casey were planning their own private CIA. He's very bright, and I'm amazed at how well he handles himself with very slick attorneys around. But that's why they must have picked him. He must have been a very highly sought-after young man when he came into the service.

D: *Back on* Golden Boy, *did you get to know Odets well during that period?*
R: We were good friends. I think when I came into the Group I was a really different element than they'd had there. With Kazan and with Odets, they liked that. I saw a lot of Odets. I remember driving in to an Equity meeting, the possibility of a strike. On the way in and on the way back, he told me about his new play, I guess it was *Night Music*. He said he'd written a part for me. When I read the play, I had one line. (Both laugh.) They had an enormous estimate of themselves and of their importance, so he didn't consider that as any kind of a comedown, for me to play a one-line part. By that time I had already been sufficiently corrupted by the Broadway scene to know that my career was not going to be enormously heightened by playing this part. I saw a lot of Clifford when I came to Hollywood. He did try to get me out here to direct . . . he was going to do a film called *Joseph and His Brethren.* The actor they were going to use at that point was a fellow who is married to Miss Ten, Bo Derek, and he was a very handsome boy. Clifford said, "He can't act at all. You'd better bring somebody out here like Marty. Marty will make it possible for him to go through the film." So they brought me out and I saw Harry Cohn, who dismissed me immediately. "Who the hell was I? What had I done?" And it was not very much at the time. But when I came out here, Clifford was working here, and he was ill. We saw a lot of each other. We went to dinner a lot, and I listened a lot. I liked him. I did not approve of the way he had behaved, and he knew that and then he disappeared from my life. I missed him. I missed him a lot when he died, because there was nobody like him around. I was in a foreign land—Hollywood. It *was* foreign, and still is in some ways. Fortunately for me, I do things by

myself a lot; I go to racetracks and play a lot of tennis still. The intellectual life of this town and the theater life of this town is *not* first-class. It never has been. I think the industry does not really allow for it; it only allows for success. If you don't understand that, you might as well leave. And if you're not prepared to fight on that level, to some degree, you might as well leave. I've had that struggle consistently in my career, because of things I've chosen to do. I've never had a runaway hit and I never will have, because of choice of subject matter. I mean, this film is about working-class people. We sold it to the first people we showed it to, because we had done another film for these same people called *Norma Rae,* which made them a lot of money, which we worked for half-salary on, because they had turned us down at first. I went in and said, "Listen, we want to make this picture." They know that in this town, they know that if I really want to make something I'll take less money. Sometimes I won't. *Murphy's Romance* did very well commercially, so I wasn't about to take less money for this. But that's the junkyard we deal in, and it *is* a junkyard. When something good is made, it's only attributable to some crazy, creative guy who has gone out on a limb—humanly, artistically, commercially—and said, "I've got to make this!" Somehow he has had enough muscle to get it made, and it worked. Because this is not a town that is interested in doing anything that is not totally commercial all the time. And with the big sums of money involved, it's really tough to blame them. But that's not what I'm interested in, and I've managed to exist out here all these years. Not too many of us have been fortunate enough to do that.

D: *Your career really is unique in that regard.*
R: In that regard it was very unique. Continuing really fundamentally . . . with *some* falling off the good street, doing pictures I felt should be made that nobody else really would make.

D: *Was Franchot Tone a vital part of the Group Theatre?*
R: By the time I got there Franchot was already in Hollywood. I met him, he's a wonderful guy, but he was not there. So I never really got to know him on a work level. I tried to hire him once. He called me and said, "You prick, now I know what you think of me. You want me to play that part?" I said, "Franchot, it's a terrific part." He said, "Yeah, but I don't want to exhibit myself in that way." And that was the end of it. So I never worked with him,

even after I came out here. I liked him, though. Funny, charming, and witty man.

D: *Was* The Gentle People *also for the Group Theatre?*
R: Yes.

D: *Was that an interesting show for you?*
R: Well, it was okay. It was okay because of the cast, the cast was just extraordinary. The play was okay. Harold Clurman directed, and I think he did a very good job with it. It was a kind of medium success, but it was not a major Group Theatre effort I didn't think. The best plays they did were Clifford's plays.

D: *Of the several shows that you did before going into the Air Force, which did you find most rewarding?*
R: Well, *Golden Boy* was easily the most rewarding. It was the first, it was the best, and the conflict that finally . . . the political thing had not really hit, so there was no discordance. To this day, there are people who hate Kazan. To this day, there are people who, if they met him on the street, would spit in his face. There are many who have not forgotten the full-page ad he took in the *New York Times*. But that didn't exist then, so it was a very harmonious, artistic attitude in which any impulse you had had a chance to grow. Anybody could be, finally, in that kind of an atmosphere, as good as they could be. Obviously, there is no getting away: if you're not gifted, you're not gifted. And talent has always been, to me, a genetic accident. One has nothing to do with it. One should bless whatever he wants to bless, if he or she is gifted, because it is accidental. I have known a few people in my life, and only a few, who really made, in my opinion, the most of their equipment. When the equipment is extraordinary, there is a tendency to piss on it; when the equipment is not extraordinary, but good, then it depends on the character of the people. I've known a few who have become, if not extraordinary, first-class, by really continuing to work and continuing to work on themselves. That, to me, short of the great talents, that's the most significant achievement in any world, and I respect it the most.

D: *You were in the Air Force when you did* Winged Victory.

R: Yes.

D: *Did you find that interesting?*
R: It was okay. My whole class went to China. I was a weather observer, and the day I was to go the orders came for me to go back to New York. I was grateful, frankly, for that. I had just gotten married. I did come back and I went into rehearsal. I felt a little out of place, I was a little heavy in that uniform. And the play was really a soap opera. The success was a testament to the American commitment to soap opera. The picture was no good.

D: *I was going to ask you what you thought of the picture.*
R: The picture was no good at all.

D: *Was it made at Twentieth Century-Fox?*
R: I don't know who made it. George Cukor directed it. He was a little out of his element, it was not what he did best. Most artists do their best work when what they're doing is right in the middle of their vein of gold; then they're free, and almost any idea they have that comes out has a chance to be first-class. I had tried to enlist five years previously in the Spanish Civil War. I had been turned down because the commitment was full. So I finally got into a war where I didn't get to fight either. All I did was go to weather school, I expected to go to China, and then I got this last minute call. I did begin to direct while I was there. I did a play that I'd always loved that Sidney Howard wrote, called *Yellow Jack,* which was a big hit. I did it to take to hospitals and places like that, with actors who were free to work. I had wanted to direct almost from the very beginning.

D: *I was going to ask if that was your goal all along.*
R: At that point in the history of the American theater and cinema, if you didn't look like Robert Taylor things were going to be tough. If you looked the way I looked, you'd have to wait at least twenty or thirty years. There were no Dustin Hoffmans and no Walter Matthaus; young character actors did not become stars—*because* of that, really, not for any other reason. I said, "I can't do this for twenty-five years, wait." I put together an evening of one-act plays, out of which *A View from the Bridge* emerged, and that was it. As I say, I didn't want to wait. I don't know how good an actor I really was. I've had a couple of chances since. I'm okay. I've worked in a couple of films—

one in which I played a character somewhat like Tommy Lasorda. And one other film. Otherwise, I don't get offered any jobs, so I assume there are not a lot of people around who think I'm first-class as an actor.

D: *Your first time to direct on Broadway was* Mr. Peebles and Mr. Hooker?
R: Yes.

D: *Was that a good start for you?*
R: Well, it was not a hit. It was an interesting play, a morality play, and it didn't quite work. I knew that when I started, but to be offered a job to direct a play on Broadway is so enormous that I took it. It was okay, it was an okay evening. It just wasn't good enough, didn't quite work when it should have.

D: *How did you feel about* The Man?
R: That was a melodrama, it worked very well. I learned a very funny lesson on that. I was directing Dorothy Gish, and I walked in one evening before the curtain went up and she was in the bathroom throwing up. She said, "I do that every show, Marty." I never really quite realized the nature of that tension. It taught me a very big lesson that I've subsequently been able to use with other people. I've worked with a lot of people who have had incredible nerves. It's easier in films. Somehow, the attitude about most films is such it doesn't quite happen. It sometimes happens in key scenes with actors who realize there are certain things that are more difficult for them to do.

D: *I've read where you said that for you live television was an adventure.*
R: It was fun. I really liked it until . . . I wasn't in it too long. At the beginning there was one studio above Grand Central Station, and one camera for every show. We never went any further west than the Mississippi River. We were totally in charge of material, so I did Saki, Hemingway, Willa Cather, anything I wanted to do. And material is the basis of all the work, it starts there, certainly I believe that. It was fun, it was really fun. There was nobody to bother you, the shows were exciting, and the material was extraordinary. And then, of course, it caught on and that was the end of it. Then the agencies came in with sponsors and they were very difficult about material. I had no restraints in my life at all, on any creative level, and I couldn't deal with it. I had a lot of fights. And then it all ended by the fact that in 1951 the

blacklist came in and I didn't have to fight anymore, that was it, they put me away.

D: *This may not be a very productive question, but I'm curious how the blacklisting in television compared to the blacklisting in the big studios out here.*
R: Well, I wasn't out here when that happened so I don't really know. In television, I knew. Just before I was blacklisted I had a very good job at CBS, I was kind of a key troubleshooter. When they had any problems with anything, I was sent. I was making a lot of money.

D: *You were doing the* Danger *series?*
R: Yes, *Danger*, it was a big hit. We had created that series, and it was okay. Fundamentally, it was a kind of shoddy series, melodrama, but it had some kind of theatric life. One day I got a call to go see Donald Davis, who was then the head of television, a very nice guy. I came in to see him and he was very upset. He said to me, "Marty, you haven't been renewed." I said, "Why?" He said, "I have no idea." I was certainly one of the top directors at the network. So I knew, of course I knew, and I told him. And Don, I'll never forget, said to me, "Marty, this is the United States of America. Those things don't happen here." I said, "Okay." Now, as I had come up to see him on the old fourteenth floor at CBS, a producer who had had a terrible show on . . . the network had called me and I went to see the producer and I worked on the show for about two weeks and at least straightened it out. It never became good. It was so full of faults and vacant at its center that there was no way it could be good. As he saw me, we were walking down that long hallway, he just disappeared. I knew before I got to Donald's office what was going to happen. Donald, later on, a year or so, called me and said, "Marty, I'm terribly sorry. I now know that everything you said to me that day was true, and I feel like the worst kind of. . . ." I said, "Donald, there's nothing you can do about it. Nobody can do anything about it. It's going to run its course." There was a guy in Syracuse who owned a couple of big grocery stores, I guess mini-markets, and he named me and all these other people, said we were sending our money to the Soviet Union and China, large sums of money. Of course we were not. Nobody would get a nickel from me at that point, on any level, much less the Soviet Union. It was all guilt by association. When I was getting ready to do *A View from the Bridge*, I got a call from CBS. I went to see a guy at CBS from the FBI, he had an office there. He said,

"Listen, everybody's trying to hire you in this town. You've got to be some kind of a fool. I know your wife is working for the telephone company, selling space, walking around selling ads. This is a job where you're going to get $1,200, $1,500 a week." I said, "Well, I'd like that. What do I have to do?" He said, "Well, I'll tell you what you have to do. I can't really tell you at this point, I want to organize it." And as I was leaving, he said, "Are you going to rehearse the Arthur Miller play soon? You can't do that." So I just walked out of the office, that was the end of that. It was just a bad time. I didn't work for six-and-a-half years. I was a young man, really at the height of my powers. I had a good wife, somehow it evened out in that case.

D: *You taught at the Actors Studio during that time?*
R: I then taught at the Actors Studio. As a matter of fact, I was there at the formation. I taught a class with Kazan, beginners. We interviewed over 2,000 kids, chose about twenty-six, eighteen of whom became stars. It was a very creative and productive time. Except right in the middle of it the whole thing broke with Kazan and McCarthyism. That was a terrific blow, because everybody was afraid to take a position against him because everybody wanted to work for him. Very complicated.

D: *When you say "the whole thing broke," could you go into that a bit more?*
R: Well, Kazan had been to Washington to testify. He came back, he was directing a play by a Hungarian playwright that Zero Mostel was in. At that time he told everybody that the one thing he wouldn't do was name names. Well, of course, he had named names. Once that broke, and the full-page ad, which I think was his price to be able to work again, that split that whole community. The whole American intellectual community was split in half. Half of them disappeared, some of them have become right-wing Jewish intellectuals, but it was never the same after that. It is true, I'm convinced, that he would not have been able to work for the next couple of years in Hollywood. He could've worked anyplace on Broadway and anyplace else in the world, as a director. We've never talked about it, he's never said why. I'm told that he has a biography coming out this fall. Joanne Woodward, who is now directing *Golden Boy*, called me to tell me that. I said, "Okay, I'd like to read what he has to say, why he did it."

D: *Joanne Woodward is one of the twenty-six that you selected?*

R: No, she was already in Hollywood I think. No, that's not right. Yes, she was one of the people. Julie Harris, Paul Newman . . . it went on and on and on.

D: *Lee Remick, I guess.*
R: Yes. Well, the people who were choosing were really good, their taste was impeccable and there were no judgments except talent. When they're that good, you see it very quickly. That was a lovely time. That and my first job were probably the two best times of my life—more than any of the successful films I've done, that's all after the fact. It's when it's happening, when you're really beginning to feel you're growing, and certain things begin to happen inside of you. That is an extraordinary experience.

D: *Was it during that Group Theatre period . . . that was the time of your Communist association?*
R: I never had a Communist association. I was always a very left-wing liberal, and I agreed with the Communists a lot of the time, but *didn't* agree with them some of the time, and that was bitter and angry. It was a great time in American history, so many good writers came out of that time. The American theater was incredible at that time, the playwrights, which is the best indication. You had Odets, you had Miller, you had Williams, you had Elmer Rice, you had Sidney Howard, you had Philip Barry, you had S. N. Behrman . . . it went on and on and on. You had a right to expect three or four plays a year from this gathering, their gifts, almost all of them very liberal—I don't think any of them Communists. Clifford may have been for a week or two, impossible for Clifford to be anything anyway which didn't relate to his work. That's another thing that is never considered: among the few genuinely left-wing liberals in the world of artists, I don't know any that I would really consider Communists. I'm sure a lot of them had left-opinions, I'm sure [Pablo] Casals did. Almost all the intellectual opinion in this country was left-of-center. Today, it's true not as largely. Buckley, who did the most reprehensible thing I've ever known, in his job . . . there's a copy of his magazine which came out some fifteen years ago, with a sketch of Lillian Hellman on the magazine cover. The heading was, "The Ugliest of Them All." You know, listening to him (and sometimes he is engaging), I couldn't conceive that he would really do anything like that. Of course inside is an attack on Lillian, saying she had no talent, on and on and on. This came

from Buckley, from Mary McCarthy, and from a lot of the people who I guess had shifted their left-wing position. Now, I'm sure that Lillian was not a Communist, I'm sure of it. Yet, she behaved . . . her opinions were very often the opinions of the Communist party. She was a funny gal.

D: *Is it true that you lost the title role of* Marty, *which Paddy Chayefsky had written for you?*
R: That's true. I had bought Paddy's first play, couldn't get it on, wasn't good enough, but it was full of his gift. Walter Bernstein had written a script that I played, in which the then-critic from the *Herald Tribune* said, "Martin Ritt is the best actor in television." It was a melodrama, kind of a Mark Hellinger story, that Walter did a very good job on. Sidney Lumet directed, who had been my assistant, and it was a big hit. So Paddy came to me, he was preparing a series of "Tales of the Big City." He said, "This is a perfect part for you." I said, "Paddy, I'd love to play it." He wrote it for me. But, of course, they couldn't hire me at that point. Many years later, on one of the television shows, Rod Steiger said, "I got this part because Martin Ritt couldn't get it." Paddy was a very unusual fellow.

D: *How did your first film directing come about?*
R: Well, I was unemployed. I was teaching, and Bob Aurthur (with whom I'd done a play) said, "I want Marty to direct this picture. David Susskind, who produced the film, said, "Well, we can't hire him." Metro is in a proxy fight, again, good fortune on my part. And I would work for $10,000 to do the film, which is what they paid me for about a year-and-a-half's work. That's how I got it. Mostly it was Bob Aurthur, the writer, who insisted that I direct the film.

D: *This is* Edge of the City.
R: Right.

D: *I'm curious about MGM at that particular time, 1957. Did you sense that the Golden Days were over?*
R: We were in New York, I didn't sense anything. I didn't see anybody, nobody talked to me, I just made the picture in twenty-eight days or something like that, which I've never done since.

D: *Did you find a big adjustment to film work?*
R: No. I knew what I wanted, and so I said to the guys, "This is what I want," and they gave it to me. But I didn't even know where to look in the camera. I've never spent a lot of time with that part of my work anyway.

D: *That was going to be one of my questions: with the interest you have in the dramatic content, did you find yourself relying heavily on the cameraman—in this case, Joseph Brun?*
R: It wasn't him so much, it was everybody. I just said, "This is what I want. He's going to be walking down here, this is what I want to see, this is the size I'd like to see," and I got what I wanted. I shot so little film that when we finished the cutter looked at me and said, "You are crazy. If you had made a single mistake we wouldn't have been able to put this one together." I didn't understand that at that time. I said, "It'll never happen again," and it didn't. Now I shoot a lot of film, because I realize how important it is. I varied my approach in terms of form very much with the content of my films. I was very preoccupied with the form of a film I did that Walter Bernstein wrote called *The Molly Maguires,* because of the period and the really extraordinary look that I felt we could achieve with the great, great cameraman, Jimmy Wong Howe. I spent a lot of time planning that picture physically. On a picture like *The Front,* on a picture like *Sounder,* I was so concerned with getting *Sounder* emotionally, getting what that film was about. I knew I was dealing with material that bordered on being soapy, that each thing had to be so powerful that it would transcend the essential soapiness of the material. And it worked, it worked extremely well on that film. Nobody got paid on that film. I did the film for $50,000; Cicely [Tyson] and Paul Winfield got $10,000 each. The film cost a million dollars, and it was an enormous hit in the United States and Canada, and, critically, all over the world. It was critically an enormous box office hit in South Africa. I just saw it about three months ago, it's a very good film.

D: *I remember when it came out I thought it was a very good film. How did you feel about* No Down Payment?
R: Well, it was my first film out here when I was under contract. I wanted to make a much more serious statement about the American middleclass than I was able to. I didn't want to shoot the end of the film, and for two days they fired me. They brought in another director and said, "He's going to

shoot the end we want." So I went back in and shot the ending they wanted. So I think the first half of that film works pretty well, and the second half is a lot of shit. But [Spyros] Skouras was then head, and he was one tough and conservative hombre.

D: *How did you find the general atmosphere around Twentieth Century-Fox at that time?*
R: It was terrible. I got a call from him three days after I came out here. He said, "I just got a call that you're a Communist. You have to go before the Committee." I said, "Mr. Skouras, I have never been named, I've never been subpoenaed, I am not a Communist, and I'm not going anyplace. I've got nothing to say to anybody. Pay me my three days' salary and let me go home." He said, "No." They wanted me, they thought they'd make a lot of money with me. And Jay Kanter, who was then an agent at MCA, and I met with Skouras every day for eight days. We walked back once, I remember, we were either at the Roxy or the old Radio City Music Hall, and Jay said, "You know, Marty, when I listen to you I believe you; and when I listen to him I believe him." The picture that was playing was *Oh Men! Oh Women!*, written by Eddie Chodorov, who was blacklisted. I said, "If they really had any feeling about Mr. Chodorov's material, they wouldn't have bought it, they wouldn't have made it into a film. All they've done is take his name off. The film is harmless. All these guys that you've been talking about, and Hollywood's been talking about, look at the films they've written! What is in those films politically that has anything to do with destroying our way of life? Not a phrase!" well, Jay didn't understand it then; I hope he understands it now. That's who I'm making this new film for.

D: *On* No Down Payment *your producer (and, I know, several times after that) was Jerry Wald. Did you work well with him?*
R: Well, Jerry was a perfect Hollywood producer. The nicest thing about Jerry was he was very enthused. And if he believed in you he really wouldn't fight, because that was not his nature. I liked him. I liked him because he was enthusiastic and because he was prepared to do material that nobody else would do. That's where I met the Ravetches, through him, and we've done seven pictures together. Now *they* are not political, but they are social. So my memories of Jerry are really quite nice. I never made a picture with him, outside of *The Long, Hot Summer*, that I felt was very good; and I didn't

think *The Long, Hot Summer* was any great film, but it was a very good commercial film. But I liked him. I felt if he was the worst I had to work with in Hollywood, I would have had a good time out here.

D: *Of course it's often been said that Jerry Wald was the prototype for Sammy Glick. Do you think that was indeed so?*
R: I think there are elements in both that would make one possibly say that, but I didn't care. It didn't affect me. Anything I didn't want to do, nobody—Jerry Wald, Jesus Christ, or Skouras—could get me to do. (Both laugh.)

D: *On* No Down Payment *and also* The Long, Hot Summer, *your cameraman was Joe LaShelle. Did you find him a good man to work with?*
R: Really a very good professional. And of course, because I was always such a hum-drum dresser, all these cameramen were so dashing and so beautifully dressed, they always amazed me. I said, "How can you come to work dressed like that?" I mean, Joe would show up on the set, virtually the leading man. He knew his job very well and he was very good. It struck me as funny. It's happened with quite a few cameramen I've worked with.

D: *I remember last summer I interviewed a director who said that cinematographers were some of the greatest prima donnas in the business.*
R: Oh, yes. The greatest advances in film have been in their work. It's given some of them a sense of themselves which is totally unjustified. They were put on their own to make a film, and the few that have done that have come serious croppers. There are one or two that have made interesting films. I guess the most interesting is the Englishman, Nicolas Roeg. Not particularly my dish in films, but at least I feel a filmmaker is at work. It's not an easy transition. Most of the directors will either come from the writing or acting ranks, that's a normal development. Editors no longer . . . very rare with the others. The minute the word became that important in the making of films, that began to disappear.

D: *Interesting that on* The Long, Hot Summer *you were working with several of your Actor Studio students: Paul Newman, Joanne Woodward, Lee Remick.*
R: And Tony Franciosa. Yes, I did. The reason for that, of course, is that there is a shorthand in the language. They understand exactly what you mean

more quickly than the other actors. But I also worked with Orson Welles, who understood nothing.

D: *How did you find working with Welles?*
R: It was a pain in the ass. Except that he was so witty and so extraordinary a human being and a persona, which is why I cast him. I was fully aware that we beat them to doing *Cat on a Hot Tin Roof*, that character. Of course Tennessee never (and this is the only thing about Tennessee that I've never liked), never really admitted his indebtedness to [William] Faulkner. We took it from the Faulkner short story, and it wasn't as good as his play *Cat on a Hot Tin Roof*, but it didn't have to be. It was a movie, and it was made for different reasons. I wanted Orson very badly, because I realized what an extraordinary persona he was. We met, we cast him. There was a big fight. Fox didn't want him at all, because he'd just done a film with Henry Hathaway in Africa, and he'd given them nothing but trouble. I forget the name of the film, but I said, "He'll be terrific in this part." Well, we get down on location and at one point I say, "Okay, Orson, get into this jeep and drive around town." He said to me, "I can't drive." I'd never heard that from anyone in California. I said, "What do you mean you can't drive?" He said, "I can't drive." I said, "Why the hell didn't you tell me this when we were back in California? Where am I going to find somebody to double for you in Clinton, Louisiana?" He said, "That's *your* job." I found somebody, and Welles and I got along very well. He kept saying to me, "You don't know a hell of a lot about making movies." I said, "I know a hell of a lot about people and about what their behavior has to be in order to make my film work." He said, "Yes, you do know that." So we had that kind of relationship all through the film. It was on a lighter level, though it was not light, because he was needling me. But I liked him and I found him funny. I said to him one day, "Don't fuck around that way with Tony Franciosa, because he doesn't understand you and he's going to knock you on your ass." He was very afraid of any physical contact. I wrote to him afterwards and we remained friendly. When we finished the film, he had just finished *Touch of Evil*, and he was crying to me that he had gone way over and they wouldn't let him cut the film the way he wanted. In one of the arguments I'd had with him I said, "You know, Orson, the difference between you and me is (or *one* of the differences) there's no way you'll hire an actor in one of your films who would give you the kind of trouble that you're giving me in this film." He said,

"That's a smartass remark. Why do you say that?"' I said, "Who is playing a Mexican detective in your picture?" He looked at me and said, "Fuck you." And that was the end of the conversation. And he hired . . . everybody adored him. I had known Mercedes McCambridge in New York. She was the girlfriend of Gary Merrill at one point, who was in the army show with me. And when I started to do *The Long, Hot Summer*, she called me and said, "You've got a big fucking nerve directing him." I said, "He needs a job, and I'm happy to have him in the picture." They adored him, and rightfully so. I mean, he made, in my opinion, the best American picture that's been made. It was a great gift—he pissed on himself. With that kind of equipment he should have done . . . God knows what he should have done! And he didn't. But he still did make *Citizen Kane*. He is one of the tragedies of American film, I guess the biggest tragedy in my opinion. We've had a few like that.

D: *It's a heavy burden, though, to have that kind of success at twenty-four.*
R: It *is* a heavy burden. But if you're that good, if you're that gifted, you owe something, too. It is a genetic accident, he didn't have anything to do with that. But he never accepted that. And he was unafraid. I mean, when he was working at WPA, Marc Blitzstein's *The Cradle Will Rock,* his politics (I don't know what they were) I'm sure were fairly liberal, but he wasn't afraid to do the work of a man he thought was a Communist. He was an extraordinary talent and an extraordinary man. Just a pretty good actor, no more than that. And that's enraged a lot of his followers who I've told that to, who asked me. I said, "Don't ask me. If you ask me I'll tell you what I think." I did that publicly a couple of places, so they were not too gracious about me.

D: *How did you feel about* The Black Orchid?
R: It was a picture with a terrific lady.

D: *Sophia Loren?*
R: Oh! She's a terrific lady. I enjoyed making it, it was an easy film to make. Tony [Quinn] and she were terrific together. I didn't have any illusions about the film. I didn't really make a film (outside of *Edge of the City*, which I liked) until I made *Hud* that I felt mirrored me almost totally. We had a preview of that film in Long Beach, which was not successful.

D: Hud, *you're talking about?*

R: Yes. The audience resisted the film, and particularly the end of the film. Marty Rackin, who was then head of Paramount, came to me and said, "What are you going to do about the end?" I said, "I love it, I'm not going to do anything about it. You've got a great idea? Tell me. If I like it I'll do it. But I'm not going to do anything about it, and I've got Paul [Newman] on my side." Before they could come up with an ending (if they could—which I doubt), the notices began to pour in and they all realized they had a big success on their hands. That was the end of that. They were scared of the picture. We did get cards saying, "Why don't you go back where you came from?" I don't even know where the phrase came, in relation to that picture, but I remember the cards. But we got a lot of cards on that picture that said to me, "Hud is right. The old man is an old fart and the kid is gay." If I'd been really smart (which I've always conceived myself as) I would have seen Haight-Ashbury right around the corner, because that's what was going on in the country. We made that picture because the Ravetches, who had worked at Metro as junior writers, it was their idea, said to me, "We have just done a big hit, *The Long, Hot Summer* was a big hit. We'd like to make a picture which says in essence that a man who is committed to his appetite above all else is no fucking good." Well, that hit an immediate chord with me. Gable always played this part at Metro for the first half of the picture, then God, Spencer Tracy, or some young girl converted him. "Let's just go through logically and say that a man who does this consistently is a prick." That was the nature of that film, that's what we started from, and it worked. It's a great screenplay, it always was. We cut about twenty or thirty pages, it was just too long. There was a love story with the young boy and girl and I said, "What the hell? That's not what it's about." They loved it, and I said, "No, it's no good. It's going to cost another half-million dollars to shoot, and it's a waste of time. Finally they agreed. I had a great time making that picture, I really did.

D: *Did you work closely with Larry McMurtry?*
R: No. He didn't see anything until he saw the picture. We shot down near where he lived. I think he was there one day, when we were shooting the scene which he liked with Pat Neal. He's certainly turned out some nice books.

D: *Pat Neal was fabulous.*

R: Oh, boy, what a lady! Terrific lady. And I didn't want her at the beginning, I was fighting it. Harriet Frank fought for her. I said, "I've seen her on Broadway, I've seen her here, she's a lady. I don't want a lady in this part." In the novel, she was black. It was too early in the history of Hollywood to do that. She said to me, "Marty, she's terrific, she will be terrific in this." And finally I saw it, I agreed with her. And then I had trouble getting her because her marriage was in some kind of difficulty, she had a new child. I made every adjustment for her: shoot for a week, go to England for two weeks. She was terrific. It's so hard to find an actress with that kind of capacity. I need one for this, and I think I've got Jane Fonda. It's so hard to just have the confidence in your own womanliness and not have to be "on" all the time, and to sense that you can still control the atmosphere in every scene that you're in.

D: *Well, she certainly did.*
R: Oh, she was terrific, just terrific. They were all terrific. Paul was terrific, and overlooked. The boy, who I never really liked. . . .

D: *Was that Brandon de Wilde?*
R: Brandon de Wilde. Paul said, "He's going to be a star." I said, "He'll never be a star. Not that he isn't a good actor—he is that—but he has no real balls." Every star, short of the actors who are comedians, must have a real dash of danger to them. You have to feel at one point that they'll kill you. Those actors become the quicker stars. Obviously, that is a dream that's close to a lot of American men and women. You know a lot about people from the films they like to see.

D: *Did you work well with Melvyn Douglas?*
R: Very well. Totally different background, but he was a very intelligent man, good actor. I liked him, he was quite a man. He had been through the thing with his wife. Quite a guy. Old Mel, he worked until he died; I guess that's what we're all going to do. Doc told me to stop working five or six years ago. I said no. I made *Norma Rae,* and I've gotten healthier in the last two or three years: walking, and really watching everything I eat, which is the key. Enough exercise . . . tennis is never enough, because it's not that consistent, it doesn't have that aerobic thing of continuous. . . . This morn-

ing I walked a mile. I can't walk quickly; quickly as I can go is about nineteen minutes. But it sets me up for the day. It's painful, too.

D: *Let's back up to a film we missed. I'm curious about* Paris Blues.
R: Well, we had no script on that picture. We had the commitment from these actors, and everybody said, "Jesus Christ, what a cast!" I said, "We have no script." We worked and posted around on it; we had an eighty-five page script finally, and I made it. It's no great shakes of a film, some people like it a lot. I always found it fairly entertaining, no more than that.

D: *Did you enjoy the association with musicians?*
R: Very much. I'm an ex-hoofer, and I enjoyed that very much. They were lovely guys. Duke Ellington had the strangest atmosphere. I went to see him many times, he lived at the Chateau Marmont or some other hotel. He'd get up late and have steak for breakfast, always be a broad around someplace. Terrific guy. Terrific guy to have all those things and still be an artist and an intellectual of sorts. I liked him a lot, I like guys like that very much. The trumpet player was a whole different dish.

D: *Louis Armstrong?*
R: Yes. (Chuckles.) He was just terrific.

D: *How did you feel about* The Outrage?
R: Well, I won't do it again. I thought the picture worked pretty well. I did it because it seemed that they had made a good transition from the Japanese story, *Rashomon*. But when I finished the film I saw *Rashomon* a couple of more times, I'm never going to try to reproduce the work of a master again. I like the film, but it wasn't as good as the other one. It suffered, I suppose, what it should suffer. There's some very good work in the film.

D: *Here again you were working with James Wong Howe. I'm curious what you felt his special genius was.*
R: Well, when I gave him *Hud* to read he came to me at our first meeting and said, "Why are you doing this film?" I thought the script was really terrific, I was amazed to hear him say that. I realized that he just didn't know how to read a script. I said, "This is terrific, Jimmy." He said, "Terrific?" "Yeah." Two weeks into the shooting he came to me and said, "I know what

you mean now, this is terrific." Jim could do anything, and *would* do anything. He would die to get a shot. We were shooting in West Texas, and I really wanted a sense of the infinity of the land. Every shot in that picture of any size is backlit, so we got that. And he fought to get it all the time, he understood what I meant. And when I shot the execution of the cattle sequence, he figured out how to get the cattle to come to the camera. I didn't know what to do. We dug that hole and we brought them in, they saw us, and they just stood away. He covered every goddamned camera with hay, and they were there. He was one of the purest artists I've ever met in my life. He wasn't too smart, but he was very gifted, and he loved to work. Crews hated him, he was very rough, he would scream at them. He and I loved each other. He understood that I understood everything he didn't understand, and I *knew* he understood everything I didn't understand. So we had a great time together.

D: *When you said a moment ago that he didn't know how to read a script, do you think he was so into imagery . . . ?*
R: I just think he was uneducated and not a theater person. He was totally uneducated. When he chose to do a film, he did it about some basketball team, and it was just a film. As a cameraman, he was terrific, just terrific. And he could figure anything out, and would do it. I remember in *Maguires* we were shooting a scene where there was an explosion, and all the operators ran out after the gas began to explode. Jimmy ran right back in and operated whatever camera he could find that was still functioning, so that I got whatever footage I needed. I loved him. He told me the funniest story about how he got his first job. He was a still photographer at Paramount. I forget the name of the actress, but somebody who had blue eyes. Blue eyes, in those days, with black and white photography, didn't come out, it came out kind of washy. She had come in and taken several photographs for her next film. About three days later she came back, screaming. Her eyes were a luscious brown. She started to scream, "What did you do, Jim?" He had no idea what he had done. Finally he got her out, sat down, and tried to figure out what it was. He finally figured out that he had drawn all the black drapes, the velvets, and the reflected light off those velvets had changed the color of her eyes. She immediately got him to photograph her next film. He built this little teepee of black velvet in which he placed the camera, and everybody in Hollywood came to see what the chink was doing—that's the way it was phrased.

And that's how he got his first job. He was really a terrific artist, he didn't think of anything else. I loved him. And then he got ill and blew up. He was on cortisone. I don't know what the hell was wrong with him. His wife is a good writer, a white woman, really lovely lady.

D: *Back on* The Outrage, *was Edward G. Robinson good to work with?*
R: Yes, but he was a little deaf. We were shooting with a lot of rain, which complicated the issue. But, like Jimmy Wong Howe, he was a genuine actor and I liked him very much. I had a very good cast in that picture.

D: *Claire Bloom.*
R: Lovely lady. I liked her very much.

D: *Did you enjoy* The Spy Who Came in From the Cold?
R: I enjoyed the film; I didn't enjoy making it too much because [Richard] Burton and I didn't get along. He was on the booze, and I'm one of those fellows who shows up early to work and works hard and goes home, goes to sleep, and gets up the next morning. I don't drink. It bothered me not quite as much, because it helped the part. Otherwise, it would have driven me crazy. There's a guy who's pissed on himself. And he's very engaging, it's difficult not to like him, but I didn't like him. Very engaging, funny, very bright, very socially oriented—everything that I would normally like very much, but he was a bum. I think he knew it himself, and I think that's why his talent never really did the kind of work it should have done. We didn't get along at all. I was making my first picture in a foreign country with a lot of actors that I didn't know. I had a terrible time convincing Michael Hordern to play a homosexual. It was not very vogueish at the time. He said, "What'll I do? I'll never get another part." I said, "You're going to be terrific in this." I had been to the theater in London almost every night and I knew that a large section of the theater was dominated by homosexuals. So I could understand to some degree, but he *wasn't* a homosexual. I could understand, to some degree, his worrying about it. I said, "Mike, it doesn't matter." And he did, he got nothing but work after that picture and was one of the most employed actors in London. I like the picture. In this town, nobody believed it, because nobody believed that a member of the CIA or any foreign service would be as duplicitous as the English were. The picture did okay, it came out, he got nominated, but I don't think it was truly appreciated. But if

you're making subject matter which is before its time . . . the best pictures I've made are the pictures that have been nominated—with the exception of *The Front* and *The Molly Maguires*, both pictures which I like very much, which did much better in Europe than they did here. I'll never understand why *Maguires* didn't, never. It's been explained to me twenty different times by twenty different people, and I'm sure that all twenty of them were wrong, but I'm still not clear on what it was. The only thing I can think about in that film is that it was too gray, that the villain of the piece I made too attractive. It was just too gray. The hero of the piece, in my mind, was the character that Sean Connery played. Now, it's interesting that the actual person after whom the [Richard] Harris character was created, went from there to someplace in Colorado, did the same thing, and was murdered there by a worker. He got a very good job, became sort of a minor executive.

D: *I found it interesting that after you made your first film you never went back to the theater.*
R: No. I've had plenty of opportunities, but I never really found anything I liked, as the theater began to diminish in its potency and playwrights began to disappear. They began to appear in regional theater, really, out of protest. That is, a young man, a young woman would appear who had something to say and there was no place to get it done but regional theater. The one thing that I was willing to do, but I was only willing to do one of them, was that Texas play, three one-act plays.

D: *Preston Jones, you're talking about?*
R: Yes. I said I would direct one. They said, "No, Marty, you've got to direct all three." I said, "I can't do that, I can't go through that. I don't have the time or the energy. Let me direct one, I'll choose the one I want to direct." They sent the three to me and I liked them all. I liked one best. But they wouldn't do it. And I've had nothing else anywhere near that class sent to me, and nothing else has appeared on the American scene. The plays of Sam Shepard I don't think ever quite work, and he has been winning prize after prize. So that tells you the state of the American theater. I hired a black writer who had written a play I liked to do *Sounder*, and that was a wild experience. A guy I heard this morning was terrific. I must find out his name and send him a note—just terrific. He spoke about patriotism, spoke about all the things that Ollie North has been espousing, only differently. I was very

impressed with him. I've been impressed with North, how smart he is, he's bright. They really chose a good guy. But I think in the last analysis they're all going to come off badly, because they have all broken the law.

D: *Of your theater work, do you feel that* A View From the Bridge *was your most exciting?*
R: Well, it was the best piece of material I had. The only problem I had was that I had to cast it for both plays. Therefore, everything was just a little less perfect. Casting is ninety percent of getting a first-class performance. If you make a mistake, you're dead. Now, if you're casting in a rep company, which was part of the problem I had in *A View From the Bridge* . . . yes, it was the best play I had. It was not quite a big hit, but it was okay, and it was an impressive piece of work by Arthur [Miller]. Even the really good playwrights, Arthur and Tennessee, they've gone way downhill. Arthur's last two plays, neither one of which I liked . . . it's very difficult on that level to tell people you don't want to do it, people you respect and admire. Particularly in the commercial sense, with nobody else around. You don't know who else is going to write something first-class. It's very difficult to do something first-class. The guys who have been around forty or fifty years and have never done anything first-class, you can forget that they'll ever do anything. Guys, on the other hand, who've done it . . . Hollywood operates, totally aware of it or not, on that basis. They keep hiring guys and directors who envy the fact that these people have gotten the job; they say, "Why do they hire him?" I say, "Well, look what he did." "But that was so long ago." I say, "What's the difference? He did it. He's not a runner, he doesn't have to be in that kind of shape." There are plenty of people in this town who never understood why [John] Huston was being hired; he hadn't done a successful picture in a long, long time. Well, he finally came up with one. But he had every right to, he made some of the best pictures that we'd ever seen. He's an extraordinary man, I like him very much. Artistically and humanly, he's extraordinary.

D: *In the film chronology, I guess we've worked our way to Hombre.*
R: I had a good time making that picture. I thought Paul [Newman] was really terrific in that film. It was a Western that we made somewhat differently, from our point of view. I don't know whether that helped it or not, but it did very well. It was a big hit commercially. As a matter of fact, I think

it was my best film commercially. It was very popular in Europe, where they like Westerns. We picked that up from one of his early, cheap paperback novels. Paul and I were in business at that time, and I was looking for a picture to star him in. That used to happen a great deal, and still does; people are looking for pictures for certain actors. Once an actor says, "Yes, it's a go," ... not the kind of pictures I want to make. But I enjoyed that film. It was a tough location. Jimmy [Wong Howe] was terrific. The whole crew wanted to quit. I finally called him in and said, "Jim, you've got to behave yourself." He said, "They're no fucking good," and started to scream. I said, "They're okay. They're professionals. They don't care like you care, like I care. That's part of why they are what they are and why we are what we are, so behave yourself." And he did finally. He hated them, he hated all crews. He said, "They're all making too much money," which was true. He was a terrific man. For a non-intellectual, he was a terrific man.

D: *Of course you'd worked with Paul Newman a long time by this point. Do you feel that he'd really grown as a screen actor?*
R: I'll say this about Paul: of all the actors that I've worked with, Paul has made the most of his equipment. He gets better and better all the time—without me, with me, without me. I know him very well. [Harriet] Frank and Irving [Ravetch] and myself noticed the cool sexuality that was implicit in that man, and that's what made him the big star that he is. He was a beginning actor, and Joanne was a much more developed actor at that point. But Paul had that thing, and we could tell right away. We kept looking, for *The Long, Hot Summer, Hud,* and *Hombre*—three H's, that's how they designated these three films—were all pictures that we . . . well, *Hud* was different. We did *Hud* second, and *Hombre* was after *Hud*. But I like the picture. I really like Westerns myself, very much. My favorite American director has always been [John] Ford—a man that I probably didn't agree with about anything else.

D: *I was going to say, coming from the theater as you did, John Ford's an interesting man to admire.*
R: Well, I thought he was terrific—terrific director, terrific mind—even though I knew we didn't agree on anything. It's very interesting to me that he did the most progressive movies in this town. Who else would do *The Grapes of Wrath* or the picture he did about the Indians, which I tried to make, *Cheyenne Autumn*. It stopped me from getting the other picture made.

Howard Fast, I think, had written a novel on the same subject, which was better. He had a better story. All of Howard Fast's novels were good stories. Howard is not a great writer, but the stories were always good. He really understood how to put together . . . and all the cheap novels he's written under an assumed name, they're all pretty good, too. I almost did one of those, too. But I loved Ford, I loved his work. It's always interesting to me that a really very conservative man would do such progressive films. But every artist is really tuned in to telling the truth, despite what he believes sometimes. Why else would he make a film like *The Grapes of Wrath*? I mean, I'm sure that if you had a political discussion with John Ford at that time he would have negated everything that that film is about.

D: *I've read, of course, where he identified the Okies moving off the land with the Irish being removed from their land. Whether that's true, I don't know.*
R: Fundamentally, what the film had to say was much too radical for him, so I don't believe those other things. I mean, I've heard them from all the old-timers. [Henry] Hathaway told me that he was making a film once in Spain and somebody came from the French cinema to see him, an interviewer. And he knew he had made a piece of shit, he had done the film with Wayne. Hathaway was an old pro, but he was no dummy, and he knew that he had made a piece of shit. And this guy started to praise the picture and talk to him about the shots. Finally he felt he was being insulted. He didn't quite understand it all, but he really chased the guy out of the hotel, he ran after him, lost his temper.

There's no question in my mind that people like Bergman, Fellini, who really are extraordinary filmmakers, who understand what they feel very deeply in terms of visual images, that, if film is an art form, it's in that area someplace. As I say, I just haven't made up my mind, I don't know. There hasn't been enough time.

Most of us who have grown up making films in this country are professionals, that's where we developed, it's very rare. Some of the early films that I've heard a lot of people blabbing about, I go to see and I don't like. I'm not prepared to discuss it. I don't have to discuss any of the paintings I have on my wall and make adjustment for the fact that they were done in the eighteenth century, and discuss it on that level. The technology of film obviously has improved so much that some of those films are at a disadvantage, unquestionably. But I don't think they're really first-class, some of them. I think in Hollywood that the directors who've done the best work are generally the best professionals, who know how to make a film, who know material, who know how to relate to people, who have a sense of the proper visuals for the kind of film they're making—all the things that go into making a film director. Some of the younger people who are attracted by certain kinds of films and some of the critics, world-class critics, who are attracted by certain kinds of films, I'm not negating that at all, that's fine. That's not my bag, that's not the world I live in. I've seen some of those films I liked, and a lot that I didn't like. And I am certainly not the definitive critic. So there is no way, except in the case of something quite extraordinary, like Orson might have been, that the American cinema can develop anything but high-class professionals. And since it is very much a commercial enterprise, our films are the most popular films in the world. And they are popular because they are highly professional, it's well done, well made, well acted. The extraordinary visions that some extraordinary artists have, that's fine. I mean, I'm a fan of Bergman's more than I am of Fellini, but I have enormous regard for both of them. I have an enormous regard for Woody [Allen], who I don't put in their class, but some American critics do. A couple of his films I have not liked, but I like him very much. He is unusual and he is his own man—all those things I respect. So I think the whole business of films and what's good and what's bad . . . I mean, I think the critics have begun to lose some of their power. First of all, there are so many of them. It's become a way to achieve a certain kind of notoriety without ever having to do anything creative. Some of the guys have made a lot of money out of it. I don't have any bitterness about that, except when they don't like my film, then I get really pissed off. So I've had my bouts with some of the critics. But I think, finally, the survivors are the professionals. And the more professional they are the better they survive. It has to be on every level; that is, dealing with the studio, dealing with the stars, all things that I've done for the thirty years I've been out here. I'm really amazed that I continue to work at my age with the kind of stuff I want to make. That only means that they think there's a reasonable chance they'll get their money back, or make a little money. Popularity is not the keynote of my success. A lot of people don't like me and don't like my films.

D: *One of the things I read described you as "an individual at odds with the system." Do you feel that's true?*

R: Well, I work in the system. Sure, I'm at odds with it, I don't agree with it ninety-nine percent of the time, but I somehow manage to work in it. It doesn't really bother me that much. They go so far with me and then they let me go. Otherwise, I won't work. The one thing I know about capitalistic society is that as long as you can make money for them they'll find a way to get you to work. And you don't have to be a red to know that.

D: *Of course, you came in on the tail end of that big studio era. I'm curious about your perception of that. Do you feel that the breakup of the big studio system allowed for more creativity, or do you think that something important was lost?*

R: I don't really know. I think it did make for some more creativity, except that people at the head of studios in those days—bastards, so many of them were—I think they were professionals. They knew the business.

D: *Zanuck knew filmmaking.*

R: Totally. He was an extraordinary professional. I didn't like him particularly, but that was because we didn't agree. I don't agree with too many people, but I do want to work. And on this picture, this last one, I was amazed that Metro bought the picture. They were the first people we showed it to, it was not complete. I was only not amazed for one reason: we had done *Norma Rae* with the same guy. They had never had a picture like that, and they haven't had anything like that since. So even if they had certain reservations about it, they decided it was worth a shot. I think this town, now, there's a better chance for a young filmmaker than ever before in the history of the game. There is so much independent money and everybody wants to get into show business, so there's a real good chance. If you really have any ability, you'll be able to make a couple of pictures. If the pictures are any good, you've got it made. Even if you don't have ability, you want to make little shitty pictures—horror pictures and the half-porno pictures—people have gotten very rich, people whose names you'll never hear of.

D: *Again, the reference point here is* Hombre; *by that time you're into producing. How did you find that experience?*

R: Well, it was no different than when I directed, except for this picture I did with [Barbra] Streisand. Nobody ever bothered me. In that case we had found the book, we had made the initial purchase for $17,000, we created the screenplay. Why do we want to pay another salary? So we just didn't hire anybody. The producer, you see, is always reserved final cut. It was never used with me until I worked with Streisand. She's a very complicated lady.

D: *How did you feel about* The Brotherhood?
R: It was a job. I liked what it was about. Kirk [Douglas] was an actor that I thought was good. There was something about him that was attractive to me, and he wanted desperately to play this part. He wanted me so that he could be as good as he thought he could be, so I did it. I had fun making the picture. It was cold in New York, I still remember that. And I enjoyed working with some of those older actors from the era before I came into this town. I enjoyed making the picture. It was a picture well-made; obviously with never the kind of success of the two films [Francis Ford] Coppola made, which were first-class. Francis, I thought, was the best of the younger guys. I now feel [Martin] Scorsese is the best of the younger guys, because he's totally unafraid. I was hoping he would make *The Last Temptation of Christ.* He's still trying to make it. [Robert] DeNiro turned him down and I really got pissed off. It's complicated, it's difficult. I don't know how devout a Catholic DeNiro is, but there is a sequence in the screenplay in which Christ was in bed with a woman. But Scorsese was willing to make it, and they had money with DeNiro; then he walked, and that was the end of that. I think he'll get it on, he's good. I sometimes wish his films had a little more mind to them, they have a lot of everything else. He's very good. Paul enjoyed working with him very much, Paul talked to me about that.

D: The Color of Money?
R: Yes.

D: *I thought Newman was good in it.*
R: Yes, so did I. I thought he was good, and I thought the boy was good—not as good as I wanted him to be. But he's a very nice kid, I really like him. I spent two or three hours with him on a plane.

D: *Tom Cruise?*
R: Yes. I was quite taken with him. But I found the film very . . . I didn't like the script. Paul loved the script, I didn't like it. It was okay. Of course it was shot very well, so it gave the picture an aspect of importance that didn't

really exist. A lot of people like the film. It was a success, it was not really a big hit. I know a lot about that because I've had a lot of pictures like that.

D: *You were saying yesterday that you didn't understand, and still don't, why* The Molly Maguires *was not a big hit.*
R: I really don't. But, what the hell, why do I have to understand?

D: *Historians loved it. (Laughs.)*
R: Terrific movie. Everything in that movie works. Except one problem, if you're going to make a film about a great character, that may be just too sophisticated for movie audiences. And the ambivalence they felt about the character Richard Harris played, which I felt was necessary for his getting into the Molly Maguires. Maybe it wasn't that, I don't know what the hell it was. I was sure I had a big hit. Boy, that was a blow. After that picture I felt terrible, I really loved the movie.

D: *How did you feel about* The Great White Hope?
R: I swore after I finished that that I would never do another play, I'd just finished one. So all the promises of filmmakers are not to be too well trusted. (Chuckles.) I never really liked the play as much as everybody else did. The two actors were terrific, and he was onto a very hot subject. I think the film suffered, it needed something that I didn't quite give it. I kept the two actors, and they were terrific, but the film was not a success. The blacks I think really rejected the film. There was a period . . . I did a film I really liked called *Conrack*, that the blacks rejected. They rejected it because there was a white Jesus Christ. At that time they were into teaching their own courses, they were into "blackness," in an extraordinary intellectual way. I said, "I've been fighting for some kind of understanding between blacks and whites since I remember speaking my first words in the English language. I'm not going to change my point of view because it doesn't suit you at this point. You're only interested in "blackness" and black historians and black teachers, and I have no objection to that. At the same time, that's not my bag." I think it's the most faithful audience in films, blacks. I think they go to see their expression more than anybody else, because there's no place else they can see it. And when they support a film, even a film that is not the normal black fare, like *Sounder*, they help make it a big hit. I mean, Eddie Murphy is a movie star unquestionably; but I'll bet that every black in America goes to see Eddie

Murphy's movies. There's no other group that is that attentive. Nobody has those problems, that's why. I mean, for a black to see him walk into a Western bar and beat the shit out of the barman, that's better than three eighteen-year-old girls. I felt I could have done a better job on that picture.

D: The Great White Hope?
R: Yes.

D: *Did you work well with James Earl Jones?*
R: Yes. He's a terrific actor. I knew his father, we were young actors together in New York. Jimmy is a terrific actor. And so is the girl, I like her very much. I thought the film would succeed, but it didn't. But when I looked at it a few years later, I just felt there were certain things I had missed.

D: *We mentioned briefly yesterday* The Front. *I'm curious about several things, including the fact that here you're dealing comically with probably the most painful period in your life.*
R: Well, sitting right here, talking with Walter [Bernstein] about the script one day, I said, "Walter, we have got to be very careful." We were telling the story of Hecky, that's how we started to write that screenplay. It bordered on being sentimental. "We're not telling it the right way. It shouldn't be Hecky's story." And we came up with this other story that we knew, we had all been there when it existed, and we decided to turn it around. I think we did the right thing. We never lost a moment of Hecky. The absurdity of the whole time in American history was caught better by that. I remember him saying, "This is not up to my usual standard, I'm not going to turn it in," and one of the guys almost killed him. "You son of a bitch, what do you mean 'not up to your usual standards?'" So it was deeply felt. But we felt that was the right way to go, and I think it was. I like that film, I think it's very good, and we did fairly well with it. It didn't do nearly as well in this country as it did in the rest of the world. Anything that has a smack of anti-Americanism, even if it's not really anti-American, they will jump on.

D: *Did you usually work closely with the writer? Did you have a hand in the writing?*
R: Yes. I doubt that anybody has done any collaboration like the Ravetches and myself. I've worked very closely with them on some, not so close on

others, but I've always kept them on the set. They've always stayed, so that if I needed anything done they would do it. I've written, myself, two plays, and that really convinced me that I was not a first-class writer. So I don't really try. But in most every case I keep the writers around. We simply pare down to what I feel is essential. I don't try to write, because I'm not really comfortable with it. But I have very strong control over the content of the material. The Ravetches and I have worked together more closely on this new one than any. When we did *Norma Rae* I sent something from *Life* magazine and they really got very excited. I had a screenplay in six weeks, a first-class screenplay. So I guess you must say I work quite closely, because we're shaping the film as we're making it. A film changes from day to day.

D: *Once you've approved the script, does it become law, or is there still some . . . ?*
R: Well, once I approve the script I regard it as more or less law, unless something genuine happens during rehearsal or the shooting. In other words, I don't like actors just hemming hawing and saying ridiculous kinds of words that they come up with because they're more comfortable, I don't like that at all. I much prefer the firm tone of a genuine writer. But nothing is sacrosanct when you make movies, because it does change from day to day. You look at the dailies and say, "I didn't realize that's what was going to happen, that that character was going to do that. If that's what's going to happen, we can do this and we can do that." It's one of the exciting things about making movies, it is the most exciting thing. It's happening at that very moment. It's not like the theater. I never rehearse so that they've already played the scene, because I'm looking for that accident. I rehearse them until I think they're ready to explode, then I stop. Then I wait until I shoot the scene, I want that first orgasm. When I have very good actors, I'll stage a scene, rehearse it, and then do something to disrupt it when I shoot. I'll drop a bulb, knowing full well that with the kind of actors I have the scene's going to go on, and that irritant in the scene is going to help. Or I'll move a piece of furniture in some way. I only do that when I have the best actors around. But it's always interesting, because actors tend to get set. When they get set they get too comfortable, that certain kind of immediacy in life is lost.

D: *I've also heard that Spencer Tracy would never do a scene quite the same way twice so there would be an element of spontaneity there.*

R: He was maybe one of the two or three best movie actors I ever saw. Yes, sometimes actors will do that for themselves, just to keep it alive.

D: *Did you enjoy the association with Sally Field?*
R: She's terrific. Flat out, she is terrific. A terrific girl, a first-class actress. I really like her very much.

D: *She was fabulous in* Norma Rae.
R: She's the only actress who ever won the Cannes Film Festival, New York Film Critics, and the Academy Award in the same year. She's a terrific girl, too. The guy who married her was very lucky. She's an ace of a girl, I really like her very much.

D: *How did you feel about* Cross Creek?
R: I liked *Cross Creek*. I grew ill during that film, and I could see that in the film. The film lacked a certain kind of dynamic. Maybe it's always implicit in that kind of material, but I like the film. I was very disappointed. Of course you're always disappointed when a film doesn't succeed. But I liked it, and I liked all the people in it. I had a good time with them. I really grew ill on that film, I thought I was not going to be able to finish. We stopped for about three or four days. I guess being as ornery as I am, everything came back. But I never really physically was up to making that film. That's happened to me, in and out, on a couple of films. There's nothing you can do about it, that's it.

D: *Looking at the sweep of your film career, do you feel like your approach to filmmaking has changed over the years?*
R: Well, I had no approach at the beginning, I didn't know what I was doing. I just showed up, I knew what I wanted, asked everybody to give it to me, and they did. I don't think it's changed all that much. In the films that I really think are my best films, where everything has come together, I just had a great time. I enjoyed making them, I knew what they were about, I knew what I was looking for, I knew I had the right actors and that they could give it to me, and I knew that I had to wait to get certain things. I waited with Cicely Tyson. I waited and waited until that moment when she ran to meet her husband, and that was the first take we printed, that's all. [John] Alonzo came over and said, "You'll never get anything better than

this in your life." It's the first time I'd used a long lens, because it was the only way I could get the shot. I was always very suspicious of all the new technologies, because they always seemed to be there to satisfy themselves. I still don't use them too much, but I'm not as bad as I was in the beginning. I was very suspicious.

D: *Do you feel like your professional life has contributed to your personal development?*
R: I think I've changed very little. I think, mostly, people change very little. I have a lot of friends who've been in analysis for thirty or forty years, and I've said to several of them, "Why? By now you should be way beyond a Ph.D." They've all said the same thing: "Marty, I wouldn't have lived, I would have killed myself." That gave me pause, so I stopped. I don't really devil them anymore, which I used to do. But I don't think people change very much. Whenever the die is cast, it is cast. And depending on how good they are, how smart they are, they change somewhat, but not fundamentally. I feel I know what to expect from Mr. Falwell for the rest of his life. And the exposure of that whole evangelical thing (which I could never understand why it existed), I could never understand the popularity and the American people giving them so many millions of dollars, and still, after it exploded, so many people still clinging to that little asshole, Jim Bakker, and his wife. But I guess that's part of living in a great country. The evangelicals to me are the biggest joke in the history of my lifetime.

D: *Have you ever considered doing a film on that?*
R: Yes. I never got a script I liked. They are a joke, a sanctimonious joke, and Falwell is the biggest joke of them all. He has not yet been caught, and maybe he doesn't have enough energy to do anything like that, but what he's about is an enormous crock of shit. I know that, and somehow I have a feeling that deep down he knows it. He's not foolish, I just can't stand him. I can't stand any of them. Some of them always attracted me because they're so theatrical. Swaggart is very theatrical, but he probably was some kind of a frustrated actor.

D: *Yes, I think historically Billy Sunday would have made a great actor.*
R: He seemed to be the straightest of the bunch. But that's all just a joke. American religion is a joke. And how carefully it's all cultivated. How many

times now has Oliver North talked about God? I have no objection to God. I'm an atheist myself, but I don't object. I've been to places and seen people genuinely moved. I remember walking into a church in Israel and seeing a woman kneeling there, crying, so deeply moved. Whatever she was moved about was obviously of minor interest to me, but she was moved. And she seemed a very nice lady.

D: *You can't help being moved by the fact that she was moved.*
R: That's right. That's what a good actor does to you, too. But it's such a joke, the religious thing is so silly.

D: *This has been fabulous. I thank you very much.*
R: A pleasure.

The Long, Hot Career

CARRIE RICKEY / 1988

HE IS AN URBAN JEW attracted to the rhythms of the rural South, a loner devoted to unionism. He is the man who, when suspected of un-American activities, dismissed charges by declaring, "I am American as chopped liver!"

Director Martin Ritt, aged 75, sturdy and bullnecked, resembles the gruffest of bookies but speaks as gently as a scholar. A relative latecomer to filmmaking—he was 43 when he made his directorial debut with *Edge of the City* (1957), starring John Cassavetes and Sidney Poitier—Ritt has enjoyed an unusually long and productive third career. (His first was acting; his second was spent directing plays and television dramas before being blacklisted, a period he later memorialized in *The Front* in 1976.) Of his generation only Sidney Lumet, ten years Ritt's junior, has worked as long—three solid decades.

This season's *Stanley and Iris*, a love story that stars Robert DeNiro as an illiterate laborer and Jane Fonda as the woman who teaches him how to read, marks Ritt's status as the oldest working director in Hollywood. It is his twenty-fourth film.

Ritt is a self-effacing man, comfortable with the fact that while many of his movies are instantly recognized (*The Long, Hot Summer*; *Hud*; and *Sounder*), he himself is not. From the Los Angeles editing room where he's polishing *Stanley and Iris*, he reflects on a career that began in 1914 on New

---

Originally published in *Fame* (1988): 35–36, 38, 40. Reprinted by permission of the author.

York's "upper Lower East Side," as he calls the 10th Street and Avenue B neighborhood where he was born.

"Yeah, Ritt was the real family name," the director says, anticipating the inevitable question. "My mother came from Poland, my father from Russia. She was totally illiterate; he had a smattering of education. She was a cleaning woman; he had been a second mate on the Hamburg Line, so he spoke a couple of languages. They met here in the States. He ran an employment agency for new immigrants, spoke to people in their own tongues. Fleeced 'em probably," Ritt adds with a chuckle.

Education was a priority in the Ritt household. "By day, there was PS 64. then in the late afternoon there was *cheder* [Hebrew school]. Having to go to school when all the other kids were out made us [the Jews] an open target. We were always getting attacked, usually by the Italian kids, and I fought as much as I could. I was a tough kid, and probably drew upon that ethnic tension when I made *Edge of the City*."

About the effect of his religious education, Ritt confesses, "I wasn't observant. I got bar mitzvahed, but religion was never an important part of my life." He admits that *cheder* may have provided his foundation in ethics, but is much more willing to credit his moral education simply to living in Manhattan during the Jazz Age and the Depression.

At DeWitt Clinton High before the crash, the mastiff-like Ritt earned a reputation as an athlete and a scholar. The official Paramount Studio biography of him, circa 1965, asserts that he was awarded athletic scholarships to various universities. Whether or not this was so, it is documented in *Who's Who* that he attended Elon College in the textile-belt capital of Burlington, North Carolina.

The choice of locale was to have a profound effect on the urban street fighter, leading him to direct the first of Hollywood's "regional" movies—the Faulkner-inspired *The Sound and the Fury* and *The Long, Hot Summer*, as well as *Norma Rae*, which is set in the Georgia textile belt.

While he claims to have studied "nothing in particular" and that his only ambition was "to get through school with the least amount of trouble," Ritt remembers enjoying his literature classes, which proved to be useful for the future director of *Hemingway's Adventures of a Young Man* and *Cross Creek*, his biography of regionalist Marjorie Kinnan Rawlings. While in North Carolina, he embarked on the first of many explorations of the rural South, storing up images of remote townships and hardscrabble lives that he would later use in *Sounder* and *Conrack,* his stories of black youths struggling for education.

Ritt graduated from Elon in 1934, returning to New York at the lowest point in the Depression. "I enrolled in law school at St. John's in Brooklyn. Didn't have to spend too much time there to know that law wasn't for me. By this time my mother had worked her way up to an agent for chorus girls. That's how I got around in show business."

A youthful activist and Work Projects Administration (WPA) proselyte, Ritt joined the Group Theatre as an actor. He was drawn to its belief that culture could transform politics and vice versa. "The Group Theatre was a great collection of American intellectuals and artists," says Ritt of the gifted cluster that included Clifford Odets, Elia Kazan, Morris Carnovsky, Stella Adler, and John Garfield.

Though Ritt would later be accused by McCarthyites of having belonged to "Communist front" organizations, his memory of the pre–World War II era is that "I was never aligned in any organized way. I was just for people working and performing politicized material." He doesn't remember having been a card-carrying member of any political group apart from the WPA, the New Deal agency that funded public art by painters such as Willem de Kooning and Philip Guston, and history-making theater organizations such as the Group and Orson Welles's Mercury Theater. But he admits, "My politics were always liberal. It was a product of my being a minority. I just didn't keep my mouth shut. I said whatever I felt. The WPA allowed me to have this attitude."

Ritt fondly remembers this period—the late '30s—as his "real education. . . . I was reading everything, seeing everything. On Broadway. Off Broadway. I was a member of a group called Theater of Action, which was where I met Nick Ray. We performed a play that Kazan directed. . . . He was brilliant to be around." Although Kazan would later "name names" for the House un-American Activities Committee during the Hollywood witch-hunts of the '50s, it was he who inspired in Ritt a passion for naturalistic and character-driven theater.

"At the same time, I wanted to be the best actor that I could be," recalls Ritt, whose fledgling career was interrupted by a stint in the Army during World War II. "Because there was no part for me in the Air Force show, I was given a chance to direct some plays." While in the Army, Ritt received orders to report to Hollywood, where he made his movie debut in George Cukor's

Winged Victory, "a lollipop patriotic story," which "wasn't up to Cukor's skills." Of his first time in the city that he would later make his home, Ritt only remembers that "I lived in the barracks, never saw much of Hollywood. My only recollection is that I played a lot of gin rummy."

A more significant event of his army career was that Ritt established his reputation as a theater director by helming an army production of Sidney Howard's *Yellow Jack*—"my first big hit critically," he remembers.

After he demobilized, Ritt immediately found work in New York in the new medium of television—both in front of and behind the camera. "I did some live dramas, hokey melodramas, mostly, but I was working." And by anyone's census, he was working a lot, making an estimated one hundred appearances and directing some one hundred fifty television episodes between 1946 and 1951. Others completing their apprenticeship in directing at the time were future movie directors John Frankenheimer, Delbert Mann, Robert Mulligan, Arthur Penn, and Sidney Lumet—for Lumet, Ritt starred in the teledrama *The Paperbox Kid*. Reflecting on this period, Ritt thinks the most important factor for him was "working with all these New York actors whose confidence I earned and who later worked with me in film." Actors like John Cassavetes, Sidney Poitier, Patricia Neal, and Joanne Woodward.

This particularly satisfying period for Ritt ended abruptly "around '50, '51. I was just doing my business—a melodramatic series, prophetically enough called *Danger*—and one day was attacked." A *Red Channels*-type publication called *Counterattack* alleged that Ritt had been involved in "Communist front" groups during the '30s. Implicit in the allegation was that since he had been a closet Communist, Ritt's television work was therefore anti-American propaganda.

"It was guilt by association I suppose," Ritt says with a sigh. "I was never subpoenaed, never named by anyone. I was told I would have a lot of job offers if I would only go in front of a committee and name a whole lot of people who had already been named or who were already dead. I thought it was all incredibly cynical on the part of the people offering me those jobs. I told them, 'If you're not looking for information, why ask me to debase myself?'"

At first, both the sponsor for *Danger* and the network, CBS, wanted to keep him. "Then CBS said that although it didn't want to lose me, it didn't want to lose advertisers. The need to make money superseded everything else. I never denounced the Group Theatre or anyone, because I loved them," he says with obvious pain. How did it affect his relationship with those who did name names? "Oh, Kazan and I still talked, but it was never the same. His behavior didn't help our relationship."

"So I couldn't get work in television and went back to work in theater," Ritt remembers. "Was in Odets's *The Flowering Peach*; that's about the only job I had, and then I taught acting professionally to anyone—and I mean anyone—who paid money. It was very hard. I knew that when I went certain places, I got brushed. I had quite a few friends in the same position—limbo." Press him for details, and he politely replies, "I don't want to talk about other people, dear." To this day, he's wary of naming names—whether they be those of the villains or the victims.

Why does Ritt think he got fingered by Commie-hunters? "Probably my affiliation with the Group Theatre and a little bit of everything. I always supported liberal causes, always have. When I had money, I gave. When I didn't, I gave what I could."

During his blacklist days, Ritt was grateful for wife Adele's staunch emotional and financial support. "She sold space for telephone books. She handled it all so well." After spending about five years in professional limbo, Ritt got a Hollywood entrée that was as abrupt as his network exit: In 1956 MGM approached him to direct *Edge of the City*, a powerful urban drama chronicling an interracial friendship between army deserter John Cassavettes and dockworker Sidney Poitier. Ask him why MGM wanted a blacklisted director and Ritt can only explain, "I came cheap."

Edge established Ritt's eye for movie naturalism, his gift for getting the most out of his actors, his ear for urban rhythms, and his gut for issues. In this little-known but well-made drama, he developed the themes of working-class integrity, racial integration, and unionism that he would return to in subsequent films.

"The reviews for *Edge of the City* were very good, which suddenly made me a viable property. Then I got offered a contract at Twentieth Century Fox." He and Adele moved to Los Angeles, where the recently unemployable Ritt plunged into what would be thirty-two years of continuous employment.

"I came to Fox on a seven-year contract and was happy to get it!" he remembers. His first Fox assignment was *No Down Payment* (1957), a suburban soaper that marked his first film association with Joanne Woodward, one of Ritt's favorite actresses.

It was in his subsequent film, *The Long, Hot Summer* (1958), starring Woodward and Paul Newman, that he realized another of his priorities: evoking a vanishing Southern rural culture. "I would say that *Summer* was Hollywood's first regional story," observes Ritt of the genre that he established by shooting on location in Louisiana thereby allowing the film its distinctive local flavor.

Unlike most Hollywood directors, Ritt never exploits a locale for its pictorialness. Rather, the authenticity can be found in the actor's honeyed dialects, the slow-dripping rhythms of the editing, the sunlight particular to the area. In Ritt's films, the regional details are implicit, the characters explicit.

And what characters he had in *The Long, Hot Summer*, an amalgam of William Faulkner's short stories *Barn Burning* and *Spotted Horses*: Orson Welles as a Southern-fried patriarch, Woodward as his virginal magnolia of a daughter, and Newman as a drifter, the Faulknerian equivalent of gardener Oliver Mellors in *Lady Chatterley's Lover*. "Directing Welles was quite an experience," allows Ritt in obvious understatement. "Welles was the greatest director of films, but as an actor he was very theatrical."

Did this make it difficult for Ritt to maintain the texture of a film where the other two principals were Method actors? "It's not hard to direct some actors who are Method along with those who are not, if you know your way around," Ritt replies enigmatically, refusing to elaborate. "As a director of actors, I know what it's about, I know how to motivate."

The Long, Hot Summer was erotically charged, hugely successful, and established Paul Newman as a star. Ritt is frequently credited for Newman's acting evolution from the ersatz Brandoisms of *Somebody Up There Likes Me* to the tough softie he patented in *Summer*. But, of the actor whom he would later direct in *Paris Blues* (1961), *Hud* (1963), and *Hombre* (1967), Ritt will only say: "I know I helped, but I also know he did it fundamentally himself by making the most of his equipment."

One part of Ritt's personality you'll find in nearly every one of his films is an affection for marginal characters who care more about getting recognized as humans than beating the system. Surely this is what makes *Edge of the City*, *Sounder*, and *Norma Rae* so emotionally powerful and so unlike typical Hollywood products.

Ritt is quick to give credit to his scenarists. You can divide the director's career between those movies written by the husband-and-wife team of Irving Ravetch and Harriet Frank—apart from the Faulkner adaptations, they are

Hud, Hombre, Conrack, Norma Rae, Murphy's Romance, and *Stanley and Iris*—and those penned by other fine writers such as Lonnie Elder III (*Sounder*), Julius Epstein (*Pete 'n' Tillie*), and Walter Bernstein (*The Molly Maguires, The Front*).

"We've done eight films, the Ravetches and I, so we've developed a collaborative shorthand. We bat story ideas around, send each other material. The idea for *Norma Rae* came from a *Life* magazine article that I was sent and the Ravetches developed; *Stanley and Iris* came from a British working-class novel called *Union Street*. The only thing I can say about our professional marriage is that as we all get older, we agree less," quips Ritt.

Another part of Ritt's personality imprinted on his films is his commitment to laborers and labor unions. If you were to program a film series about Hollywood's view of workers, virtually every movie would be by Martin Ritt: *Edge of the City* deals with dockworkers and a corrupt foreman; *The Molly Maguires*, with coal miners organizing in western Pennsylvania in 1876; *The Front*, with blacklisted writers trying to make a living during the witch-hunt; and *Norma Rae*, with a union organizer in a Georgia textile mill.

"Nobody else cares that much about the subject of unionizing," Ritt admits. "I'm just naturally interested in the fight for something that nobody believes in—interested in it politically as well as cinematically." A union man from way back, Ritt sounds positively Tom Joady when he lists his affiliations. "Actor's Equity, the Screen Actor's Guild, the Director's Guild of America . . . wherever there's a union, I join."

"Along with unions, racial issues were always significant for me," says one of the few Hollywood directors who consistently directed movies about blacks, whether it was Sidney Poitier in *Edge of the City*, domestic Ethel Waters in *The Sound and the Fury*, jazzman Poitier in *Paris Blues*, tenant farmers Paul Winfield and Cicely Tyson in *Sounder*, or the barrier-island schoolchildren of *Conrack*. Occasionally attacked by those who say a white director can't direct a black film, Ritt shrugs that logic off with, "That's the worst kind of racism. If you believe that, you also have to say a black director can't direct white actors, and I don't believe that."

Why is Ritt virtually the only Hollywood director who has consistently addressed social problems? "Like my wife, they've always been around me," he jokes. "And besides, I only believe in making films that move me to tears or make me laugh to tears." His unusual comedy *Pete 'n' Tillie* (1972), cast with Walter Matthau and Carol Burnett as the offbeat love objects, did both.

His reputation for getting the most out of his actors, most of whom get Oscar nominations and some of whom—like Patricia Neal in *Hud* and Sally Field in *Norma Rae*—take home Oscars, helps him attract a stable of stars, which in turn gives his socially-conscious films market appeal. "My relations with actors have always been good enough to get them to do things they wouldn't do otherwise," he says.

When he's not making movies, Ritt is busy at the racetrack. He is known by most racetrack habitués as "the best handicapper in the business." Wags dub Ritt and his sometime star Walter Matthau "The Odds Couple," for if Ritt is the best handicapper, Matthau is by common consensus the worst. (Their obsession was satirized in Ritt's lackluster comedy *Casey's Shadow*.)

Ask Ritt what distinguishes him from the other directors in his generation, and he takes an actorly pause.

"I'm still alive."

True Ritt

JULIA CAMERON / 1989

IT IS FOUR O'CLOCK in the afternoon in a damp, chilly garage in Toronto, Canada. Director Martin Ritt, one baleful eye on his watch, is doing his job. Since he is still hoping to catch an outdoor shot before they lose the light, his job right now is to push.

Between setups, Ritt asks, "How long on this change? Ten minutes?" Pause. "Is that 10 *real* minutes or 10 of the other kind?" The crew gets the point.

At 75, director Martin Ritt resembles a sharpei dog. His great rumpled face, set crease on crease between outsize ears, looks like the mug that it is. His eyes are lively—quick and instantly judgmental—but not without humor.

A short, squat man who looks much larger, Ritt styles himself a member of the working class. His couture owes more to grease monkey than clotheshorse. His trademark jumpsuits run to seersucker stripes in navy or muddy-pond brown self-belted, baggy, they look like overgrown Oshkosh kids' clothes. It's appropriate gear.

When Ritt works on a movie, he is half kid, half grease monkey and *all* business. Relaxed and relentless, he's a veteran who has learned to pace himself and a crew. There is no wasted motion.

To him, moviemaking is a job and a damn good job, "the only one I ever wanted."

Good thing he's damn good at it.

Originally published in *American Film* (November 1989): 42–48. Reprinted by permission of the American Film Institute.

Although less famous than many younger, showier talents, Martin Ritt has worked far more consistently than most American directors. This fact is particularly interesting given his political leanings: ruggedly leftist.

Blacklisted from television in the '50s, he was able to keep working in the theater, which saved his sanity ("that and a love of the horses and an understanding wife"). The blacklist wound down as his film career wound up, but Ritt still has a quiet rage at being denied the right to work at his trade.

Given the shadowboxing involved in studio politics and his own outspoken politics, he is more than lucky. He's downright blessed. Ritt's gratitude is understandable. So is his mirth. "I couldn't believe they let me make *The Front*," he chortles. (Ritt's angry film dealing with blacklisting could once have been blacklisted itself. He may have called it *The Front*, but it is a movie about backstabbing, a skewering of McCarthy-era hypocrisy.)

Ritt is an old-style radical, endowed with a strong and determined social conscience. His movies show it. While they are seldom inflammatory or "on the money" about a hot issue, they often make statements through character development and casting that showier *issue* movies merely exploit.

Edge of the City, Ritt's first feature, centers on a black-white friendship. John Cassavetes plays an army deserter, an edgy, driven and ultimately destructive man who is befriended by Sidney Poitier, a steadier, hardworking dockhand. With the roles and personality traits reversed, the movie would have been far more conventional—and far less revolutionary.

First and foremost, Ritt's movies are about people. These people, not coincidentally, are caught up in the issues that fire Ritt's social conscience, but the issues generally take a backseat to the people. As a result, Ritt's work is *quietly* revolutionary.

Consider *Hud*. It is not only Paul Newman's and Patricia Neal's performances that are breakthroughs. It is the whole blue-collar, sweat-soaked, musky atmosphere of the piece which was a breakthrough. Ordinarily, when Hollywood turns to the "lower classes," the scent of slumming rises from the films like cheap perfume. The filmmakers are all too apparently taking a "walk on the wild side."

Not so Ritt. He never distances himself from his material with the obtrusive camera work that announces of the director: "I am an artist examining this milieu." Instead, his hand is invisible. We do not glimpse a foreign world, but rather we inhabit it. This holds true film after film.

In this chilly Canadian garage, Ritt is at it again.

The garage is the natural habitat of Stanley, hero of *Stanley and Iris*, a blue-collar film about illiteracy. Stanley is played by Robert De Niro, Iris by Jane Fonda.

Question: Why would two stars of such voltage choose to make a small, quiet movie about love amid the ruins of the working class?

Answer: Martin Ritt.

"Let the actors act" is the unspoken motto behind Ritt's quiet hand. Not for him the jerk to sudden close-up that says, "Get it?" Instead, there is a moderation in his filmmaking technique that allows the actor to achieve effects through acting instead of the director achieving effects through showy shooting or clever cutting.

Ironically, this respect for the actor's craft may have gained Ritt some of his best performances while costing him a more estimable reputation of his own.

Because he does not sign his films visually, Ritt has become an anomaly: One of the most productive and accomplished American directors, he has nonetheless remained far more anonymous than his body of work would merit or suggest.

"A worker among workers," not to mention a veteran of the estimable Group Theatre, Ritt has preferred to let the projects and their ensemble members shine rather than doing a star turn himself. It is not the case—as is sometimes naively suggested—that he has no visible aesthetic. It is his aesthetic to remain invisible.

Take the matter of lighting. Ritt lights with a quiet, relatively even hand. He eschews the drama of high-contrast lighting in favor of the drama of the drama itself. To him, this means naturalistic acting in naturalistic light. This choice costs him the easy score of immediate visual impact and aims for the long ball of emotional impact.

Actors love Ritt for this. Because he respects their craft, they have aided and abetted his. One secret to his productivity is the willingness of great stars to work for a director who can help them be still greater ones. As a result, Ritt's repeating ensemble includes some of the biggest names in the business.

This is a man whom actors like and trust. An actor, wanting to expand his craft or hone it, is apt to turn to Ritt with some relief. And so, megastars Fonda and De Niro are shivering their way through a no-frills-just-chills shoot. But let's get to the plot before the thickening.

Travis Bickle was a cosmopolitan lady's man compared to Stanley. As De

Niro manifests him, Stanley does not so much define bachelorhood at its worst as refine it into a whole new category.

Just look at his digs. There's your drab cot. Your drab shirts hung on a pole. Your entire drab bachelor life style with the bloom off the rose . . . until Stanley meets Iris.

Iris does not so much enter Stanley's life as invade it. (Like most permanent bachelors, Stanley has drawn the line . . . and he lives behind it.) Stepping where angels fear to tread, as Fonda herself always has, Iris enters the *sanctum sanctorum* of Stanley's cave. That's the scene of the day. It's a good scene.

Iris takes in the masculine impoverishment of the "room" and notes that stubborn Stanley makes no apologies for himself or his environment. Why should he? Domestic aesthetics are not his bailiwick. He is an inventor, not an interior decorator.

Located smack in the middle of Stanley's cave is a culinary contraption aimed at rendering burned and underdone cookies a thing of the past; Stanley has devised a cookie tree that will abolish uneven baking by its gradual rotations.

A baker herself, Iris is impressed. Quite impressed. But Stanley is not auditioning for this damn woman. Women . . . who needs them? True to his closed-mouthed code, he shows no emotion. He acts like a rat—a very well-acted rat—but a rat.

It's a good scene, and Ritt aims to make it a great one. Hunched over the end of Stanley's workbench, he tinkers with it the way Stanley tinkers with one of his gadgets.

"I want the machine whirling. I want the steam. I want Jane. I want a couple of angles. Right, right. Where are you going to crop?" (this last to Australian director of photography Don McAlpine).

"OK . . . right. But I want the left hand in."

A stickler for realism, even in romance, Ritt doesn't go in for the prettification of factory life to fit Dream Factory images. Let Taylor Hackford stage love scenes where the hero, dressed in white, swoops into the filthy factory and sweeps the heroine off her feet. Love in Ritt's terms starts more quietly: as a click behind the eyes. That's the click he wants from Fonda now. Quiet on the set.

"Ready?" Ritt asks.

"Ready," Fonda nods. Ritt signals action. Fonda is to take in Stanley and his invention, then . . . click.

As the camera rolls, Fonda's face registers a fluid mix of wonder, sorrow and tenderness. Click. She's found her man. Any woman would see herself in this archetypical female response to such heartbreakingly male self-sufficiency. Men! Can't live with them and they can't live without us!

"What about a couple of glances toward Our Man?" McAlpine asks. It's more on the money than what Ritt had in mind, but he listens carefully before nixing the idea.

"Sorry, Marty, we're out of steam," interrupts crack first AD Jim Van Wyck. Ritt grimaces.

"Exactly five minutes and 40 seconds to get it back up," Van Wyck promises.

Ritt puts a hand over his eyes.

"The Thinker," Fonda jests.

Ritt looks up. "Print that first one. When we get steam, we'll go ahead right away."

This time there's no chatting as Fonda and the machine both gather steam.

"Ready? Steam? Let's go!" Ritt wants to get the shot.

They go again. Fonda is brilliant. Ritt is pleased. They move on.

With the skewed logic that makes the movies, Ritt has needed to film Fonda's reaction shot prior to filming the De Niro action that cued it. McAlpine will now light for the master shot, the bassackwards of logic.

A movie kid long before she was a movie star, Fonda is at home on the set. Between setups, she chats with technicians and wardrobe people like the trooper that she is—"That's nice, what you did with your hair. . . ." She knows that good morale makes for good films. She's been a producer herself.

De Niro, the consummate professional when the camera rolls, prefers to hold a certain reserve between takes. He doesn't want anything to split his focus. This unremitting concentration can make for a certain edginess in those around him.

"Why are we *whispering*?" waggish stagehands have been known to whisper on De Niro shoots.

Taxi Driver's most famous sequence—"You talkin' to me?"—began as an inspired improvisation. The joke is that if De Niro was talking to anybody, it was to himself. Unlike Fonda, he does not make small talk. In fact, even normal conversation seems to be miniaturized into trivia by his single focus: *nothing personal.*

Fonda has no problem with rehearsals. In fact, she likes them. She likes to stretch and loosen up between innings. She enjoys a game of catch, hitting a few practice flies. In this, De Niro does not play ball. "Don't worry. It will be there," he once assured her.

Among actors and directors, acting is often talked about as a game of catch. There is no such thing as a great line reading unless it is also a great catch for the line preceding it and a good toss to set up the actor who must follow it. Acting is all about connecting. Catch the ball; get it in the right ballpark when you toss it back.

For any director, it is always a balancing act. Actor A likes rehearsals. Actor B hates them. Actor A is red hot after five takes. Actor B starts at a boil but cools off further with every single roll.

How do you mix and match?

"I never like any of them to get comfortable," Ritt mumbles. "I like to keep them all a little off-center. It makes the work better. If you do take after take, they just get worse. . . . You ready yet?"

(Sometimes Ritt-the-producer eggs on Ritt-the-director. Especially when someone is asking pesky questions.)

The crew is ready. The set is lit for De Niro's master.

"Send in Robert," comes the crisp directive from Ritt.

"They're on their way in. De Niro's coming in," comes the instant response via walkie-talkie.

Outside the garage, a relay of crew members stands sentinel along the hillside that is passing for a small industrial New England town. Today, the glorious Canadian maples are standing in for glorious New England maples. The stalwart saltbox houses climbing the quiet residential hill are passing muster as American workers' homes. The big white movie trucks along the curb look like American movie trucks—just cleaner, like all of Canada.

De Niro emerges from a truck and heads uphill toward the garage. He walks head down, hands plunged deep in his pockets. Except for his (now) salt-and-pepper hair, he could be the same shy, pixilated Travis Bickle on date night that he was 13 years ago in *Taxi Driver*. This is not a star who is easy with his celebrity. This is not a star who is easy with much of anything.

An actor whose core is solitary, De Niro is a profoundly physical actor, connecting best with things, not people, finding in the act of physical contact with objects a spark of connection that the camera records as truth.

"It is a perfect part for him," Ritt volunteers, noting that Stanley-the-inventor demands a great deal of the detailed physical action De Niro excels at.

"He likes to have something to *do*," Ritt understates.

De Niro arrives and goes straight to Stanley's invention. He is looking for a small, precise action, a "thing to do."

De Niro sets to work, talking under his breath, half to himself and half to Ritt: "So, let's see, let's see. Is it going to be a problem if I do this? So . . . so . . . I don't do this? Gonna be a problem my doing this? Ah, this is a problem. As long as I stay in? . . . OK, OK, I got it."

Quickly and methodically, with fierce determination, De Niro is filling in the scene, making it indelibly his—and Stanley's. For De Niro, concentration is everything. Each roll of the camera is a roll of the dice. He eschews rehearsals, feeling they dull his edge. He likes the added adrenaline of shooting from the hip.

Ritt lets De Niro find his beats. He gives him time but not leisure. When De Niro nods readiness, Ritt signals "roll camera."

"One hundred-sixty Mary, take one," intones the first camera assistant, smacking together the striped sticks.

As the camera rolls, Robert De Niro rolls the dice.

"In the side door, then down some stairs to the church basement. You'll find it. . . ."

The directions are for crew lunch, not an Alcoholics Anonymous meeting, but the space and goal are the same: Some soul food to help cope with an addiction.

In some circles, moviemaking is elevated to an art form—just like ritzy boozing—but its heart remains the same: the intoxicating dream of creating an alternative reality scripted as you see fit. And so, yes, the AA comparison is appropriate.

"Matter of fact, they do hold those meetings here," a Toronto crew member antes up. "What they don't hold is those Overeaters meetings!"

Good point. The trestle tables are high-calorie glories, incongruously presided over by a wasp-waisted beauty. "No doubting her gender, is there?" Ritt jokes.

The food, however, is no laughing matter to him: creamed, not steamed; buttered and battered; sautéed and sauced....

"I am a full-blown diabetic," Ritt announces, not without defiant pride. It's as though he's staking out turf: I ate like a horse, or at least a man, and I've got the disease to prove it! This remark is accompanied by a sidelong glance to his wife, Adele, who has traveled to location with him. She doesn't bite, just listens. Ritt cares for his health seriously now—and deeply resents doing it.

Ritt does not so much watch his diet as glare at it. Heaven help the salad with oil, the vegetable with butter, the dessert with hidden fats. Movie food is traditionally stultifying. The whole point of a trestle table of doughnuts is to bribe a crew into sufficient sugar stupor to artificially ignore fatigue. In fact, the food served on *Stanley and Iris* looks, for movie food, healthier than usual. That is real fruit. Those are recognizable vegetables.

"It's still got stuff on it," Ritt growls. "There's butter on those beans."

"Butter on those beans" comes out as a blistering indictment. Gravel-throated, Ritt's rasp is the kind of voice that can be seen as well as heard. Martin Ritt, director, owes part of his efficacy to Martin Ritt, actor. Not for nothing did he act in more than 150 episodes of vintage CBS TV.

True, most directors are actors and certainly characters. Their hyperbolic certainty and dread posturing around "questions of artistic integrity" whenever their will is crossed can routinely be Oscar-level performances. Still, Ritt is an actor among actors. Nurtured in the early moment-to-moment truth of the Method, he has never lost touch with the importance of honesty in acting. He brings to his role as director his own full bag of actor's tricks.

In 1943 and '44, Ritt acted under George Cukor's direction in *Winged Victory*. By '46, he was back in New York and a director himself.

1948 brought Ritt to CBS TV to both act and direct. His career flourished until 1951, when a Syracuse grocer fingered Ritt like a rotten apple for his political sympathies.

Nearly 40 years later, sitting in a Canadian church basement, disgruntled by lunch, the mere mention of blacklisting turns his stomach sour.

"It was bad," he says dourly. He glances toward his wife. *"Bad."*

How did he survive it emotionally?

A second quick glance to his wife. "With some difficulty."

But how?

"The racetrack and a very understanding wife." Ritt laughs. "I am a sports enthusiast." This is true, but make no mistake, he is not talking athletic aesthetics. He is talking about stress relief via an alternative addiction.

A director who is not directing is a miserable creature. Most of them should be given small countries to run—and not peaceful ones, either.

Akira Kurosawa, so "American" he was out of favor with Japanese financing people, created 400 paintings to approximate *Ran*, until he could shoot it. Billy Wilder turned his visual obsession into art connoisseurship. Ritt considers himself lucky to have been able to make his movies instead of turning to origami "or the bottle."

Speaking of horses, Ritt enjoys the analogy that directors as animals are very much like show jumpers—those crazy horses that are only happy when they are trying to leap something high enough to kill them.

"That's us." Like many directors, he enjoys a good, solid, adrenaline high.

Ritt is a man's man. Sports, sex and the concept of appetite in general pervade his conversation. He is an earthy man. When he talks about working with actors, he puts it colorfully, to say the least.

"They're all different," he says. "Just like women. Just as, when you are a young man and have a healthy appetite, you do not approach each woman in the same way, as a director, you approach each actor according to what will work in each case."

That he has just described direction as seduction doesn't phase Ritt in the least. He is a pragmatist and a plain-spoken man. He knows that the "art of direction" is quite often the "art of manipulation," which boils down to seducing someone to *act* the way he wants.

"It's an interesting thing," he ruminates, interested himself. "There are a lot of great actors who are not, never will be, *movie stars*. Want to know what makes a movie star? It's *fuckability*. It's having what I call a high fuckability quotient. Without that, no matter how good you are, you'll never be a movie star.

"Take Marilyn," he continues. "Now, I never thought much of her acting. But when she came into a room, the men came to attention—know what I mean?"

Yes.

"That's what it takes to be a movie star."

Ritt says "movie star" with an extra ounce of reverb, as though he's reading it off a mental marquee. He is talking cultural archetype.

"An awful lot of young people will go see young Cruise in anything. He's become a genuine *movie star*."

Ritt's appetite for life, for work and even for food are still very much with him. Ritt is ruminating on the business, and it is ruining his digestion.

"I saw that new Eddie Murphy movie," he says dyspeptically. "You know, in the old days, you couldn't do a really *bad* play. Oh, once in a while, one crept through, but so many bad films get through!"

"I enjoy being able to travel with him," Adele says of her peripatetic life with her husband, "now that the children are gone."

The children are not *quite* gone, however—although Ritt would bristle at any hint that he is now sulking over his dessert deprivation. Like most directors, this is not a man who takes easily to a "no." "What about that thing you made the other day," he badgers the caterer. "It was kind of crispy and had chocolate, and it sort of crunched. That wasn't too bad, was it?"

(Ritt is describing every two-year-old's favorite, Rice Krispies surprise. When the caterer tells him as much, he's chagrined—but briefly.)

"I don't know how a serious young filmmaker can make it today," he declares dourly. "I don't know how they can do it."

Do what? Keep the faith?

The phrase "keep the faith" elicits a small, wry smile—*wince* might be a better word. Ritt's faith in the movie business has long since been lost—unless you believe, as all true believers do, that doubt is an essential tenet of faith.

Ritt goes on, "I saw a good, well-made, serious movie last year. *Orphans*. It was really good. Know what it did? *Nothing*. I didn't think it stayed open two weeks. Know what *Cocktail* did?—$80 million. I'll settle for that."

If he would really settle for that, why not make something more commercial than a movie about illiteracy among bakery workers?

"Nobody knows what's commercial," Ritt says—actually growls.

As Ritt well knows, what he's just said is true and not true. He amends himself.

"Spending a year on a bad picture strikes me like spending a year with a hooker who's a bad piece of ass," Ritt says between low-cholesterol mouthfuls.

By nature expansive and forward-looking. Ritt regards younger filmmakers with a fatherly concern. The young bucks do not threaten this old bull. On the contrary, he sees himself in the best of them.

A born gambler, Ritt nonetheless dislikes the box-office odds these days. Long odds are one thing, rigged races are another. "With the two people I've got, I might have a shot," he ventures. "He's very good in this picture."

"He" is De Niro.

Ritt chuckles. "I don't know De Niro that well, but I like him. He's an actor to the core. I asked him what he was going to do with his downtime in New York, and he said, 'Party.' That's an actor for you."

Now that the conversation has come around to acting, Ritt visibly brightens. Ritt's got a theory about casting actors. He's expounded it before, so there is now a recognizable Marty Ritt monologue: "The Vein of Gold."

Holding his hands wide apart so they create a channel in midair, Ritt explains. "It is very hard to lie to a camera. It cannot see what isn't there, and it does see what really is. You can't fool it about your true nature for very long. If you're doing something very stylized, like a restoration comedy, you can deflect it briefly, but not for long. Now, every actor has a vein of gold. . . ."

Ritt jigs his hands. The hands indicate the vein of gold.

"When you cast an actor in his vein of gold, he will be terrific, always terrific. With craft, he can add something to his territory on either side. . . ." Ritt moves his hands an inch or two further apart. "But you can't move too far. You must always try to cast within that vein of gold."

Take the casting of Sally Field in *Norma Rae*. Prior to her tutelage with Ritt, Field was regarded as a light comedienne of some merit who had turned in some very nice dramatic work on television and was just beginning to make a name for herself in films. Under Ritt's guidance, she became *Norma Rae*. The part fit her like a (work) glove. "I wanted a kind of mutt. A very attractive girl, but not beautiful in a movie way. She had to be feisty and fierce. When Sally talked to me about her kids, I saw that she had that in her. And Sally's a worker."

When Ritt uses the word *worker* or *pro* to describe someone, it is shorthand for a larger compliment. Field is a worker. Fonda is a pro. Both women do something Marty Ritt approves of. They work.

Work is central to Ritt's personal ethos. *Work* is even central to his work.

"I don't have a lot of respect for talent, Ritt grumbles. "Talent is genetic. It's what you do with it that counts.

"Dessert?" he asks his wife plaintively. She doesn't say "no" but she doesn't need to say it. That half-acre of desserts will just have to be ignored

... another grueling day and another day of gruel. "The lentil soup's good," he notes reluctantly.

Neatly disproving the popular theory that participants in a long-running marriage grow to resemble each other, Martin Ritt and Adele, his wife of four decades, resemble not each other, but two highly individuated characters from a medieval stone frieze. She is the traditional bird figure: quick-eyed and quick witted, the vessel of feminine intelligence that misses nothing and cuts straight to the quick Ritt himself is the male beast: half mastiff, half lion, bristling and brindled as a Paleolithic pit bull.

Adele Ritt excuses herself. Her husband grumbles after her—fondly: "That crispy thing was good."

What about some more talk about his art.

"Art?" Ritt enjoys making a reading that makes it sound like *Art* is someone his sister dated. "What can I tell you?" he asks. He gets to his feet.

"Art?" (An even broader reading.) "You just do it."

That's all? No further ... thoughts?

"Cerebration is the enemy of originality in art."

Back to the set.

INDEX

Actors Committee, 131
Actor's Studio, 3, 4, 32, 50, 61, 63, 65, 116, 121, 138, 150, 160, 165
Adams, Don, 55
Adler, Luther "Buddy," 56, 122, 132, 152–53
Adler, Stella, 56, 126, 127–28, 138, 188
Aldrich, Bob, 40
Alger, Horatio, 10
Allen, Woody, 24, 26, 57, 67, 96, 177
Alonzo, John, 31, 58, 79, 146, 183
Altman, Robert, 50, 117; *Streamers*, 113
American Graffiti, 24
Anderson, Max, 98
Armstrong, Louis, 170
Aurthur, Robert Alan, 110; *A Very Special Baby*, 57
Awake and Sing!, 86, 124, 133, 140, 141

Bakker, Jim, 184
Balzac, Honoré de, 139
Barn Burning, 191
Barry, Philip, 161
Battle of Algiers, The, 119
Beethoven, Ludwig van, 9
Behrman, S. N., 161
Belafonte, Harry, 37, 40
Belasco Theatre, 123, 138, 152

Bennett, Richard, 141
Bergman, Ingmar, 176, 177
Bernstein, Walter, 34, 41, 46, 57, 60, 100, 113, 134, 163, 181, 192
Bertolucci, Bernardo, 55
Bickle, Travis, 196, 199
Black Belt Jones, 21
Blacklist period, 34–37, 53, 54, 95, 96, 99–100, 110–13, 132, 137, 153, 181, 189–90, 195
Blitzstein, Marc, *The Cradle Will Rock*, 167
Bloom, Claire, 172
Bludorn, 41–42
Bogdanovich, Peter, 27
Bohnen, Bud, 133
Boy Meets Girl, 151
Brando, Marlon, 140, 145
Bratsburg, Henry Morgan, 123, 153
Brecht, Bertolt, 135
Bromberg, Joe, 132, 136, 137
Brown, Clarence, 116
Brun, Joseph, 163
Brynner, Yul, 4
Buckley, William F., 161–62
Burnett, Carol, 192
Burton, Richard, 53, 58, 61, 63, 145, 172
Bustin' Loose, 79
Butch Cassidy and the Sundance Kid, 33, 48

Canby, 48
Carlyle, Brooke, 71
Carnovsky, Morris, 128, 129, 131, 188
Casals, Pablo, 161
Cassavetes, John, 15, 57–58, 63, 96, 186, 189, 190, 195
Cat on a Hot Tin Roof, 166
Cates, Gil, 152
Cather, Willa, 97, 98, 158
Chaplin, Charlie, 59
Chayevsky, Paddy, *Marty*, 99
Cheever, John, 98
Chekhov, Anton, 124
Chodorov, Edward, *Oh Men! Oh Women!*, 164
Chosen, The, 85
Cheyenne Autumn, 175
Cimino, Michael, 55
Citizen Kane, 167
Civil War, 40
Clark, Susan, 51–52
Clarke, Arthur, *Childhood's End*, 40
Clayburgh, Jill, 55
Close Encounters of the Third Kind, 129
Clurman, Harold, 56, 121, 122–24, 127–28, 133, 141, 150, 152, 156
Cobb, Lee J., 56, 144
Cocktail, 203
Cohn, Harry, 154
Cold War, 99
Colman, Ronald, 74
Color of Money, The, 179
Communist Party, 91, 130, 136, 161–62
Conformist, The, 55
Connery, Sean, 68, 89, 90, 173
Conroy, Pat, 27
Conway, Curt, 139
Cooper, Gary, 74
Coppola, Francis Ford, 24, 179
Cosby, Bill, 101
Coyote, Peter, 63
Cronkite, Walter, 34
Cronyn, Hume, 22

Cruise, Tom, 179, 203
Cukor, George, 156, 188–89, 201

Da Silva, Howard, 35
Danger, 134, 159, 189
Davis, Donald, 109, 133, 159
Davis, Owen, 109
De Kooning, Willem, 188
De Laurentiis, Dino, 54
De Wilde, Brandon, 169
Dean, Jimmy, 140
Death of a Salesman, 8
Deer Hunter, The, 55
Deering, Olive, 134
DeNiro, Robert, 179, 186, 196–200, 204
Derek, Bo, 154
DeVore, Gary, 61
Diller, Barry, 80
Douglas, Kirk, 179
Douglas, Melvyn, 53, 65, 169

Eisenhower, Dwight, 135
Elder, Lonnie, 192; "Ceremonies in Dark Old Men," 72
Ellington, Duke, 170
Elon College, 56, 69, 148, 187
Epstein, Julius, 192
E.T., 129
Exorcist, The, 18

Falwell, Jerry, 184
Farmer, Frances, 125–26, 153
Fast, Howard, 176
Faulkner, William, 4, 5, 115–16, 166, 191
Fellini, Federico, 5, 176, 177
Ferrer, Joe, 142
Field, Sally, 61, 62, 64–65, 71, 87, 94, 96, 100–01, 106, 115, 143, 144, 145, 183, 193, 204
Fifth Season, The, 142
Finney, Albert, 43
Fitzgerald, F. Scott, 33
Flowering Peach, The, 109, 141, 190
Fonda, Jane, 169, 186, 196–99, 204

INDEX   209

Force of Evil, 37, 39, 48
Ford, John, 139, 175–76
Franciosa, Tony, 165, 166
Frankenheimer, John, 189
Friedkin, Billy, 18, 43

Gable, Clark, 66, 168
Garfield, John, 48, 95, 122, 137, 152, 153, 188
Garfield, Jules, 136, 153
Garner, James, 71, 96, 101, 106, 144, 145
Genet, The Blacks, 21
Gentle People, The, 156
Gish, Dorothy, 158
Gladiators, The, 4
Glick, Sammy, 165
Golden Boy, 56, 63, 95, 122, 125, 136, 138, 149, 152, 154, 156, 160
Goldwyn, Sam, 92
Grand Central Station, 97, 158
Grapes of Wrath, The, 139, 175–76
Great Gatsby, The, 33
Green Berets, 19
Group Theatre, 65, 99, 105, 116, 121, 122–28, 130, 131, 132, 133, 135, 136, 138, 139, 140, 142–43, 145, 149, 150, 151, 154, 155, 156, 161, 188, 189, 190, 196
Guston, Philip, 188
Guthrie, Tyrone, 49

Hackford, Taylor, 197
Hall, Conrad, 40, 51
Hamlet, 73, 143
Harris, Julie, 161
Harris, Richard, 42, 58, 89, 90, 180
Hathaway, Henry, 166, 176
Hellinger, Mark, 134
Hellman, Lillian, 98, 161
Hemingway, Ernest, 31, 98, 158
Henry V, 20
Hill, George Roy, 128
Hill Street Blues, 101
Hodern, Michael, 172
Hoffman, Dustin, 84, 157

Hollywood, 35, 38–39, 63, 154
Hook, Robert, 73
Hooks, Ken, 11
Hooks, Kevin, 146
Hope, Bob, 66–67
House Committee on Un-American Activities, 57, 91, 109, 110, 135, 188
Howard, Sidney, 157, 161, 189
Howe, James Wong, 58, 60, 163, 170–72, 175
Huston, John, 117, 174

Ibsen, Henrik, 124
Intruder in the Dust, 116
Iron Petticoat, The, 66

James, Henry, 23
Jarnegan, 141
Jewison, Norman, 113
Jones, James Earl, 58, 63, 81, 84, 181
Jones, Preston, 173

Kael, Pauline, 46
Kanter, Jay, 135, 164
Kazan, Elia "Gadge," 5, 56, 105, 112, 122, 125, 128–29, 130, 131, 132, 138, 149, 150–51, 154, 156, 160, 188, 190
Keaton, Diane, 94
Kelly, Gene, 32, 36
Kerwin, Brian, 96, 101
Koestler, Arthur, 4
Kramer, Stanley, 120
Kroger, Tony, 146
Kubrick, Stanley, 29
Kurosawa, Akira, 202

Lady Chatterley's Lover, 191
Landau, Mr., 20
Lang, Jennings, 39, 40
Lashelle, Joe, 165
Lasorda, Tommy, 158
Last Picture Show, The, 27
Lean, David, A Passage to India, 81
Lee, Will, 124, 125, 126, 133, 138, 142, 153

Left-militant Group Theatre, 56
Lewis, John L., 43
Lloyd, Norman, 129
Loren, Sophia, 167
Losey, Joe, 38
Lucas, George, 68
Lumet, Sidney, 97, 134, 186, 189
Luna, 55

Maddow, Ben, 116
Madigan, 38
Madison Square Garden, 99
Malden, Karl, 123, 152, 153
Mann, Delbert, 189
Manoff, Arnold, 34, 134
Mantle, Burns, 140
Mario and the Magician, 43
Marshall, George C., 135
Martin, Ross, 55
Marx, Karl, 92, 144
Matthau, Walter, 157, 192, 193
Mayes, Wendell, 62
Mean Streets, 29
Meese, Ed, 110
Mellors, Oliver, 191
Mercury Theater, 188
Merrill, Gary, 167
Miller, Arthur, 3, 5, 86, 91, 98, 136, 160, 161, 174
Monroe, Marilyn, 202
Moscow Art Theatre, 130
Mostel, Zero, 91, 100, 113, 131, 160
Mozart, Wolfgang Amadeus, 11
Mulligan, Robert, 97, 189
Murphy, Eddie, 75, 180–81, 203
McAlpine, Don, 197, 198
McCambridge, Mercedes, 167
McCarthy, Joseph, 25, 29, 100, 111, 135
McCarthy, Mary, 162
McCarthy period, 17, 24, 37, 91–92, 96, 129, 130, 133, 153, 160, 188, 195
McMurtry, Larry, 14, 26, 65, 168

Neal, Patricia, 15, 33, 53, 61, 65, 168–69 189, 193, 195
New York, 29, 34, 47, 56, 57, 66, 67, 86, 95, 110, 115, 123, 148–49
New York Times, 48, 87, 116, 131, 132, 156
Newman, Paul, 12, 14, 15, 22, 29–30, 32, 33, 38, 48, 53, 58, 61, 63, 65, 84, 115, 140, 143, 144, 145, 146, 161, 165, 168, 169, 174–75, 179, 191, 195
Newsweek, 33
Nicholson, Jack, 145
Night Music, 126, 154
North, Oliver, 154, 173–74, 185

Odets, Clifford, 56, 63, 86, 95, 109, 124, 126, 128, 129, 131, 132, 133, 141–42, 152, 154, 156, 161, 188, 190
Office of Strategic Services (OSS), 38
Olivier, Laurence, 20, 49, 61, 145
Outrageous, 46

Paper Box Kid, The, 97, 134, 189
Penn, Arthur, 98, 189
Petrie, Dan, 109, 134
Pierson, Frank, 62
Poitier, Sidney, 4, 9, 15, 57, 63, 81–82, 96, 186, 189, 190, 192, 195
Polonsky, Abraham, 34–52, 62, 134
Pryor, Richard, 75, 79

Quinn, Anthony, 167

Rackin, Marty, 168
Radnitz, Robert, 72, 80, 89
Rainbow Group, 80
Ran, 202
Rashomon, 35, 170
Ravetch, Irving, and Harriet Frank, Jr., 15, 27–28, 60, 61, 65, 66, 115, 116, 164, 168, 169, 175, 181–82, 191–92
Rawlings, Marjorie Kinnan, 63, 187
Ray, Nick, 188
Ray, Satyajit, 107

Reagan, Ronald, 75, 110, 149
Red Channels, 137, 189
Red Scare, 99
Redford, Robert, 33, 40, 51–52, 84
Remick, Lee, 124, 125, 126, 133, 138, 142, 161, 165
Renoir, Jean, 59, 129
Rhinoceros, 131
Rice, Elmer, 98, 161
Risky Business, 68
Ritt, Adele Cutler, 59, 95, 109, 136, 190, 201, 204–05
Ritt, Martin: on acting, 16, 60–61, 116–17; on adapting plays, 20; on the American filmmaker, 44, 177; on appetite, 145, 146; on being blacklisted, 56–57, 62, 67, 91–92, 99, 108–09, 159–60, 195, 201; on being Jewish, 85–86; on the black experience, 72, 75, 77, 84, 114–15, 180; on Broadway, 3, 56, 57, 63, 95, 96, 158; on capitalism, 117; on casting, 15, 49, 59–60, 63, 64, 72–73, 93–94, 143, 145, 174; on cinematographers, 31, 60, 163, 165, 171; on commercial success, 22–23; on the creative process, 6–7; on critics, 46–48, 152, 177; as a dancer, 32, 34, 36; on directing, 83, 149; on the editing process, 28, 82; on education, 187, 188; on feminism, 115; on filmmaking, 19, 83, 176–77, 182, 183–84, 194; on first films, 23–24; on going on location, 29, 69–70; on Hollywood, 4, 96, 108, 110, 117; on horses, 42, 55–56, 202; on the human condition, 36, 37, 59, 107; on the labor movement, 88, 115; on novels, 22; on period films, 28–29; on political films, 68, 92, 118–19; on politics, 7, 117; on post-production, 26; on preparation, 17–18; on racism, 75, 192; on regional theater, 173; on rehearsal, 30; on religion, 184–85; rural films, 115, 144, 191; on scriptwriting, 27–28, 60, 182; on serious films, 25, 93, 117–18; on social commitment, 78; on the South, 69; on storyboarding, 18; on suicide, 24; on survival, 36–37, 62; on talent, 156; on teaching, 145; on television, 56, 66, 82–83, 95, 96–99, 101–04, 158–59, 189; on unions, 80, 88; on unity of opposites, 14, 32; on video technology, 108; on writers, 65, 119, 181–82

Works: *The Black Orchid*, 167; *The Brotherhood*, 179; *Casey's Shadow*, 113, 193; *Conrack*, 6, 7–14, 15, 19, 21, 22, 27, 28, 42, 53, 58, 60, 64, 69, 76, 113, 114, 180, 188, 192; *Cross Creek*, 63, 64, 69, 78, 95, 115, 146, 183, 187; *Edge of the City*, 3, 4, 15, 57–58, 63, 66, 82, 96, 109, 110, 134, 135, 167, 186, 187, 190, 191, 192, 195; *First Blood*, 17, 18–19, 23, 31, 32; *Five Branded Women*, 53–54, 62; *The Front*, 26, 34, 42, 46, 53, 57, 58, 60, 67, 90–91, 93, 95, 96, 100, 103, 113, 133, 150, 163, 173, 181, 186, 192, 195; *The Great White Hope*, 21, 53, 58, 63, 81, 82, 180; *Hemingway's Adventures of a Young Man*, 31, 187; *Hombre*, 27, 29–30, 33, 58, 60, 61, 63, 115, 144, 174, 175, 178, 191, 192; *Hud*, 12–15, 17, 27, 28, 37, 53, 60, 61, 63, 65–66, 84, 95, 113, 144, 167–68, 170, 186, 191, 192, 193, 195; *The Long, Hot Summer*, 3, 4, 5, 27, 58, 61, 63, 95, 115, 132, 144, 164–65, 167, 168, 175, 186, 187, 191; *The Man*, 3; *The Molly Maguires*, 16, 21, 26, 41–42, 58–59, 60, 63, 67–68, 81, 89–90, 93, 95, 113, 163, 171, 173, 180, 192; *Mr. Peebles and Mr. Hooker*, 3, 158; *Murphy's Romance*, 71, 95, 96, 100, 106, 115, 144, 155, 192; *No Down Payment*, 3, 5, 163, 164, 165, 190; *Norma Rae*, 53, 54, 59, 60, 61, 63, 64, 67, 68, 69, 82, 84, 87–88, 92, 93–94, 95, 106, 113, 115, 116, 155, 169, 178, 182–83, 191, 192, 193, 204; *Nuts*, 152; *The Outrage*, 170, 172; *Paris Blues*, 58, 60, 170, 191, 192; *Pete 'n' Tillie*, 192; *Set My People Free*, 3; *The Sound and the Fury*, 4, 5, 27, 116, 187, 192; *Sounder*, 11, 20–21, 37, 41, 42, 46–47, 53, 54, 58, 63, 68, 69, 72, 75, 76, 77, 78, 79, 80, 82, 84, 89, 95, 113, 114, 143, 163, 173, 180, 186, 188, 192; *The Spy Who Came in From the Cold*, 35, 53, 58, 61, 63, 89, 95, 113, 145, 172; *Stanley and Iris*, 186, 192, 196, 200–01; *A View from the Bridge*, 3

Robeson, Mark, 43
Robinson, Edward G., 172
Roeg, Nicolas, 165
Romance of a Horsethief, 41
Rosenberg, 38

Saki, 97, 98, 158
Saroyan, William, *My Heart's in the Highlands*, 138
Sarris, Andrew, 466
Schickel, Robert, 100
Scorsese, Martin, 29, 179
Siegal, Don, 39, 120
Shakespeare, William, 20, 102
Shaw, Irwin, 97
Shepard, Sam, 173
Sherwood, Robert, 98
Simon, Neil, *Slugger's Wife*, 85
Siskel and Ebert, 75, 77, 152
Skouras, Spyros, 57, 110, 135–36, 164, 165
Skulnik, Menasha, 141–42
Soldier's Story, A, 77, 113
Somebody Up There Likes Me, 191
Spielberg, Steven, 68; *The Color Purple*, 114
Spotted Horses, 191
Stanislavsky, Konstantin, 50, 130, 138
Steenburgen, Mary, 63, 64
Steiger, Rod, 99
Steinbeck, John, *The Grapes of Wrath*, 119
Stilwell, Joseph, 55, 61, 62
Strasberg, Lee, 150
Streisand, Barbra, 178–79
Stulberg, Gordon, 80
Sunday, Billy, 184
Superfly, 77
Susann, Jacqueline, 31
Suspense, 97
Susskind, David, 57, 96
Swaggart, Jimmy, 184

Taj Mahal, 22
Taxi Driver, 198, 199
Taylor, Robert, 157

Ten Days That Shook the World, 25
Tender Mercies, 85
Thackeray, William Makepeace, 29
Theatre of Action, 105, 188
Three Men on a Horse, 151
To Sir, with Love, 9
Tone, Franchot, 155–56
Torn, Rip, 63
Touch of Evil, 166
Tracy, Spencer, 74, 168, 182–83
Trumbo, Dalton, 54, 57
Tuchman, Barbara, 55
Turman, Larry, 81
Turner, Lana, 145
Tyson, Cicely, 21, 22, 32, 63, 72–73, 74, 79, 114, 143, 146, 163, 183, 192

Union Street, 192
Updike, John, 98

Van Peebles, Melvin, *The Story of a Three-Day Pass*, 78
Van Wyck, Jim, 198
View from the Bridge, A, 136, 157, 159, 174
Voight, Jon, 15, 17, 19, 28, 64, 143

Waiting for Lefty, 140, 141
Wald, Jerry, 164, 165
War and Peace, 151
Wasserman, Lew, 38, 39, 40
Waters, Ethel, 192
Way We Were, The, 25
Wayne, John, 176
Weinstein, Paula, 43
Welles, Orson, 4, 143, 144, 145, 166–67, 177, 188, 191
Wexler, Haskell, 40
White, Teddy, *Thunder Out of China*, 55
Whitehead, 141, 142
Wilder, Billy, 93, 120, 202
Williams College, 128
Williams, Tennessee, 5, 98, 129, 150, 161, 166, 174

Willie Boy, 39–40, 41, 51
Winfield, Paul, 21, 63, 73, 163, 192
Winged Victory, 56, 156, 189, 201
Wise, Robert, 38, 120
Wiz, The, 77
Woodard, Alfred, 78, 84, 146
Woodward, Joanne, 5, 143, 144, 160–61, 165, 175, 189, 190, 191

Works Progress Administration (WPA), 188, 189
Wyler, Willie, 5

Yellow Jack, 44, 56, 157, 189
You Are There, 34, 134

Zanuck, Darryl, 118, 132, 178
Zinnemann, Fred, 93, 120

www.ingramcontent.com/pod-product-compliance
Lightning Source LLC
Chambersburg PA
CBHW021838220426
43663CB00005B/297